World of Risk

*Next Generation Strategy
for a Volatile Era*

This publication is designed to provide accurate and authoritative information in regard to
the subject matter covered. It is sold with the understanding that the publisher is not engaged
in rendering professional services. If professional advice or other expert assistance is
required, the services of a competent professional person should be sought.

Other Wiley Editorial Offices

John Wiley & Sons, Inc., 605 Third Avenue, New York, NY 10158-0012, USA
John Wiley & Sons Ltd, Baffins Lane, Chichester, West Sussex PO19 1UD, England
John Wiley & Sons (Canada) Ltd, 22 Worcester Road, Rexdale, Ontario M9W 1L1, Canada
John Wiley & Sons Australia Ltd, 33 Park Road (PO Box 1226), Milton, Queensland
    4064, Australia
Wiley-VCH, Pappelallee 3, 69469 Weinheim, Germany

Library of Congress Cataloging-in-Publication Data
Daniell, Mark Haynes, 1955-
    World of risk : next generation strategy for a volatile era / by Mark Haynes Daniell.
        p. cm.
    Includes index.
    ISBN 0-471-84085-8
        1. Strategic planning.   2. Leadership.   3. Risk.   4. Competition, International.
    I. Title.

HD30.28 .D36 2000
658.15'5–dc21   99-055797

Typeset in 11/14 points, Adobe Garamond by Linographic Services Pte Ltd
Printed in Singapore by Craft Print Pte Ltd
10 9 8 7 6 5 4 3 2 1

World of Risk

Next Generation Strategy for a Volatile Era

by

Mark Haynes Daniell

John Wiley & Sons (Asia) Pte Ltd
Singapore   New York   Chichester
Brisbane   Toronto   Weinheim

*"...But the sky knows
the reasons and the patterns
behind all clouds,
and you will know, too, when
you lift yourself high enough
to see beyond
horizons."*

Illusions by Richard Bach

Contents

Preface

WORLD OF RISK was inspired by a set of personal experiences and observations that took place over a uniquely turbulent and troubled time in Asia. Because my family and I had moved to Singapore in the summer of 1997, we were able to experience at first hand the "haze" and the Asian economic crisis, and could follow daily press coverage of a fatal viral outbreak in Malaysia.

Other catastrophic events taking place in Asia over that period provided further headlines and instructive stories in the regional media: the flooding in China that killed 4,000 people and led to a ban on deforestation activity; the continuing decline of the Japanese economy; the spread of the Asian economic contagion to other emerging markets and an increase in poverty and economic disparity as a result of the crisis; acts of piracy in the South China Sea; and corruption and crime amounting to billions of dollars in Indonesia, China, Vietnam, Burma, and other emerging Asian nations. Tensions between Taiwan and China, and between the US and China had a direct impact on local capital markets and were the chief topics of conversation for many weeks across North and Southeast Asia.

Each of these events and the implications of their common patterns would not have been so clearly visible from either of the two countries of which I am a citizen and a former resident—the US and the United Kingdom. In this sense, an Asian perspective truly carried with it a unique opportunity for learning amidst the turbulence of the end of the 20th century.

I was also privileged to attend and address a number of high-level forums in the region during 1997–99, including the World Economic Forum, the Economist Conference Unit's Heads of Asia Pacific Operations gathering, the Business Week CEO Forum, the Harvard Asia Pacific Business Forum, and a major Conference Board meeting, which further added to my understanding of the economic crisis in particular during those troubled years.

Also, as a corporate strategy consultant and managing director of Bain & Company (Asia), Inc., I was able to observe a broader application of Next Generation Strategy to the unfolding events during this period. The strategy framework revealed gaps in the global architecture and weaknesses in the strategic approach adopted in critical areas of societal challenges in Asia.

The application of that model of global strategy also highlighted some of the practical actions that can be taken to improve considerably the current state of global affairs and to better manage future risks. Unless we develop and implement a better approach to managing these risks—which were clearly visible in Asia during the two-year period prior to the drafting of this book—they will invariably spread to the rest of the world.

My hope is that learning from this set of past crises will provide a useful platform for the development of a better approach to the problems and risks they represent today and in the future.

* * * * *

This is my first book. As such, I am particularly cognizant of all of the teachers, friends, authors, guides, and family members who have been supportive through the years leading up to this effort, as well as those who have helped to make this book a reality.

Of past and present teachers, I would single out for particular acknowledgement, Henry Ploegstra and Robert Gray at Exeter; Henry Steele Commager, Jeffrey Carre, and Joseph Epstein at Amherst; Roger Hood, John Finnis, and Adrian Zuckerman at Oxford; Louis Franke and Mme Burgess at "Sciences Po;" Raymond Aron at the College de France; and Professors Weinstein, Brudney, and Tribe of the Harvard Law School. Directly or indirectly, they and their colleagues have contributed immeasurably to the development of this book.

Many books over the years have contributed to the overall content and thought process of this book. The attached bibliography does not do full justice to the many contributions made to this one book over years of reading and observation. For further reading and a deeper analysis of the topics addressed here, I would recommend the following and recognize their particular contributions to my own understanding of these issues.

On societal and economic development, and the trends and currents therein, Peter Drucker's *Post-Industrial Society*, Samuel Huntington's *The Clash of Civilizations* and *The Remaking of World Order*, Paul Kennedy's *Preparing for the Twenty-First Century*, Hamish McRae's *The World in 2020*, and Kenichi Ohmae's *Borderless World* are all essential reading. *A History of God* by Karen Armstrong is informative and comprehensive. A fresh and alternative view on religion and spirituality is provided in *Spiritual Politics* by Corinne McLaughlin and Gordon Davidson. Bruce Hoffman's *Inside Terrorism* and Paul Stares' *Global Habit: The Drug Problem in a Borderless World* provide key sources of data and interpretation of these vexing problems. Matt Ridley's short but powerful book, *The Future of Disease*, from the *Predictions* series, provides a succinct and clear summary of a complex phenomenon.

Vital Signs from the Worldwatch Institute provides a clear summary and useful scorecard on performance and risk in many of the basic elements of the environmental system.

On the business side, any of the works of Prahalad, Doz, Hamel, Porter, Hax, Ohmae, and Drucker are worth reading and re-reading.

In the drafting and editing of the manuscript, I benefited from the wisdom, information, and editing skills of many friends and colleagues. Jennifer Jacobs of Malaysia's *Business Times* provided overall reviews, advice, and encouragement. Les Nemethy, formerly of the World Bank and now CEO of Matev, provided valuable advice on international institutions and insights into the world economy. Chandrashekar Gupta, banker and nuclear physicist, kept me honest on scientific theories and their application to a wide range of dynamic systems. Lady Patten provided welcome words of wisdom and encouragement from her experience as a director of many large, publicly quoted companies. Steven Green, US ambassador, entrepreneur, and philanthropist, provided encouragement and valuable commentary on risk pricing, and the economic implication of risk at a systemic level. My partner, Paul Wilson, contributed extensively to the section on banking consolidation. Andrew Mitchell of Earthwatch helped enormously with the section on the environment. Kannan Chandran, managing editor of *The Peak* in Singapore, chipped in from a hectic international schedule. The courageous Lorenzo Matassa, prosecuting magistrate in Palermo, helped to clarify and expand on the issues of global crime and policing. Steve Coltrin and Krystyna Stachowiak of Coltrin & Associates in New

York helped to structure and edit these contents. Colleagues and friends at Bain & Company—Orit Gadiesh, James Gilbert, Spencer Low, Mike Garstka, Jim Hildebrandt, Jean-Marie Pean, and Tom Tierney—provided valuable ideas and encouragement. Alexandra Holmes, from conceptualization through to final editing provided guidance, wise counsel, inspiration, and direction. For her invaluable contribution, I cannot thank her enough.

At a practical level, many individuals contributed to the research, typing, and editing of the endless sets of drafts, corrections, and redrafts. Louise Kow, Tina Sim, Elizabeth Giles, Doreen Fernandez, and an army of part-time typists in Singapore were magnificent in their cheerful support of the production process. Anja Wittrup was, throughout the project, a great support and dear friend. From the publishers John Wiley & Sons, Nick Wallwork, Gael Lee, and Elizabeth Daniel were a great team which was always responsive and friendly despite a few missed deadlines, many last-minute changes, and an elusive author.

I would like also like to thank Matthew Siva and Michael Lafferty, the editor of the *Singapore Economic Bulletin* and owner of Lafferty Publications, for their consent to incorporate material used in Chapters 2 and 3 which was originally drafted for their highly respected publications.

This book, as a result of its broad coverage and synthetic content, is inevitably a bit like an Impressionist painting—a series of colorful dabs and individual brushstrokes which only make a fully coherent picture when viewed in its entirety. Each reader will draw his or her own conclusions and come away with a unique interpretation of the content. I hope that these individual perspectives can, over time, be shared to extract value that goes well beyond the covers of this book.

Of course, the most important source of support comes from my family, whose positive attitude, covering many months of late nights and weekend labors on this project, is fully understood and appreciated. Ivana, Vinci, and Christian could not have been a more supportive or more patient family during the writing and production of this book.

* * * * *

Mark Haynes Daniell

1
A World of Risk in the 21st Century

Our modern world of risk and volatility has evolved to the point where we need different and more effective solutions to global problems. Old risks and problems can no longer be mastered with our current set of strategies, institutions, standards, and attitudes. Existing response and control mechanisms—national and international—have failed to generate acceptable results in the newly globalized areas of crime, disease, terrorism, environmental degradation, economic inequality, deculturalization, and other threats to the quality of our lives. Even the brand new cyberworld has created risks that we have failed to master.

Global performance to date in these areas could be labeled as satisfactory underperformance—generating a continuing state of outcomes, which by objective assessment is not acceptable, but which over time has become accepted as the prevailing norm.

Looking ahead, the risks we face are increasing in scale and complexity. Unfortunately, our ability to respond has not kept pace. The nation state on its own is too small and often too fragmented to provide an effective response to problems of an international dimension. International and intranational institutions are often slow to respond as they are hampered by restrictive charters and underfunding, and are driven by a need for broad consensus. As a result, they may only accept a lowest-common-denominator outcome. The results from this current global architecture are, on the whole, unacceptable.

However, within our collective intellectual capital we have a depth of knowledge for a better approach to resolve problems of a global nature. This approach—called Next Generation Strategy—can provide a valuable guide to improved strategy, structure, leadership, and results for tomorrow's world.

The most advanced model of global strategy has evolved through a tough selection process at the cutting edge of international business, distilling the learning from years of expensive experience and millions of hours of management attention. The best ideas in the global business world are tested, refined, applied, and replicated. Weak ideas fail and are analyzed for applicable learning, then discarded. The result is the creation of a dynamic model of best practice global strategy that can lead to a far better outcome in areas of personal and professional concern, as well as in the sphere of international business competition.

The application of this state-of-the-art business model to global challenges outside the commercial sphere could contribute significantly toward reducing risk, stabilizing volatility and mastering the spiraling challenges we will face in the next century.

By avoiding compartmentalization and by applying our best knowledge and capabilities to the most critical challenges to our collective well being, we can indeed make this a better world for the next generation.

Statement of Purpose

As we step forward into the new millennium, we have often questioned the nature of the civilization we are building. What legacy are we leaving behind for the next century and the next generation? How can we build a better world—how can we design and implement the changes that will make the most positive impact on our lives and the world in which we live? We focus more on description, diagnosis, and prognosis than on prescription for change.

Today's era of increasing volatility and escalating risk can in fact provide a platform from which to drive positive change for tomorrow. But we can only drive fundamental change if we are prepared to take full advantage of our best knowledge and improve our approach to the collective management of global affairs.

An Unsatisfactory State of Global Affairs

Past results in almost every critical area of societal performance can only be characterized as unsatisfactory. The approach to date has failed to address critical risks, to capitalize on valuable opportunities, and to capture the full potential for positive change inherent in the modern world. In this volatile era, the stabilizing effect of a successful global strategy has long been missing. Opportunities abound but are not captured to create more ambitious visions and goals. An improved approach to the management of critical global challenges could lead to a new and more creative set of initiatives for change, a new global architecture, and far more effective leadership.

As risks become larger in scope and more global and complex in nature, our ability to manage them becomes more critical. Gaps in the global architecture become more acutely felt, yet prove even more difficult to identify and to address. The challenges of leadership and motivation grow ahead of our apparent ability to respond.

Today, pure theory and even well-thought-out strategic designs are not enough. Ideas need to be implemented. As John Gardner stated: "In this era of complexity, great enterprises are designed and carried forward by the kind of man who has a vision of what might be and a practical strategy for getting there, a man with an idea in his head and a monkey wrench in his hand."

A New Model of Global Strategy

This book describes in a practical way how to design and implement solutions that will address these critical issues on a more effective basis. From the cutting edge of global business, a new and more comprehensive global strategic model has dramatically improved the performance of enterprises and collective initiatives that cut across borders and embrace multiple countries. The application of this state-of-the-art strategic model could considerably improve the current level of underperformance in many areas of critical global challenge outside the commercial world as well. Risk and volatility can be reduced. Many more opportunities for improvement can be captured. New levels of operating excellence can be achieved. New and more aspirational visions for the future can, in fact, be realized. Capabilities to respond to future challenges can be enhanced. Individuals and collective enterprises can be motivated and engaged. Gaps in the global architecture can be rectified. Results can be improved.

Rising Levels of Risk

We are now living in a world of rising risk and increasing volatility. Everywhere, we seem to encounter increasing and intensifying risk. Business risk. Economic risk. Environmental risk. Political conflict and risk of military engagement. Risk of unforeseen harm from criminals and disease. Risks to the retention of our unique cultures and to the spiritual foundations of our lives. We even run the risk of unpredicted new catastrophes as complex new systems interact, such as distributed computer networks, the Internet, and modern capital systems. These new points of intersection can increase volatility, compound individual risk, and magnify potential damage in ways we are just beginning to understand.

Poor management and lack of leadership have unnecessarily increased the risks and volatility of this turbulent era. Many risks at a world level are now characterized by a recurring pattern of newly globalized threats, unmatched by any effective national or international response capability. If risk is measured as the threat we face net of our capacity and preparedness to respond, then recent events can only raise the level of concern over the future we are now facing as we move forward into the 21st century.

An Era of Opportunity

On the other hand, we also live in an era of great opportunity. Time and time again, we have proven that we are capable of rising to the most challenging tasks where we have the will and the knowledge required. In the management of global challenges, there is much we already know from the most advanced sources of information and application. A new strategic approach to the management of global challenges has emerged from the best practices of successful global businesses. As global business systems and risks have grown and evolved, the field of international business strategy has similarly evolved and developed.

A new state-of-the-art approach to strategy—elaborated here as Next Generation Strategy—has changed both the content and process of strategy as applied by leading international business enterprises. Next Generation Strategy provides a better approach to managing risk, capturing opportunity, directing complex dynamic systems, and building the human and organizational elements of strategy on an integrated basis. It addresses both the "hard" and the "soft" elements of strategy and accomplishment. In addition, it provides an approach that can lead to the design and implementation of an improved architecture at all relevant levels. Furthermore, it contains an integrated model of solutions that leads to improved results in the real world.

The application of the core principles of this approach has already generated dramatically better financial results for international businesses in a wide variety of circumstances. The lessons learned from this strategic evolution and application can provide many effective responses to the new global risks that we face outside of the business sphere as well.

Trillions of dollars of accumulated experience in global problem solving within and across national borders have led to the creation of a new state-of-the-art model of global strategy in the business world. Good approaches are proven in the market place, built upon, and applied successfully. Others are found wanting, analyzed for lessons learned, and rejected. The result of this Darwinian process of selection is a survival of the strongest model of problem solving and results creation.

Good strategy bridges an aspirational vision to results in the market place. The product of strategy is an effective plan of action that links an aspirational vision to the achievement of improved results which are aligned with the overall vision and supporting imperatives. This plan of action is driven by a clear set of priorities, accountabilities, resource allocations, and timetables. It will encompass all elements of risk, opportunity, and the full business system in an integrated program of change.

The quality and value of each strategy can only be measured in the real, tangible results it creates. Where results are unacceptable, a new approach to the diagnosis, design, and execution of strategy is required.

Shared Elements of Global Strategy

As we step back from the major challenges of our era, look afresh at the current state of global affairs and critically assess the results of existing strategies, it is clear that there is much room for improvement. The application of our best learning and most skilled response in global management could make a significant contribution to the management of risk and the realization of opportunity in the highest priority areas that increasingly threaten our collective well being.

Although the cutting edge of competition in telecommunications, financial services, and other turbulent areas of global commerce may seem light years away from the management of the environment or patterns of organized crime, the modern world has brought them closer together. The same issues of globalization, complexity, risk, and dynamic systems behavior are common to both. As the fundamental characteristics of commercial and societal problems reflect surprisingly similar patterns, the best solutions in both areas also have much in common.

Global business, as is the management of global affairs outside the commercial sphere, is as much about process and politics as it is about substance. The resolution of major challenges in the business world also has to do with scarce resource allocation, governmental relations, the politics of large and numerous organizations, and the oversight of a complex process of change and transformation.

Most importantly, businesses, like governments and countries, are collections of individuals who need to be led, directed, engaged, and inspired. Failure to reach the individuals who are involved in a collective enterprise—commercial or societal—will ensure that even well-thought-out strategies fail to achieve the full potential inherent in the system they are attempting to change.

Need for A New Approach

"If we are to achieve results never before accomplished, we must expect methods never before attempted." – Sir Francis Bacon

Looking objectively at our current approach to global strategy, the results to date, and the state of world affairs today, one is forced to conclude that we can indeed do much better. Current results in global management are unacceptable. But our capability to respond is not. The set of unrealized risks we face is increasing exponentially. The approaches we have taken to date, on the whole, have not led to a satisfactory state of affairs in the critical areas of global challenge and risk management.

A more comprehensive and creative approach to societal issues could improve dramatically on our current levels of underperformance in critical areas such as crime, disease, the environment, terrorism, economic disparity, and the cultural integrity of our various civilizations. Old models of strategy and fragmented approaches are no longer sufficient to master the mounting and very modern problems of the next century.

Ironically, most of the major threats to our collective well being are man-made. The globalization of old problems is often driven by newly developed channels and systems of distribution and delivery. It is thus not surprising that we already have, in our collective intellectual capital, a strategic model and approach that would help us manage better the risks we have created.

These global risks are greater than ever before, and are accelerating with time to make our world more dangerous than it has ever been. Yet our capability to manage these risks is also much more powerful than we know—and fully capable of reducing risks and capturing opportunities as never before.

Programs of large-scale change and transformation are never easy to design or implement. Longstanding traditions, habits, and standards of performance will be difficult to recast and reform. The effort will inevitably provide new challenges—individual and collective—as well as new opportunities for growth and fulfillment.

The Greatest Risk

The greatest risk of all to our collective well being may be to compartmentalize our experience and fail to apply our most advanced knowledge to the most critical challenges of our time. If we avoid this risk, and learn from our own best and worst experience, we can improve results dramatically in those areas that most affect our lives as businessmen and as individuals. A thorough understanding and thoughtful application of the principles of a new generation of effective strategy could indeed make this a better and safer world in which to live and work.

A Higher Synthesis

Ultimately, this is a book as much about hope and the potential for positive change as it is about risk. Through an improved approach to global strategy and through the renewal of effort to achieve the full and positive potential inherent in the systems of risk and opportunity we face, together we will be able to lift the boundaries on what is truly possible.

Through the synthesis of individual effort and collective potential in the pursuit of that higher level of shared accomplishment, we may also rediscover that greater sense of purpose and belief in our lives, which has proven so elusive in the modern world. In the shared pursuit of a better world for others, we may also recover, as individuals, a better part of ourselves.

Summary of the Argument

Many global systems, including most businesses, now operate at a level best called satisfactory underperformance. Ordinary results, when viewed objectively from a fresh perspective, are unacceptably low. Yet years of unacceptably low performance have worn down standards and sensitivities to a level where consistent underperformance has become, in a perverse way, satisfactory.

Many new risks fall into the same recurring pattern that leads to a state of continuous underperformance. The pattern usually develops as follows. An unexpected crisis or growing problem surfaces somewhere in the world. Modern interconnected distribution and delivery networks spread the problem rapidly to other nations and regions. Because the nature of the problem now involves many nations, individual states are incapable of responding effectively on their own.

International institutions (G7, G24, European Union (EU), International Monetary Fund (IMF), World Bank, United Nations (UN), World Health Organization (WHO), Interpol, etc.) fail to stand up to the challenge or are conspicuous by their absence. A leading institution taking center stage or co-operative action among nation states is presented as the most appropriate remedy. High-profile conferences are convoked with much fanfare. After much discussion and publicity, the co-operative effort rapidly finds the lowest common denominator. Weak solutions are proposed. Even fewer are implemented. In some areas where its national interest is affected, the United States (US) attempts to project its strength internationally, with mixed results. The problems spread or fester. After a while, the media loses interest and the world moves on— time bombs continue to tick, risk piling on risk.

This repetitive pattern erodes standards and sensibilities alike to a point where the unacceptable becomes, through repetitive exposure or through neglect, a newly accepted norm.

Recent challenges and crises in the economy, the environment, disease management, criminal interdiction, and other critical spheres of global action have followed this now predictable pattern with frightening regularity. The Asian economic crisis, the larger emerging markets crisis, Acquired Immune-Deficiency Syndrome (AIDS), the drug trade and money laundering, terrorism, degradation of the ozone layer and global deforestation, the loss of sustaining local cultures, and the growth in the gap between the haves and the have-nots have all followed this same pattern of accelerating global risk and diminishing capability to respond.

Fortunately, not all the news is bad. Over time, we have managed to reduce a number of threats to our well being. We have increased our capacity to respond in many areas. The Cold War is over. International trade and related employment has risen dramatically. Many life-threatening diseases have been eradicated. Major terrorist groups have been crippled and their leaders jailed. Crimes of violence, in some areas, are receding. Most of the world has been on a path of increasing literacy, expanding economic growth, and rising capital market values for decades. Hundreds of millions of citizens around the world have climbed out of the poverty trap for the first time. Women are, in most countries, more empowered than ever before. Children have more protection and a valid expectation of a better life than their parents in many developing countries.

Yet a dispassionate review of our current situation will identify a new set of challenges and risks we have created for ourselves, but which we are far from mastering.

Systemic Nature of the Challenge

The risks that are emerging from these recent developments are showing a common pattern of behavior. The major risks we now face are becoming consistently more global, more complex, and more dynamic over time. They have taken on a life of their own and can now be seen as the "living" systems they have become. As the new systemic nature of these risks becomes clear, the nature of the challenge and the content of solutions also change.

The precise nature of each challenge will differ as each system follows its own unique path of development. However, a number of common patterns have emerged that can help us to understand, and eventually to manage, the risks and opportunities created by these complex systems. Some of the common elements of evolution, or paradigm principles, can be seen across many apparently dissimilar systems, reflecting a high degree of pattern integrity where they appear. The common principles of relevant systemic behavior would include visible increases in globalization, complexity, turbulence within systems and at their intersection, dynamism, acceleration in the rate of change, continuous obsolescence and reinvention, connectivity, convergence, and con-solidation and rationalization.

These recurring characteristics can be seen as common elements in the evolution of many of the systems that pose the greatest challenges and present the highest levels of risk in the current global paradigm.

These 10 elements of commonality are themselves increasingly interconnected, creating even more systemic risks and opportunities for positive change. Developing and implementing a strategic model to understand and master these systemic patterns and characteristics is a necessary step in shaping a more positive landscape for the future.

Rising to the analytical challenge, designing effective strategies, and implementing measurable change must rest on an improved understanding of each of these systemic characteristics. State-of-the-art international business strategy is increasingly about the analysis and management of complex systems and a mastery of the imperatives they mandate. New solutions are usually necessary to respond effectively to the new and more complex challenges these systems create.

Results in the international business community now depend upon the design and implementation of action plans that simultaneously address similar issues in numerous distinct countries and contain effective responses to the challenges of integrated global operations. A multinational strategy only addresses operating challenges in a set of distinct national markets. In today's world, this is not enough. A simultaneous approach to individual country markets and global-scale operations is required. This co-ordinated approach is known as a *transnational* approach. It is also the most effective approach to societal challenges that have become transnational in nature.

As in general business practices, effective practices to master transnational challenges are carefully designed, tested, implemented, reassessed, fine-tuned, and replicated across national borders. Ineffective initiatives are swiftly discarded. This process of selection and refinement has yielded a depth of knowledge on the content and process of global strategic development. It has generated a model which is well-suited to respond to the challenge of transnational problems—old and new. This approach, best captured in the model of Next Generation Strategy, can lead to far better results in the interlinked national and global systems it addresses. It can also lead to a visible reduction in risk and increased capture of opportunity in a wide range of global systems.

Risk and Opportunity Defined

There are, of course, many types of risk. Although risk analysis can be applied to neutral and even positive future eventualities, this book focuses primarily on the negative concept of risk. This captures the commonsense use of the word as well as its precise mathematical content. The quantification of any type of risk can be broadly described as a function of four interrelated variables. For risk, at its core, is a simple four-element system in its own right. The quantum of actual total risk can most simply be described as:

1. the scale of the potential harm *adjusted by*
2. the likelihood of that harm occurring *net of*
3. the ability of an effective response to be put in place *adjusted by*
4. the likelihood of that response mechanism being deployed effectively

The result of the application of the two halves of the equation—risk and response—will yield a net risk assessment that can be used to calibrate risk on a fully informed basis.

A corollary of net risk assessment is net opportunity assessment. Instead of a four-element risk system, a similar allocation of value and probability can be spelt out in a positive, rather than negative, four-element system. The calculus applies where there is an opportunity for positive improvement in a situation—with or without an offsetting risk element.

The net opportunity assessment would be similar in structure and content to its more negative relative of net risk assessment, but a similar calculus would work with new variables as follows:

1. the value of the opportunity *adjusted by*
2. the likelihood of that opportunity eventuating *net of*
3. the ability to capture the opportunity *adjusted by*
4. the likelihood of that ability being deployed

As we step back from the combination of risk and opportunity in many critical global systems, the overall picture that emerges from the detail is deeply worrying. We are creating ever more dangerous threats to our own well being, and the likelihood of that harm occurring is rising. The net increase in threat comes from both risk elements—a growing scale of potential harm and an increased likelihood that harm will come about. Our ability to respond to risk and the likelihood of deployment of this response are also of legitimate concern. There are indeed gaps in the global architecture. Many efforts to respond to global crises have failed to rise to the full magnitude of the crisis. Even where we do have a proven capability, it may not be applied effectively or on a timely basis.

In many of the areas critical to our businesses and to our lives, the negative aspects of risk are increasing faster than the positive aspects of response—the net risk assessment is moving ever more negatively.

At the same time that the risk is spiraling upward, we are not taking advantage of the offsetting opportunities to improve the overall state of affairs.

Strategy, at its essence, is the approach we adopt to the allocation of resources to the risks and opportunities in a defined system. With a more quantified, and hence clearer, perspective on risk and opportunity, we can approach the issue of prioritization and resource allocation from a fresh perspective. By quantifying risk and opportunity, and by quantifying the impact of investments and initiatives on the balance of risk and opportunity, we can provide a clear framework for the allocation of scarce resources to improve the overall results on the most effective basis.

From that clearer perspective, we can assess our performance to date more realistically, quantify initiatives better, set new standards for achievement and even define a new concept of success. With a full application of our best knowledge, we can create an integrated strategic approach that realizes a far more ambitious vision for the future.

Rising Stakes of Global Strategy

The challenges of modern strategy are rising in proportion to the scale of the risks and opportunities we face. One of the major challenges of strategy at the highest levels is the challenge of globalization. The phenomenon of globalization carries with it increases in personal, business, and societal risk, as well as opportunities for consumer or corporate benefit.

The increasingly global nature of the capital system is characterized by new and fully interconnected distribution systems. Proprietary telecommunication networks and leased lines deliver digitalized voice, data, and images on a virtually instantaneous basis around the world. Billions of dollars can move in a few seconds at the touch of a button. Interbank systems, wire transfers, fax confirmations, satellite link-ups, video conferences, and highly automated trading systems all combine to create a vast, complex web of electronic distribution systems.

However, just as these distribution systems can transfer funds in the blink of an eye halfway around the world, they can also multiply the negative impact when economic crises hit. Funds can be withdrawn instantly as well as invested. Demand for a currency can shift from orderly buying patterns to panic selling. "Hot money" from global hedge funds can move as a pack to depress targeted currencies, decrease the value of shares, and even collapse vulnerable markets. Global asset managers move on short notice to shift billions of dollars of portfolio money to higher return activities in alternative world markets. The growth of complicated products, such as derivatives and electronically driven asset allocation models, dramatically increases the scale of potential economic damage and the likelihood of a catastrophe occurring. Uncontrolled program trading, improperly managed portfolios of derivative instruments, proxy hedging, and concentrated flows of speculative capital can trigger a full collapse of an economic system.

The new global pathways of the capital world also create the potential for catastrophe should a small subset of the potential risks become real. As the interconnected nature of the financial world accelerates, the potential for global collapse of the capital system mounts.

Global systems of distribution and delivery are not confined to new forms of electronic money and investment. Information flows, international trade, economic growth, transnational corporations, and capital markets have all contributed to a new set of interlinked global distribution capabilities. The global flow of information, goods, and people as well as capital has created a whole new set of financial opportunities for investors around the world. It has also created a whole new set of risks of massive proportion.

Complex Systems and the Catastrophe Model

This risk of economic crisis and related societal aftershock can best be described, in mathematical terms, as a catastrophic event—an apparently unpredictable and discontinuous event rapidly changing the fundamental behavior of the system in question.

Complex systems behavior, at its core, is driven by a number of interacting variables that exert influence over the whole of a dynamic system. In the absence of a material change in one or more of the variables, systems by and large retain their original shape and momentum. And in that respect, status quo rules.

On the other hand, small changes in one or more variables can swiftly and disproportionately change the fundamental direction and velocity of such a system. In any global system, there are a large number of relevant variables. Some are determining elements in the systems equation. Some are consequential. Many are both inputs and consequent outputs—driving change and, in turn, affected as a result of the change process. Actions, reactions, and resultants are contained within a single dynamic environment.

Although the standard rules of science and nature apply to any dynamic system, the most relevant technical area of mathematics to apply here to describe this pattern would be classical catastrophe theory.

Although chaos theory is a more popular topic of discussion these days, (and more complex to understand and apply) the classical multivariable model of systems behavior captures the essential insight; complex systems behave as a direct function of the number of inputs. A three-variable model results in a three-dimensional construct for analysis. The three-variable system's operating characteristics can be visualized as a three-dimensional piece of cloth with bumps and folds. Discrete phenomena track along the surface, moving in three dimensions along the surface of the cloth. Viewed from a three-dimensional perspective, the line moves in a consistent pattern along the surface of the cloth—up, down, under, and over. Viewed from a two-dimensional perspective, however, the line appears to disappear (as it enters into a fold in the cloth) and shortly reappears elsewhere in an unpredictable fashion. This apparent dislocation is called a catastrophe in mathematical terms—an unforeseen discontinuous or non-linear event with significant impact on unwitting participants in the multi-variable system.

Unfortunately, the real world too often sees only a limited view of complex systems and is caught unaware when apparent discontinuities appear along critical dimensions or other fault lines. Inadequate understanding, monitoring, and response capabilities can turn complex system "catastrophes" into real world disasters.

Risk Becomes Reality

The likelihood of risk becoming real was fully realized in Asia in 1997 and 1998 in aspects of the economy, the environment, and disease control. All three systems exhibited "catastrophes" that were unexpected, deep, and prolonged. None of the three was effectively managed. Each catastrophe was triggered by a different source. Each failure to respond effectively can trace its roots back to different causes.

Yet each stands to prove how exposed we are to the vulnerability created by undermanaged systems of risk. Together, they stand as a warning of what may lie in the future if we are not better prepared to deal today with the causes and effects of systemic risk.

Crisis I: Emerging Economies

Threats of global damage are not purely theoretical, as two recent crises in Asia have shown. Following the collapse of the Thai baht on July 2, 1997, currency after currency in the non-regulated emerging markets collapsed under heavy pressure from international and domestic sellers. Growth faltered in these countries, where citizens had enjoyed rising standards of living for over a decade. The contagion spread rapidly across Asia and traveled to Russia, Brazil, and beyond. Millions lost jobs. Thousands of businesses closed their doors forever. Hundreds of banks and finance companies collapsed into insolvency. The financial systems in South Korea, Thailand, and Indonesia were bankrupted. The reconstruction process was slow to start and the costs incurred will reverberate for years to come.

Fragile economies and social structures in emerging markets are perhaps the most vulnerable to global attack and the most sensitive to economic damage. New, large, and fragile economies like Indonesia's created an opportunity for subsequent social and human damage on a very large scale indeed. As a result of the Asian crisis, its own weaknesses and its unique political and social system, Indonesia collapsed as the crisis bit deep into the social fiber of the country. The rupiah fell from 2,200 to the dollar, to a low of 16,000 in less than one year. As a result of this collapse and subsequent aftershocks in the economy, 20 million Indonesians fell below the poverty line again.

The value of the stock market, measured in US dollar terms, fell 85 per cent in one year. Hundreds of large businesses were unable to pay billions of dollars in unhedged US-dollar denominated debts. Millions of workers suddenly lost their jobs. Prices of staple food products skyrocketed. The banking system, public and private, was made deeply insolvent. Violence erupted in Ambon, Aceh, East Timor, and Jakarta. Newspaper photographs of rioters carrying the severed heads of tribal rivals served as a grisly reminder of the potential cost as the fabric of social order unravels in countries ripe with unresolved tribal conflict.

A Lost Generation

As the economic structure was collapsing, the impact on social structure and human lives was devastating. Millions of jobs were lost. Children were forced out of school, many never to return. In Thailand, the crisis forced 130,000 children out of the educational system. In Indonesia, many elementary schools in Jakarta were forced to close due to crisis-related withdrawals.

In West Sumatra alone, 40,000 children quickly developed signs of malnutrition. In Central Java, 65 per cent of children under the age of three were diagnosed as anemic in 1999, a 25 per cent increase from 1997. The number of children suffering from diarrhea has doubled.

These human costs will continue to be felt long after the capital markets and gross domestic product (GDP) figures return to positive trends.

The World Bank speaks of a "Lost Generation" of children in Asia— unable to afford adequate housing, medical care, minimal nutrition, or basic education. Spousal abuse, family breakdown, and suicide rose dramatically. Full economic recovery receded into the future as social order in the country spiraled out of control at a dangerous rate. Foreign and domestic capital raced out of the country and has been slow to return.

Risk became reality for Indonesians, its Asian neighbors, and residents of other stricken emerging economies alike in a sharp cyclical reversal of past positive trends. The increasing complexity and interconnectedness of global financial systems only raises the probability of this kind of damage replicating itself across an ever more volatile world.

Crisis II: The Nipah Virus

Pig farmers and abattoir workers in Malaysia were struck down by a deadly pair of viruses at the end of 1998 and the beginning of 1999. A Hendra-like virus (previously found in Australia) and a separate strand of Japanese Porcine Encephalitis emerged simultaneously in agricultural areas a few kilometers from the glistening new Kuala Lumpur International Airport. Although over a hundred deaths had been reported, the risks of a broader crisis were eventually averted by the effective response from the Center for Disease Prevention and Control (CDC) in Atlanta. However, the CDC was not called in until six months after the initial outbreak, by which time the local authorities were wrestling with a problem well beyond their capability. Malaysia's six-month delay in calling in global experts may have cost scores of lives. But in the end, a major tragedy was avoided. The lethal virus seems to have been confined to a limited geographical area, and primarily to workers in a particular economic sector. Although apparently constrained by the two-kilometer range of the mosquito that transfers the virus from animals to humans and between humans, the proximity of a deadly twin viral outbreak only 15 kilometers from a major travel hub gives cause to reflect on what could have been.

Crisis III: The Haze

As the capital crisis unfolded across Southeast Asia in 1997, thick smoke —euphemistically known as the haze—arose from the fires of uncontrolled clearance burning of the tropical rainforests in Indonesia and spread across

Brunei, Singapore, Sabah, Sarawak, and Peninsular Malaysia. In this environmental area, there was no relevant global institution capable of assisting the stricken countries. There was no international court, convention, or international body capable of providing adequate redress for the catastrophe. Residents in the worst hit areas were encouraged to stay indoors, breathe filtered air, and avoid driving in a hazy pollution that reduced visibility to a few meters at its worst.

Eventually, the fires burned themselves out. Bits and pieces of assistance had come from Malaysia, Singapore, and Canada. A few of the miscreants who started the burning were identified and local court actions launched, but little came of it. A year later, the haze was again drifting across Southeast Asia, although not as dense this time, and so invoking less public outcry, but equally unmanaged. There had clearly been no reduction in the threat, and the ability to respond had remained at a minimal level should the burning have blazed out of control once again.

By April 1999, yet another year later, the haze once again wafted across Southeast Asia. By August, the air pollution was so dense that it contributed to the deaths of at least 10 people as an oil tanker, blinded by poor visibility, collided with a barge and tugboat on a river in Indonesia's Riau province. Children in the areas closest to the fires were advised to stay at home. Some collapsed and had to be hospitalized. Authorities in Riau closed all kindergartens and advised citizens to wear protective masks outside.

While residents in Riau were advised to stay indoors, the number of uncontrolled fires rose to over 400. In Kalimantan (the Indonesian part of a large island adjacent to Malaysia), another 300 fires burned out of control. The Pollution Standard Index (PSI), which registers air quality with a level of between 0 to 50 indicating a safe level and 100 indicating a dangerous level of pollution, was closely monitored. The prime minister of Malaysia, a medical doctor by profession, once said he would evacuate areas where the PSI exceeded 200. The peak PSI level in Riau in the summer of 1999 reached 978.

A Volatile Era

These catastrophes are only the beginning of the result of risk becoming real in our complex world. Worse may yet come.

One new source of risk is not found in any individual complex global system or inadequate responsive mechanism. It may well lie in the uncharted compounding of risk created when more than one system intersects and interacts—creating turbulence, compounding risk, and increasing the impact of any failure to respond effectively.

As global systems evolve, there are more and more variables intersecting from newer and less understood complex systems. The inevitable result is an increase in unexpected catastrophes and apparent discontinuities. Some will be positive. Many neutral. Some dangerous. This increase in the potential number of global systemic catastrophes lies at the root of the increased volatility of the era in which we now live and work. In the business world, there are technological, organizational, and competitive discontinuities that increase volatility and risk. In non-business areas, in the most critical challenges to our collective well being, the volatility and risk multiplies, and the potential human cost of a catastrophe mounts even higher.

The volatility of our era—the increasing potential for catastrophic events actually occurring—flows from this combination of risks and complexity within dynamic systems and in the destabilizing turbulence at their intersection. In this turbulence, risk compounds and increases at a logarithmic rate.

Risk Compounded

An example of this compounding of risk is the interconnection of the computer web with the global capital system. A catastrophe in one system can spill over directly and immediately into another. A virus, Y2K failure, or catastrophic computer systems behavior could have a major impact on both the capital markets and vulnerable operating and control systems.

Just as old-fashioned power shortages would have a direct negative impact on dependent factory operations or hospital operating theatres, a computer virus can now attack the central nervous system of factories, hospitals, and emergency mobile dispatch systems. A single virus can trigger catastrophes at thousands of new points of contact and intersection.

For example, given the fragility and lack of understanding in dramatically adverse environments of the behavior of the world's $51 trillion of financial derivative instruments the element of risk is compounded. The full systemic impact of isolated events is unpredictable. In 1987, program trading nearly drove the New York Stock Exchange into an electronically driven free fall. Now carefully controlled, the old program trading meltdown risk may find a new future in unmonitored Internet transactions, global hedge fund behavior, or management of large, highly leveraged derivatives portfolios.

Interacting systems can easily generate an unforeseen event for which there is no monitor or control. The economic crises in the emerging markets were detonated by a complex set of intersecting variables, including unsustainable currency values, corporate leverage, banking system weaknesses, hedge fund behavior, investor confidence, and interest rate policy. Each variable and subsystem operated rationally and predictably from its own perspective, but the intersection of variables and subsystems created a systemic whole that generated an unexpected catastrophe of vast proportion in the emerging markets.

Not all dangerous intersections of global systems are electronic or economic. The modern world of travel and systems of disease are a natural pair to spread infections around the world rapidly. Reuters reported on August 6, 1999 that doctors and staff in hermetically sealed suits in a special isolation ward in Germany were treating a patient returning to Berlin from the Ivory Coast. A six-meter high fence was erected around the hospital. The suspected cause of his symptoms was the killer Ebola virus. Germany's widely read *Bild* newspaper summarized the concern: "…will his fellow passengers spread the virus around Europe; could tens of thousands of people already be affected?" Travel, migration, and military conquests have spread infection and disease for years. The new world of global travel only accelerates this phenomenon.

Deliberate Catastrophes A Greater Concern

The more worrying compounding of systems risk in the economic area may lie in the intersection of the electronic capital trading system and the systems of international criminal or terrorist organizations. The new reliance on computers in the defense area also escalates the issue of risk management in this sphere to global proportions. Large-scale fraud, tampering, or stoppage of electronic systems could have disastrous and long-lasting effects.

At the beginning of 1999, it was already clear how vulnerable our defense and capital systems are to cyber-attack when a critical defense communication satellite was hijacked and a ransom demand tabled. For the first time, a major cyber-attack became a reality. One recent estimate on the global vulnerability created by the rise of the Internet estimated that 30 well funded computer experts could quickly take over the entire global electronic trading system.

Experts now claim that it is also only a matter of time before terrorist or criminal organizations access weapons of mass destruction—chemical, biological or nuclear. That deadly combination, coupled with systems of cross-border travel and distribution, will raise the scale of potential harm from deliberate release of toxins or massively powerful explosives to unprecedented proportions.

The real world is turning mathematically comprehensible catastrophes into the potential for disasters and crises of increasing harm with an uncontrolled likelihood of occurrence.

Chaos and Catastrophe

Going beyond simple catastrophe and discontinuity, chaos theory brings with it a more sinister message. Chaos theory holds, essentially, that all systems tend toward chaos. Crudely summarized, there are two sorts of chaotic systems—deterministic and non-deterministic. Systems behavior consistent with deterministic chaos will reflect an unpredictable pattern of events within a set of broadly predictable parameters. Individual events are not predictable, but the general shape and direction of the composite system is. A non-deterministic system would reflect an evolution that is inherently unpredictable. Thus, systems in a non-deterministic mode have no predictable order, and forecasting is neither useful nor meaningful at the level of an individual event or at a systemic level.

Under both types of chaos, minor events can have major, unexpected consequences.

The impact of adopting the full implications of deterministic chaos theory is that the risk of unpredictable events occurring—negative or otherwise—may be far greater than that reflected here. Under a non-deterministic model, not only is there a greater risk of catastrophic development of individual events, there is an expectation of realizing the risk of entire systems tending toward chaos. This could trigger negative events and systemic responses with effects that could reverberate across all or many implicated systems.

These chaotic tendencies only serve to underscore the need to develop effective monitors and response mechanisms to manage risk as best we can, to avoid catastrophe and chaos where possible, and to prepare ourselves for the inevitability of the unexpected.

Unpredictable change is inherent in the evolution of many natural, and even many artificial, complex systems. Constant and unpredictable change will require us to respect and adapt to new rules of the game— and to realize that strategy, to be effective, is as much process and preparation for the unexpected as it is prescription for the predictable.

Catastrophe, Turbulence, and Opportunity

This is a turbulent era. Vast changes are taking place in the world around us at an astonishing rate. The economy, and the businesses that compete within it, are globalizing at an accelerating rate. International airline travel and modern infrastructure have made it easy and increasingly affordable to travel within a country and even to circle the globe in a few hours. Computers, and the systems that connect them, are rapidly redefining the way in which we work, purchase, communicate, and even socialize. The Old World order is making way for the new in a turbulent flow of catastrophic change, evolution, and transformation.

In turbulence, there are great opportunities. At the outset of the Asian crisis, pundits often mentioned the fact that the two Chinese characters that make up the ideograph for the concept of crisis—*Wei Ji*—are separate characters which, individually, mean danger and opportunity. In every crisis, there are harmful changes or events transpiring. In every crisis, there are also unprecedented opportunities.

Detailed management studies show that in every period of turbulence, there are new opportunities for leadership. In an era of turbulence, there are constant opportunities to redefine goals and set new strategies for positive change. Turbulence and discontinuity provide opportunities to accelerate and shape positive change in all operating environments. Good strategy in turbulence addresseses both risk and opportunity on an integrated basis.

Response Capability Not Keeping Pace

As risk accelerates across global systems, corresponding monitoring and response mechanisms have not kept pace. Opportunities are missed. Given the failure of existing strategies, turbulence and evolution have created more danger than apparent opportunity in most areas of societal challenge.

The drug trade continues to grow through shifting sources and channels of distribution around the world with no international police force or co-ordinated approach capable of turning back its universal presence. Other criminal activities such as money laundering and the distribution of pedophilia spread across the world, fueled by the unmonitored growth of electronic communication systems and the Internet. The degradation of our environment continues unpoliced and the effects of failed policy travel around the globe, fall as acid rain, are inhaled in a dangerous haze, and reflected in a perforated ozone layer.

Species critical to the balance of the delicate biosphere are disappearing at an accelerating rate, with no official tally or effective response to counter the wave of irreversible extinction.

Risk compounds as problematic systems intersect. Sometimes the response merely magnifies the problem. Hemorrhagic fevers like Ebola are distributed by the systemic poverty—the have-not factor in economic disparity—and resulting lack of quality health care systems in Africa. Victims of some fatal diseases are actually more likely to be infected by needles reused by well-intentioned staff in impoverished hospitals than by contact with the disease outside of the hospital environment.

To date, we have not developed an offsetting capacity to identify and respond to most of the newly globalizing and escalating risks we have created for ourselves. Opportunities for improved responses are not realized. The recent crisis that hit emerging markets, and which began in Thailand, famously demonstrated that "there are no firewalls in the global economy." It also demonstrated that there were no smoke sensors, no fire alarms and, unfortunately, no firemen capable of putting out the fire.

Gaps in the Global Architecture

The major sources of risk in the new century will be global problems like these, where there is as yet no adequate global capability to respond. By the nature of the problems, no nation on its own can act effectively to resolve them. Ad hoc co-ordination of response between a collection of nation states is extremely difficult to organize in the middle of a crisis, and even more difficult when multiple crises are unfolding. Existing international institutions and intranational models of co-operation are often not up to the task of crisis management or problem resolution.

The International Monetary Fund (IMF) obviously failed to respond effectively to the Asian crisis and to prevent the crisis from spreading beyond the borders of the region. Other national, international, and regional organizations proved similarly unsuccessful in preventing fragile economies from tumbling into deep and painful recessions.

The same pattern of new systemic global challenge and an insufficient capacity to respond can be seen in critical area after critical area. A great part of the problem is due to gaps in the global architecture—structural gaps in the institutional approach to risk reduction and implementation of effective response capability. The decline of the power of the nation state relative to global challenges has yet to be balanced by a rise in our transnational capability to respond.

In the wake of a crisis or in the absence of a high profile event that focuses public attention, political will ebbs, media concern fades, and needed change moves quietly off the agenda.

The US, as the last remaining superpower, can, in some cases, act as a *de facto* international institution of last resort. But, this rests upon the continuing goodwill of the American taxpayer (which is far from assured), a direct interest by the US (which was absent in the recent environmental crisis in Asia), and an ability of the US to muster international support for its leadership efforts where it cannot act alone (which, again, is often far from assured). Although not a universal solution to global challenges, US leadership, focus, and action can provide a powerful contribution to resolving global problems.

Three Fundamental Weaknesses

The lack of responsive capability at a global level can be attributed to a number of interrelated failures in the foundation of our global architecture. The first is the failure of established international institutions to have an impact on the risk event once realized, or even to identify the true probability of a major risk event actually occurring. This was true in the recent economic crises of the emerging markets. This is also the case of, for example, Interpol in the criminal arena. The drug trade has flourished for decades, with little effective interdiction or suppression. The same is tue for money laundering.

The second is weakness in the intranational model of co-operation. Asean's impotence in the face of the economic crisis and the haze, arising from the Indonesian forest fires, is a stark reminder of the inability of a high profile co-operative forum to resolve critical problems created by recalcitrant member states. Asean has stepped up its criticism of uncontrolled clearance burning, but little progress was seen over two years as new "hot spots" blossomed every summer on the region's maps, and air quality deteriorated on a cyclical basis.

A Pollution Standard Index (PSI), which reduces a compound formula of eight noxious elements to a single consolidated number, became as common in Asian conversation as the temperature. Slipping quickly into the daily vocabulary of residents in Southeast Asia in particular, the PSI reflects how easily satisfactory underperformance can be accepted even when accurately measured and communicated. A similar lack of impact could be ascribed to the G7, G24, and other international cornerstones of the global architecture during the financial crises.

A third failure results from the lack of any institution of relevance at all. This would be the chief characteristic of the environmental area, for example, where there is no effective court for environmental issues or alternative responsive mechanism. There is thus no one to react to reduce the harm caused as airborne or waterborne pollutants drift across borders and into the vast and interconnected ecosystem of our world.

In critical periods of environmental challenge, there was no proliferation of unco-ordinated and ineffective institutions falling over themselves to offer conflicting advice, dangerous guidance, or inadequate funding. There was no US to step in and act in lieu of an appropriate international institution to prop up the world economy. Here, there is no relevant international agency or forum with a capability to respond to international environmental crises at all. The lack of any international institutional capability leads each nation to pursue its own remedies, prolonging and deepening crises. The annual reappearance of the haze in Southeast Asia only underscores the need for a fundamental review of the practices and powers of international bodies in the area of cross-border environmental management.

Some of the foundation stones of our global architecture are flawed; the cement that joins others together is weak, and some critical elements are missing altogether. The potential for strengthening, binding together, and filling in the gaps is obvious. Over time, continued weakness and erosion in the strength of this foundation, relative to the stresses placed upon it, could result in a wholesale collapse of systems and structures that need to rest on firmer foundations in order to withstand the storms and strains of modern development.

The Cost of Satisfactory Underperformance

In a business situation, results to date in the areas of the environment, disease, crime, decultralization, economic disparity, and other critical societal challenges would clearly fall into the dangerous category of *satisfactory underperformance.*

Satisfactory underperformance results from a set of measures showing satisfactory results relative only to past unsatisfactory performance or relative to performance benchmarked against equally underperforming alternatives. Satisfactory underperformance is most frequently present in the absence of an immediate crisis that can draw out the best from individuals and groups affected by more highly charged events.

In times of crisis, men and women can reach new levels of collective will and performance. But, if we wait for risks to become real in the areas of greatest threat before we engage our best response capabilities, it will be, for many of us, too late. Costs, like risks, can escalate on an exponential basis.

Risk carries with it potential cost. Realized catastrophes generate very real and painful costs and consequences. The resulting costs of undermanaged risk and satisfactory underperformance are human as well as economic, and long term as well as immediate.

Avoiding or suppressing the risk of crises is far less painful and costly than resolving conflict once forces have spun out of control or even engaged in battle. As Sun Tzu says, true victory in the art of war and in superior strategy results in obviating battles and conflict, not winning them. The best victories are from battles that never had to be fought. The cost of satisfactory underperformance may best be addressed through effective strategy and proactive initiatives, not through responsive investment once a risk has become a costly reality.

Loss of Faith in the Old Holy Trinity—Church, Family, and State

The globalization phenomenon has not just created specific problems and increasing risk in the "hard" areas of the environment, crime, the economy, disease, and terrorism. It has brought with it systematic erosion in the emotional, cultural, and spiritual foundations of our lives as well. Around the world today, we can see a visible decline in sustaining values and an unmet need to believe in something greater than ourselves. A sense of isolation, a lack of a larger purpose, and a dissatisfaction with material life—whether affluent or impoverished—is causing millions of individuals to look afresh at the spiritual foundation of their lives.

Solutions are less and less available through traditional channels and institutions. The rise of cults, fundamentalism (Christian, Jewish, Hindu and Islamic) and even of militant fundamentalism is the inevitable response to a lack of sustaining cultural, spiritual and individual values. By failing to move forward in a sustainable manner, the disaffected are forced to look backward to find usable systems of values, belief and meaning upon which they can build their lives.

Partially as a result, the nuclear and extended family structures, which supported our development as individuals and as collective communities for centuries, are breaking down rapidly across many countries and cultures. Divorce is rising. Single parenthood is becoming a fashionable lifestyle. The extended family as a meaningful social unit is dissolving in many countries. Most children in developed countries no longer grow up in a multi-generational environment. Families and communities dissolve and reform constantly.

The quality of the emotional and spiritual education of our children is declining from an already low base. Attendance at traditional religious establishments and belief in their value is in secular decline. Only one in 50 visitors to the Notre Dame cathedral in Paris now goes in to pray. Less than 4 per cent of Parisians regularly attended church in 1998. As for the English population, *Newsweek* magazine reports that 99 per cent did not attend the Church of England regularly in 1999. The drop in attendance over the last 10 years in England reflects the sharpest decline since the formation of the Church in the 16th century.

The lack of a sustainable social and religious institutional model is not confined to Western nations. Many of the same issues in some form or other are present in the East. The iron rice bowl continues to turn up empty in the search for spiritual nourishment.

The rise of over 10,000 cults in China and the surprising power of the Falungong movement are only two of many reflections of a lost set of moral bearings in this ancient and complex country. The same sense of unmet deeper need in China is driving a search for spirituality outside the secular state mechanisms and away from a limiting set of approved religious institutions. Resurgence in old religious and spiritual traditions, from ancestor worship to village gods to *feng shui* geomancers, has not only spread across China, but even begun to make incursions into Western consciousness as well.

In a world of volatility and spiraling risk, we are no longer able to take refuge in the arms of institutions that once made us feel safe. An increasingly marginalized church, or its equivalent in other religions, collapsing family structures, and an increasingly impotent and/or indifferent sovereign state are no longer capable of solving the most vexing issues we face. They no longer can protect us from the fears that inevitably arise from the risks inherent in a system of crumbling and weakening foundations.

The loss of faith in the family, traditional religion, associated values, and the state has not been replaced by anything tangible to give us a sense of security, purpose, belonging, or transcendence. This new set of unmastered global risks has now filtered into the spiritual side of our existence as well as our professional and personal lives.

Valuing Risk, Investing in Opportunity

Although many of the risks and opportunities set out here are difficult to quantify with precision, the allocation of resources between them, implicit or explicit, reflects our valuation of each very clearly. This allocation of scarce resources also reflects our overall values as a country or as individuals, as real world actions indeed speak louder than words.

Today's spending of hundreds of billions of dollars on military weaponry while the UN cannot raise the $500 million it needs to eradicate polio through a global vaccination program is a clear statement on societal priorities. According to UN Secretary General Kofi Annan, Europe's annual $40-billion expenditure on cigarettes would provide the world's poor with clean water, sufficient nutrition, and a basic education. The large amounts we spend on prisons, compared to the smaller amounts on improvements in schooling and policing in troubled neighbourhoods indicate where our priorities truly lie.

How we price risk, how we invest in opportunities, and how we determine the trade offs between them reflect the true sense of our collective values and societal priorities.

Reviewing our real collective priorities (to be expressed in actions, not words) and resetting our allocation of resources between them can begin to address risk and opportunity on a proper strategic foundation.

Opportunity for Improved Global Risk Management

As we assess our capacity to respond (or not) to new threats and opportunities, we are forced to the realization that existing approaches to risk management are increasingly impotent in the face of the new complex nature and escalating scale of global risk.

We need to understand far better the changing and systemic nature of risk—and to put in place a new approach that minimizes the threat and improves our capability to respond. Minimizing the threat will require an approach to diminish the potential impact of the harm and to put in place an approach to decrease the likelihood of the harm occurring. Improving our response to real threats will require an improved capability to respond and an increased likelihood that response will be deployed.

Capturing global opportunities to offset risk will require an improved focus and capability along all four elements of the opportunity calculus as well.

Although we are living in an era of turbulence, risk, and volatility, we are also living in an era of great opportunity. Many of the challenges posed by the evolution of this new paradigm of globalizing risk and challenge have already been mastered by international businesses.

Reducing risk, capturing opportunities and mastering dynamic systems behavior will require a new approach to strategy. A state-of-the-art model of global strategy, which achieves both of these objectives, is, in fact, available.

Next Generation Strategy

The cutting-edge model of global business strategy—elaborated as Next Generation Strategy—contains the elements of improved solutions to many global challenges. A transfer of knowledge and relevant best practices from the world of international business could provide a practical guide to the development of an effective strategic response in areas outside of the business sphere as well.

The most successful global companies increasingly use a similar approach to the determination and execution of strategy. Companies that have gone through turnarounds and those that consistently outperform competitors often follow a similar approach to the definition and execution of a global strategic program. From decades of intensive (and expensive) learning in the business world, a reliable model of global best practice in international strategy has emerged. Adherence to this set of proven principles can now provide a useful architecture for the crafting of effective transnational solutions beyond business strategy.

At an institutional level, the application of a state-of-the-art strategic approach could well provide substantial progress toward the development of a truly effective global architecture. The elusive concept of a new global architecture has been often mooted and never, as yet, defined. The definition of an appropriate institutional structure to drive positive change and to realize new visions is an integral part of Next Generation Strategy.

The approach and content of state-of-the-art strategy brings a focus and intensity of effort in areas most relevant to the design and generation of an effective structure for change. Next Generation Strategy can guide the development of a truly effective global architecture that can master complex systemic challenge, reduce risk, capture opportunity, and make satisfactory underperformance a relic of an unsatisfactory past.

Positive Results are Possible

Time after time we have shown that we are indeed capable of uniting to address clear and present dangers on an effective and co-ordinated basis. The coalition response to Iraq's invasion of Kuwait, the dramatic decline in chlorofluorocarbon (CFC) usage, the near-complete eradication of polio and smallpox, and the containment of Ebola and other hemorrhagic fevers on numerous occasions, have shown the depth of our collective capability when faced with urgent challenges.

The challenge we face now is learning from past successes and failures, and from these lessons, prepare ourselves to avoid or respond to tomorrow's crises. Satisfactory underperformance and lack of readiness may result in catastrophes and disasters that could well have been avoided.

Superior performance in the future is not out of the realm of possibility. After all, we created many of these problems ourselves. We have learned much on how to manage the creatures of our own invention. We have the tools, the models, and the resources to drive effective change. Our challenge now is more of a challenge of vision and strategy, than of possibility. It is a challenge of leadership, values, priorities, and organization. It is, at its root, a challenge simply of our individual and collective will.

The Structure of Next Generation Strategy

The objective of Next Generation Strategy is to master the full set of risks, opportunities, dynamic systems characteristics, and human elements that make up a global enterprise. It is a comprehensive approach, driven by best global practices, aimed at achieving the full potential of a given enterprise, including global human endeavors.

Although it is important to retain the concept of an integrated and comprehensive approach, a global strategy can also be unbundled into its full set of constituent elements to improve current understanding and inform future action. The most effective strategies can be disaggregated to reveal four interlocking components.

Each of these four major elements comprises three supporting elements that can be separated for dissection and analysis. But these elements can only be fully understood in the context of a fully integrated and functioning anatomy of the whole.

1. *The Visionary Element*

The visionary element of strategy comprises an inspiring future view of the enterprise, drives a higher level of excellence in performance, and provides leadership that captures the hearts and minds of the individuals and teams involved. Often, the most powerful visionary content is driven by a new concept of what is possible, breaking away from the past and setting new standards in a given industry or defined area of competition. Visionary content takes into account the resources, creativity, skills and capabilities of individuals and teams, and maximizes the use of physical, financial and intellectual capital of the collective enterprise.

A natural outcome from this first element of strategy is a vision statement that transforms initiative and activity into a united supporting effort to achieve the greater goal.

2. *The Approach to Strategy*

The element of approach to strategy comprises a diagnostic phase, a design phase, and an implementation phase. The imperatives of the design phase, for example, are directly relevant to an improved response to the major global challenges outside of the business world as well as to the commercial sphere, namely:

- leading or actively managing institutional restructuring
- increasing focus on the true drivers of results (i.e. the most important contributors to results) to achieve new standards of operating excellence
- implementing new measures, and systems of value and reward
- structuring the most effective model of organization, developing an integrated strategic design, and aligning all aspects of the operating system to implement the chosen strategies effectively and efficiently.

This design element is preceded by a new diagnostic model and given life by a full model of effective implementation.

The final stage of the design phase translates the vision and supporting actions into a concrete plan of action. This is implemented in the market and supported by all elements of the business system.

3.   *The Content of Strategy*

The content of strategy consists of a net risk element, a net opportunity element and an element, of systemic management. The net risk element captures the threats to achieving a vision, and sets out potential responses to reduce the impact of realized risk. The net opportunity element identifies positive initiatives toward realizing the vision and capturing the full potential of a defined system. A systemic understanding captures the complex, dynamic and interrelated nature of challenge. This can be positive, negative, or neutral within the parameters of a defined system. It is important that these initiatives are not limited by past models of understanding or past levels of performance. All elements need to be looked at afresh, and strategic management needs to be adjusted to take into account the true potential of a clearly perceived situation of systemic behavior and associated risks and opportunities.

The natural output of the content of strategy is a list of priorities— the highest value actions, initiatives, and investments that can drive most effectively and efficiently toward the achievement of the vision of the enterprise.

4.   *The Human Element*

The human element is often neglected, yet critical, in the strategic mix. Three core areas need to be addressed on an integrated basis above and beyond the vision, the approach, and the content of strategy. To be fully successful, a strategy needs to address the deeper nature and needs of the individuals engaged in the effort specifically. The three core areas are:

- capability, comprising the resources, creativity, and skills of the individuals and teams within an organization
- internal practices to develop and exploit the intellectual capital of the staff and teams of the collective enterprise
- motivation of individuals and teams, which is essential for full performance; the highest levels of performance require engaging the whole of the persons involved in order to capture the full potential of the enterprise.

Any effective approach to strategy must include all of these four elements on a properly phased and integrated basis. The full potential of the whole can only be captured by an approach that captures full potential at every step.

The New Characteristics of Global Strategy

The evolution and flow of global systems have now changed the nature and content of good strategy. The more complex nature of problems and their larger scale have raised the level of strategic demands. Past generations of static models, uninspiring visions, and fragmented approaches are no longer sufficient to master the complex and dynamic challenges of this new era. A new model of strategy is required to take advantage of rapid changes in the environment. This will help us understand the increasingly interconnected nature of enterprises and operating systems and master a new set of risks and opportunities.

The key characteristics that separate the new model from past models are that it is more comprehensive, more flexible, more integrative, more motivating, more creative, and most importantly, more effective.

More Comprehensive

Strategy now needs to understand dynamic systems behavior, risk, opportunity, and a fuller human dimension. Strategy is now as much about capability, knowledge, skills, teamwork, communication, influence, and motivation, as it is about market share and simple capital investment.

More Flexible

The business landscape is littered with the carcasses of dinosaurs that were unable to adapt to a new world of risk, opportunity, and rapid changes. Linear change is more accelerated; non-linear shifts appear abruptly and unexpectedly. The global strategic world is now more than ever a world of the quick and the dead.

Turbulence has often replaced stability as the operative environmental characteristic. Strategies need to be able to keep pace with or even to drive rapid and unexpected change. To respond to this challenge, leaders will have to address issues of capability and resource as well as structure and systems in the future.

One leading European software company, whose products institutionalize a pre-set approach to business management, has been recently described to be "pouring concrete around the pilings of an outdated business model." Constant vigilance at all levels of the business system will ensure that enterprises do not suffer from hardening of the arteries or inflexibility in the operating model.

More Integrative

Although the elements of strategy can be isolated and analyzed separately, they should be consolidated and integrated into a single model in order to be most effective. The whole must be worth more than the sum of the parts. Resources and initiatives should be integrated with a full understanding of changes in the industry or regulatory structure. A program to enhance capabilities needs to be integrated with a future view of the relevant systems of risk and opportunity that will have the greatest impact on the organization.

Elements of diagnosis, design, implementation, skills development, resource allocation, and motivation need to be consolidated into one indivisible whole.

Meanwhile, vision, strategy, and tactics need to be reviewed to be coordinated, integrated, and aligned in a unified approach to achieve full potential in the real world.

More Motivating

The old model of an hour's labor for an hour's pay is no longer sufficient to retain employees or to inspire them to achieve their own full potential. Leadership now has to engage individuals on a deeper level. The motivation of teams and organization requires a demonstration of a different set of values from the past and the mastery of a more complex set of challenges and opportunities in the future. In a more individualistic world, leadership must respond more to individual needs and aspirations in order to inspire stakeholders to rise to the challenge of achievement of the full potential of the collective whole.

More Creative

Many old strategies suffer from a "me too" syndrome, an uninspiring replication of past practices and results and/or an encumbering protection of old business models. Fresh and creative approaches to mastering risk are highly valued. An original view of relevant structures—internal and external—and a plan to create a better order are required to develop and implement more inspirational visions of the future.

More Effective

Businesses and other global enterprises often fail to live up to expectations or to achieve full potential. Strategies are only valuable in so far as they create value in the real world. The full measure of a new approach to strategy is whether that approach is more effective than alternative models—whether the results achieved are greater than in the past, and whether the investment in achieving these results is justified by the return.

Results, Results, Results

It is striking that not one of the traditional models of strategy—3Cs, 7Ss, and others—described later in this book, contain the key R word—results. Traditional models are all about inputs and elements of design. Little attention is paid to output, action, implementation, and results. Good strategy forms the bridge from an aspirational vision to effective action in the real world. No more, no less. Many old models of strategy focused solely on the design of the bridge and so paid scant attention to a stretching set of goals and targeted results, which made the whole exercise meaningful in the first place.

Monday Morning at 8am

For a strategy to be effective, it must set out a concrete program of change that begins with a different set of supporting actions. In the business world, the operative question is whether it is clear to all participants what they need to do differently on Monday morning when they come to work. If it is not clear what they need to do, or need to do differently, then the strategy process has either been incomplete or incorrect. Good strategy and effective action go hand in hand.

No Easy Answers or Solutions

Implementing any global strategy or solution is never easy in today's world. One part of this book is dedicated to debunking the myths of single-shot strategies, i.e. strategies that can be neatly captured in a word or theme, but do not lead to capturing the full potential of a single business unit or corporate whole. Adherence to a theme in lieu of a strategy will inevitably lead to a state of satisfactory underperformance— achievement of goals that understate the true potential of a business or limit the opportunity for effective change. Similarly, acceptance of the status quo approach in a situation of clear underperformance leads to an untenable outcome.

There is no simple answer to complex global problems. Nor is there any single analytical approach that can yield the correct answers or anticipate every event.

We cannot know all of the future no matter how good our forecasting. All we can do is respond to the known and be prepared for the unexpected. Preparation for the unknown element of the future is much about building capabilities to set and reset responses once unforecast events unfold.

In addition to making educated guesses, future strategy is about capabilities as well as content. It is as much about a continual building process as it is about a set plan of action. The best models of strategy are flexible and adaptable and respect the ever changing nature of systems, the flow of events, and inevitable change in the operating environment.

Creativity, Intuition, and Understanding

Traditional mechanical strategic planning processes can often lead to inadequate solutions, or navigate quickly to the lowest common denominator rather than to higher levels of understanding and achievement. One of the reasons so few businesses break out of the box of satisfactory underperformance is that their entire approach to operations and strategy is limiting, rather than liberating. Many flawed strategic processes never even address the human element or support the exploration for alternative ideas. The capabilities and inspiration of individuals and the group as a whole are often only given a passing mention, and valuable sources of ideas and initiatives are never allowed to flourish. It is the risks, rather than rewards, for creative efforts that are highlighted in most business cultures.

In the next generation, and in Next Generation Strategy, we will need to nurture, value, and manage intuition and creativity as never before. Experimentation will have to be encouraged. Some failure will need to be tolerated. Even the most brilliant of scientists proceed, in most part, by trial and error. There is no example of any enterprise achieving the highest level of performance solely on an expectation of trial and success.

Much of creativity is, in fact, free thought inspired by different perspectives. It often results from a different way of seeing things leading to a different form of description, expression or action. That moment of creative inspiration—the moment when a fresh perspective or unprecedented work is born—can lead to new levels of understanding, application and results. The exercise of the creative faculty, linked to

intuition and inspiration can emerge from many sources. Rational linear
thought alone is not always the chief source of inspired, ground-breaking
insights or results. In capturing the leading edge of advantage, creative
thought has become even more important and ever more valuable.

New insights, understanding, ideas, and approaches will create
differentiated performances in the real world. They will increasingly
become key success factors in the competitive business environment and
in the improvement of societal conditions. Effective strategies will need
to reflect the value of fresh insights on a greater basis in the future.

Old Problems, New Paradigms

Although the challenges of mastering a complex business system and the
difficulties of managing the most appropriate response to disease or the
drug problem appear light years apart, the modern world has brought
them much closer together.

There is now a set of visibly recurring patterns that underpins many
similar strategic problems in different disciplines. Old problems reflect a
set of new paradigms.

The standard pattern of global crisis now usually unfolds as follows:

- a national disaster or recurring problem emerges with
  international or cross-border implications
- an ineffective national response is made
- an inadequate or non-existent international response follows
- confusion arises since there are no clear metrics to monitor either
  crisis or recovery
- insufficient resources are made available and political will falters
- there is no agreed plan, so implementation progress stalls or
  fades away
- leadership is distracted as the crisis loses its headline intensity
- the usual unsatisfactory *status quo ante* is resumed

The common element in the pattern is the role played by rapid
evolution in global channels of delivery and distribution, and by shared
characteristics of dynamic global systems. The elements of risk,
opportunity and dynamic systems behavior are common to all. As the
pattern and systemic content share many elements, the solutions can also
rely extensively on the same proven approach to the development of
strategy.

Universal Application of Strategy

Although the fully elaborated model of Next Generation Strategy is best articulated in the business world, the key elements of strategy are applicable to non-commercial areas of global challenge as well. The same approach, which can overcome satisfactory underperformance in the business world, can be applied beyond its borders as well. The integrated approach to vision, strategy, leadership, and capability can be applied to critical societal issues as well and could contribute to a significant improvement in the state of global affairs. In each area of complex strategy, there is a common set of needs.

Vision

Vision is the aspiration of the leadership and the enterprise as a whole. It is qualitative as well as quantitative. Vision is a long-term objective that is translated into results through effective strategy, tactics, and execution.

Management of Risk

Systems of risk are complex and dynamic entities that can be disassembled, analyzed, understood and, in most cases, managed. Risk and opportunity can be quantified. Investments in the management of both can be specified, and return on investment forecast, calculated, and audited. The systems underlying net risks and opportunities are in constant flux and evolution. Risk and opportunity, however, have recurring patterns, and are governed by understandable laws of dynamic systems behavior. By better understanding the nature and behavior of dynamic systems, and by constantly readjusting choices and investment decisions to reduce risk and take advantage of opportunity, scarce resources can constantly be applied to the highest priorities. Strategic investment is governed by priorities to drive systemic behavior through careful allocation between opportunities to protect against the negative while building on the positive. The most effective strategies address both positive and negative initiatives with a long-term view in mind.

Effective Structures and Enabling Architectures

These are structures by which situations are monitored and change is made. They are both internal to an enterprise—the legal, organizational, business unit, and asset structures in a global business system—and external. The external components are made up of regulatory, supervisory and collective organizations, and entities that can create, or prevent, constructive change. The combination of the two—internal and external structures—creates an enabling architecture. Through this architecture and respecting the principles of its design and operation, effective strategies can be developed and implemented.

US President Bill Clinton spoke often of "gaps in the global architecture" during the economic crises of emerging markets during 1997 and 1998. This is an accurate description of the structural model of global management. This insight can provide the platform to launch a program of constructive change in the structural, or institutional model, of governance in the many of the most critical challenges of our time.

Organizational Capability

Organizational capability is made up of individual skills, group assets, organizational efficiency, cultures and affiliations, limits on action and capacity to respond to risks, and opportunities now and in the future. Capability is increasingly at the heart of strategy. The ability of individuals, teams, and whole organizations to create results and realize visions is one of the irreducible elements of strategy. As complex and dynamic systems present an ever-changing list of priority risks and opportunities, an organization's ability to master these priorities and the systems underlying them will be a critical element in the design and implementation of successful strategy.

Resources

Prioritized resource allocations will alter the actions taken on the relevant set of risks and opportunities. The level and allocation of responses is inextricably intertwined with the element of capability, and will focus and guide the deployment of that capability on a prioritized basis. The allocation of scarce resources among competing claims will set the balance of action between them. The allocation of resources will be guided by the overall vision, and should lead to the achievement of results on the most effective and efficient basis.

The principles of that allocation, explicit or implicit, will reflect both the value system and the true objectives of the enterprise.

Leadership

Leadership influences all elements of strategy, yet goes beyond vision, structure, action plans, and capability. The best leaders get the best results through connecting with something deeper, more personal and more human, which engages the whole of the individual in the purpose and objectives of the enterprise.

Now more than ever, leadership is about engaging the whole of the person—the heart, the mind and the soul—in a fully integrated effort to achieve the full potential inherent in a collective strategic challenge and to achieve the full potential of the individuals engaged in that effort. Not every effort will inspire the full engagement of human will and individual effort, but the greater the engagement at an individual level, the better the collective results will be.

Results

Achieving results needs to be an integral part of strategy. Severing results from the other elements of strategy will sharply reduce the likelihood of their achievement. All elements of the new model of strategy need to lead to the achievement of tangible results. Each element of strategy—vision, systems of risk, enabling architecture, capability, resources, and leadership should be assessed against the results they create.

Strategy forms the bridge between vision and results. A failure to achieve results or to realize a vision is a true failure of the active strategic engagement. A successful strategic program, fully elaborated, can be measured in the reduction of risk, in the realization of opportunity, in the mastery of complex systems, and in a strengthened capability to respond to future risks—known and unknown.

Strategic Challenges for the 21st Century

As we step into the 21st century, a number of strategic societal priorities have yet to be fully and effectively addressed. Each of the nine areas highlighted below represents an issue where our strategic approach to date has generated unsatisfactory results. Net risk assessments are increasingly negative. Salient systemic characteristics have yet to be mastered. Response capability has lagged behind the escalating risks.

Strategies to date are far from achieving full potential results or realizing an aspirational vision for each area of challenge.

1. The Environment: The sources of pollution and environmental damage are multiplying, and the scale of this problem is rising at an accelerating rate. Global warming, acid rain, holes in the ozone layer, depleted biodiversity, deforestation, and other global problems go unaddressed. Although the Rio Convention and the Kyoto Accord have generated publicity and some progress, they have achieved far from satisfactory results in almost every area of environmental management. The UN now predicts a shortage of fresh water in 20 years—the beginning of a long list of inevitable future crises as the destructive behavior of the past creates a future of increasing shortage and accelerating risk of systemic crises.

Despite a general awareness of environmental issues, the overall situation is degrading rapidly, and today's state of underperformance is worsening rather than improving, or even stabilizing. Standards and target control measures are, on the whole, neither agreed nor implemented. Industrialization, population growth, urbanization, economic growth, and inadequate control capabilities have all contributed to new levels of concern in this area. The unbundling of multinational companies and relocation of production facilities to low-cost countries have transferred some of the environmental risk to less environmentally sensitive developing nations at a rapid rate, making monitoring and rectification even more difficult.

Nature's global distribution systems—the trade winds, streams, rivers, and seemingly unlimited oceans—have been with us forever but are rapidly becoming established conduits of chlorinated hydrocarbons, sulphurous and other noxious compounds, and other harmful content. Abilities to stem the distribution of environmental pollutants, particularly those released into the oceans or the atmosphere, are limited. As an increase in the global population from 5 billion in 1990 to 9 billion by the middle of the next century seems possible, and with over half of the world's population living in poverty, and striving for higher levels of wealth and consumption, unmanaged pressures on the global ecosystem may reach a breaking point early in the new century.

2. *Crime*: Although the majority of crime is of a local disorganized nature, organized international networks distribute drugs and illegal arms, manage prostitution, corrupt officials, distribute pornography, and launder money through a set of highly sophisticated global networks. Criminal organizations have taken advantage of virtually all aspects of global distribution channel development. Drugs travel the world in ships, aircraft, and even through the post. Money laundering is expedited by interbank electronic transfer systems and protected by secrecy laws in offshore tax havens. Pornography and pedophilia are readily available on the Internet, to be downloaded easily using modern telecommunication technologies. The content of these and other criminal activities have not changed dramatically over recent years, but the distribution capabilities have changed the magnitude of the problem.

Interpol and other co-operative cross-border police organizations, and preventive initiatives, have not made much progress as modern criminal organizations have grown across the globe, increasing in complexity, wealth, and power. The US Drug Enforcement Agency (DEA), Federal Bureau of Investigation (FBI), and other national organizations that attempt to project their capabilities across borders, have had little effect on the overall scale of the problem.

3. *Terrorism*:   Although related to the issues of crime, terrorism is characterized by substantively different roots, motivations, and behaviors. State sponsorship of terrorism and the political nature of the objectives of terrorism change the nature of the problem, and hence, the required solution. The next generation of terrorist attacks is already brewing—with cyber-capabilities, and biological, chemical, and even nuclear weapons of mass destruction. These risks are becoming real within the borders of hitherto safe countries. Even the US is no longer a safe haven from foreign or local terrorists. As the threats, risks and scale of potential harm increase, the transnational policing and response mechanisms remain at low historic levels. The UN and other international organizations have not been able to do enough to drive collective responses to terrorism. Similarly, the extra-territorial projection of judicial systems and US policing has done little to limit the operations of terrorist Osama bin Laden and other terrorist groups. The rise of religious fanaticism, ironically, has increased the lethality of terrorist events. The vulnerability of large government and civilian buildings and even military targets has also contributed to an increase in the scale of potential harm. The rising risks in the future from attacks on even larger targets with more powerful weapons of mass destruction are obvious, as is the need for more effective response.

4. *Disease*:   From the fatal global peregrinations of Patient Zero to the unfolding tragedy in the developing world, AIDS has demonstrated that the global response to a life-threatening disease exhibits the same behavioral characteristics as the ineffective response to environmental, economic and sociological threats set out elsewhere. Unchecked by an initial response that could best be compared to the response to leprosy in the past century, AIDS continues to spread through Africa, Asia and the rest of the world. AIDS is not the only global concern in the area of disease and infection—resurgent influenza, increasingly drug resistant tuberculosis or a virulent and more enduring cousin to the Ebola virus could be the next unchecked epidemic that will not settle so quietly in the underprivileged parts of the world. The Centres for Disease Control (CDC) in Atlanta and related global organizations have been successful so far in containing outbreaks of particularly virulent strains of infection and disease. But its track record may be tested by less controllable viruses in the future. As the Nipah virus epidemic in Malaysia showed, even world-class capabilities in medical response may be worthless if local politics and dithering delay deployment of that capability. Over 100 deaths were recorded in Malaysia from a pair of fatal and complex viruses—and the authorities in Kuala Lumpur waited six months before calling in global experts.

5. *Economic Disparity and the Emergence of a Global Underclass*: According to medical experts, denizens of the poorer quarters in Paris now have more in common with the residents of the South Bronx, 4,000 miles away, than they do with their elegant compatriots a few kilometers away in the 16th *arrondissement*. Drugs, AIDS, malnutrition, violent crime, poor education, racial discrimination, and the deterioration of the nuclear family, with its attendant social and mental health problems are common problems shared among the underprivileged in all major capital cities of the world. Similarly, an international privileged elite is emerging, with their identifiable shared affluent behaviors, as seen from their jobs, attitudes, international purchasing habits, travel, dress, and a whole range of lifestyle attributes.

The obvious risk of a global privileged class living alongside a global underclass within a single society brings the potential for explosion between the two. The resulting social and economic damage could be extensive. Catastrophes are easy to foresee. Triggered by an economic recession or other event that widens or increases the sensitivity to this gap, a violent future attack on the rich by the poor is far from impossible.

At a wider level, three billion people, half of the world's population, live on $3 per day or less. The gap between the haves and the have-nots is widening and will, eventually be unsustainable. Often perceived as a local problem, the similarity around the world of the problem of economic disparity creates an opportunity for a shared resolution once the common nature of the problem is recognized.

It is obviously far more effective to pursue a strategy to narrow the gap and reduce the potential for a dangerous social short circuit than to attempt to respond effectively to pent up emotions and resentment once they are released in the form of violent antisocial behavior at any level.

6. *Deculturalization*:   Culture is the link to the place where we come from. It defines, in great part, who we are. It gives us a sense of uniqueness, of history, and of difference. It also provides the framework of values according to which we lead our lives. A range of cultures makes the world a more interesting place and a richer environment in which to explore who and what we are, and to redefine who and what we can be. Cultures and traditions keep families together, and ensure that children receive the wise lessons of older generations—lessons that have endured for centuries. However, global distribution systems are increasingly creating a global similarity in dress, behavior, hair styles, ideals of beauty and appearance, musical tastes, cuisine, and aspirations. A continuing and measured process of deculturalization is leading generations successfully toward the lowest common denominator of international culture, at a cost of declining local values and connections. Although cultural evolution is an inexorable sociological phenomenon, cultural preservation can be a complementary, rather than conflicting, initiative.

Unfortunately, the international organizations and initiatives with the greatest potential impact in this area—General Agreement on Trade and Tariffs (GATT), WTO, and others—are actually accelerating the deculturalization process, without pursuing a more thoughtful strategy to protect the cultural differences that make our world a rich source of diverse experience.

7. *Technology and the Cyberworld*:   Various aspects of applied technology in the areas of materials, medicine, food production, aviation, the media, military weapons, transportation and countless other areas have contributed to a new age of technology. Among these, the rise of the cyberworld stands out as a source of universal change and also as a new source of risk and opportunity. The increase in computing power coupled with an explosion in interconnection and low-cost communication options, have created a whole new set of opportunities and risks in the cyberworld. Primarily an American phenomenon of the past decade, Europe and Asia are rapidly joining the growing reach of the Internet, the Web, and other aspects of the computer age. The ever more powerful and portable personal computer (PC) is changing the way we work, learn, shop, communicate, and even think. The systems underlying this phenomenon—hardware, software, telecommunications, graphics, training, servicing, upgrading, and learning—are evolving and expanding at extraordinary speed. With the boom in Internet stocks such as amazon.com, buy.com, e-Bay, and others, capital markets have also been influenced by the impact of information technology and its applications to almost every aspect of modern life.

So far, the development of a cyberworld has been relatively benign. But this will not last. To date, we lack the relevant tools and techniques to monitor and respond to the abuses in the cyberworld. This, too, will not last. As in so many other areas, only a crisis or catastrophe of significant proportion will draw sufficient attention to the potential risks, thus driving action and the creation of an effective responsive force. Already, the Federal Bureau of Investigation (FBI) is developing this capability in the US. As necessity is often the mother of human invention, only a major problem may drive the development of tools, techniques, and a willingness to improve management and oversight capability to the full risk and volatility inherent in the new world of applied technology.

8.   *Global Trade and Finance*:   The risks and opportunities of the new global systems of trade, finance, and capital markets have been highlighted by the boom and then rapid devastation in the emerging markets. The borderless world of money and goods is here to stay. Companies are now run globally. Managers move between jobs and countries regularly. Markets and market makers work around the globe, 24 hours a day. Capital moves in and out of investments with instant reference to alternatives thousands of miles away. Currencies are bought and sold in great quantities far from their home markets by financiers, speculators, and businessmen through global brokerages and financial institutions.

Global trade grows even faster than the overall economy. The flow of goods and shares is chaperoned by the WTO and other organizations whose sole purpose is to ensure the continuing flow of goods and services around the world, removing barriers and obstacles wherever possible. Although not a new phenomenon, the fully global nature of many implicated systems and organizations, and the rapidity of reaching the far flung corners of the world, have created a new economic and commercial model of seamless, virtually instantaneous globality on an unprecedented scale.

9. *The Military*:   Although a full development of risks and opportunities in the military domain falls outside of the scope of this book,
many of the insights described here would apply in the martial world as
well. The scale of potential harm is increasing in many parts of the world
as India, Pakistan, North Korea, China, and others reach nuclear power
status. The probability of that harm occurring, below superpower level, is
increasing geometrically with the graduation of many new players to the
nuclear club, and the loss of the stability of the old bipolar world. In a
multipolar world of shifting alliances and conflicting objectives among a
larger number of parties, the probability of catastrophe increases.

The institutions that have for so long upheld global peace—Nato,
the UN, and even the Warsaw Pact—are undergoing a crisis of identity
or fundamental change. They are functioning in a world that demands
greater flexibility of response than ever before. A wide range of shared
systemic characteristics, namely, of consolidation, convergence,
obsolescence, turbulence, and other visible trends of the post-Cold War
era makes the area ripe for further, if independent, analysis using many of
the elements of Next Generation Strategy.

***Other Challenges*:**   The above list of nine selected issues is far from
exhaustive. There is no shortage of systemic behaviors that fit the
paradigm. Neither is there any shortage of opportunities to improve the
management of global issues by using a better approach to strategy and
execution. Other global systems reflect many of the same challenges:
changes in the political world, the evolution and extinction of languages,
the performing and plastic arts, systems of thought, and even the realm
of human consciousness. These and other areas of inquiry can provide a
depth and breadth of examples that reflect the same patterns and can
benefit from the same strategies' approach to positive change.

China on My Mind

In his book, *The Clash of Civilizations and The Remaking of World Order*,
Samuel Huntington described the next great risk threatening world order
as the clash between Muslim and Christian civilizations. He describes a
great conflict arising from the "fault line" separating groups with
fundamentally different and irreconcilable world views. In many ways,
Huntington's conclusions are well founded. The risks of the simmering
Middle East and crisis in Kosovo bear out their validity. However, based
on the analysis of the critical challenges set out above, China will also

play a key role in determining global performance in numerous critical risk areas—creating another great potential faultline between and across competing civilizations.

China will play a key role in the areas of environment, population control, economic growth, crime, cultural preservation, advances against poverty, crimes against women, disease control and health management. If one were to prioritize risk factors in the military area as well, the Spratlys, Taiwan, and other potential flash points related to Chinese policy would rank as high as the Middle East and the Balkans as potential detonators of the next regional or global military crisis. China's nuclear capability, coupled with a new long-distance delivery capability dramatically increases the scale of potential damage from unmanaged risk or realized catastrophe. These developments will require thoughtful analysis and action for the risks to be managed and the gap between civilizations to be bridged successfully.

At the same time, a stable and responsible China can contribute significantly to a new world order in which the risks of global conflict are abated. Engagement which encourages the desire to participate as a constructive member of the global community can support the emergence of a more positive vision and objective for China's emerging policy structure. Failure by the West to engage with the complex Chinese system will unnecessarily create increased risk, and contribute to a certain failure to capture opportunities to improve relations between the East and West.

Understanding the Chinese Perspective

China is the beneficiary of a 4,000-year-old civilization which differs in almost every aspect from its Western counterparts. As one of the world's great societies, China cannot be fully understood or engaged in constructive dialog without a full understanding of the Chinese complex perspective—past, present, and future.

Similarly, it is important that China understands fully the Western perspective. Failure to engage the West from an equally thoughtful perspective will increase the risk of the emergence of another destabilizing global duality. The last Cold War cost trillions of dollars, redirected a high proportion of scarce global intellectual capital into unused weapons research, and contributed to a climate of fear that spanned an entire generation. Comprehensive engagement on both sides will be necessary if a repeat of the Cold War is to be avoided.

The risk of a disengaged or threatened China is easy to see. A recent book entitled *Unrestricted War* by Colonels Wang Xiangsui and Qiao Liang spells out the potential for deliberate detonation by China of many of the most critical global risks to combat a more powerful adversary. Future conflict, according to the authors, will be fought out along new dimensions. Among their proposals for dealing with a powerful adversary are terrorism, drug trafficking, environmental degradation, and computer-virus propagation. As they concluded: "...unrestricted war is a war that surpasses all boundaries and restrictions. It takes non-military forms and military forms, and creates a war on many fronts. It is the war of the future."

It is also the full realization of some of the worst risks facing us as a united humanity. A better approach that diminishes this risk, through the application of the best available strategy, is a need of the highest priority. It is both urgent and important.

To build a bridge over this potential fault line will require a clear understanding of the two perspectives and the creation of multiple points of contact and numerous channels of communication. The goal of a fuller strategic engagement is to gravitate toward an agreed vision of deeper understanding, reduced risk, and realized opportunity for harmonious coexistence and mutual benefit.

An Architecture for Solutions

This book provides a practical approach to solving global problems. It is as much about engineering (or even carpentry) as it is of grand architecture. The specific content of any business strategy and of policy in the non-business areas set out above, must be guided by a clearly articulated long-term vision that is shared by all who would benefit from its realization. It will also need to include the elements of management of risk, opportunity, systemic behavior, positive and negative initiatives, and the drive to enhance capabilities to respond to unknown future events. At all times it will need to be diagnosed, designed, and implemented by inspirational leaders and engaged individuals. Hopefully, this book will provide some of the content for that vision and also put forth a useful model for positive change. By applying the best of our strategic knowledge, we can drive toward far better results. By applying the full program of Next Generation Strategy and implementing more creative responses we will be able to realize far more ambitious visions for the future.

To achieve this ambitious set of objectives and to realize our vision, we must extract the full value of state-of-the-art strategic thinking, and apply it where we can to create tangible, improved results in the real world.

Win-Win Options

The later chapters of this book explore the application of the best practice of business strategy to broader areas of social and economic concerns. The model of advanced strategy is tested against challenges that go well beyond the borders of our businesses and into the societal areas of greatest concern to us as individuals. Although far from the competitive battlefields of telecommunications, financial services, consumer goods, and other areas that are at the cutting edge of business strategy, the highest-priority societal and environmental issues can also benefit from the application of state-of-the-art transnational thinking on vision, strategy, systems, solutions, and effective implementation.

Although there are many similarities between the business and non-business challenges as set out above—similarities that can be bridged by effective application of Next Generation Strategy—there are many differences as well. In the area of business strategy, there are clear winners and losers. The relative scorecards of shareholder value, financial results, and market power and influence are easy to assess. The profit pool is finite, with winners taking the largest share. Losers take second best, slide into marginal returns or even disappear altogether.

In other complex systemic areas, such as disease, crime, terrorism, the environment, deculturalization, and economic disparity, unlike the business world, success is not limited to one player or set of players. A successful strategy in these areas of shared concern means that we will all be winners.

All of us will benefit from an environment with less crime and terrorism, and with cleaner air and water. Friends and adversaries alike would prosper in a world that has preserved its cultural heritage, giving us more diversity and opportunity for self-exploration.

True success means that we will have removed a high degree of risk from our lives. We will have succeeded in both reducing the net risks to our well being and increasing our ability to capture opportunities to improve the overall state of affairs. If net risk is defined as the gap between a threat and the ability to respond to it, then we will indeed have removed much of the risk in our collective world and in our individual lives.

Hope for the Future

The broader vision implied here is one of a dramatically better world to which we can realistically aspire. This vision can be realized through developing more thoughtful strategies, setting more ambitious goals, and designing a more effective global architecture to implement those strategies. To create a better world, we will have to discard old models and look afresh at solutions to the problems we face. If we unite to achieve all that we are capable of, we can make major strides toward realizing a more aspirational vision for the future. By implementing the best available strategy, tactics, structure, and organization in areas of greatest challenge, we will be able to achieve the vision of a better future for us all.

The final section of this book, A Message of Hope, is not a statement of blind optimism that ignores the risks and examples of the collective underperformance stated earlier in this book. It is instead a statement of hope that we can achieve more than we have to date, by sharing more ambitious visions, designing new and more effective strategies, and implementing more concrete action plans. Businesses around the world, which have mastered the new models and principles of Next Generation Strategy, are living proof that it can be done.

In the non-business world, we have shown that we can work effectively together to respond to challenges of our own creation as well. CFCs, which threatened the protective ozone layer, have been reduced by 85 per cent in five years. A coalition of nations banded together to oust Saddam Hussein from Kuwait and stop the pillage and rape of an independent country. A similar effort was undertaken to rescue Kosovo in 1999. Although AIDS has not been eradicated, smallpox, polio, tuberculosis and other once fatal diseases have been contained. Effective responses to starvation, refugee flight, disease, and other social crises by the UN, WHO, Atlanta's CDC, and UN agencies have saved millions of lives across the world.

With a model of the most effective approach to strategy and an understanding of how to change a complex world, we can make great progress against much higher standards of performance. Those high standards will need to be set collectively for the leaders we elect and for ourselves as individuals. Ultimately, the legacy that this generation leaves behind will be determined by our capability to understand and implement new strategies for positive change. Our legacy will be measured by the vision we share, the depth of change we pursue, and the strength of our commitment to make them happen.

A Challenge of Global Leadership

The central question that follows an understanding of what is truly possible is now clear: Are those with the power and influence to bring about needed change up to the task of creating new visions and realizing them in a complex modern world? There is clearly a way to make things better. Do our leaders have the will to bring about the full set of changes that are possible? Are they content to drift along in a state of satisfactory underperformance? Or are they capable of rising to the challenge of fundamental change and dramatic improvement?

We live in a world of risk. We live in a volatile era of systemic turbulence, and of rapid and dramatic change. We also live in a world of great opportunity. As we face a future in great part of our own creation and shaped by our own endeavors we can go much farther toward the goal of achieving our true full potential. Ultimately, achieving that vision is what Next Generation Strategy is all about.

2
Systems, Risk and Global Strategic Challenge

Telecommunications networks are now capable of transmitting voices, data, and images across the world in a split second. International air travel has made far away places accessible in a few comfortable hours. Technology and its spread of the English language have created new platforms for enterprise, commerce, and communications across national borders and around trade barriers which historically limited possibilities and curbed aspirations. An overlay of international law has now eroded national legal structures and contributed to the evolution of the concept of national sovereignty. The global systems that shape our world are developing and evolving at an extremely rapid pace.

Risk and Opportunity

Yet these systems can carry risk as well as opportunity. The global nature of the capital system and electronification of distribution has led to currency crises, economic collapse, and the brutal dashing of the economic aspirations of hundreds of millions of the world's citizens. The international banking system has created an enabling structure for international business transactions, but simultaneously provides the channels for drug dealers, corrupt officials, and various other felons to launder money and escape detection and prosecution.

The Internet has created a whole new and exciting cyberworld well ahead of the most ambitious of predictions, spawning millions of web sites and e-mail locations. Unpoliced, it has spun off a market and distribution vehicle for child pornography, right-wing hate messages, and unauthorized access to computers linked to defense systems, medical establishments, and sensitive personal data files.

Inexpensive international air travel has opened up the world to individuals whose parents never dreamt of even a fraction of today's holiday and business travel possibilities. But this global opportunity has also hastened the spread of terrorism, AIDS, and other life-threatening diseases.

To see these reflexive systems for what they are—dynamic, complex systems which are like living organisms in a constant flow of growth, transformation and interconnected influence—is to begin to understand their impact and the opportunities to influence their behavior to our advantage. Simply put, all these systems merely provide means and opportunities. Depending on the intentions and results of the actions of the users, the same source of opportunities can be converted into threats.

We can prevent some of the potential harm they can create by thoughtfulness and action. We can also, if properly directed, profit from their predictable patterns and emerging opportunities through astute investment and intervention. We can influence them to improve the quality of our business operations and personal lives, if we can understand and act in a manner consistent with the opportunities, as well as the risks they present.

New Sources of Risk and Opportunity Unmasked

It is essential for the development of good strategy and certainly for breakthrough strategy, to capture and process the content of systemic thinking and the related elements of risk and opportunity on an efficient and effective basis. This requires an ability to capture and distill knowledge in a consistent process and employ that knowledge to the pursuit of a defined end.

The Risk Calculus

Within each system, there is a set of risks and opportunities that can be clarified to illuminate the optimal strategic path forward. This set of risks and opportunities needs to be broken down into the elements which constitute the full nature of the net risk or opportunity created.

In the risk area, the four elements are scale of potential harm, likelihood of occurrence, capability to respond, and probability of effective deployment of that capability.

Scale of Potential Harm

The scale of potential harm can range from the overwhelming to the negligible. At the upper end of the systemic or societal scale are true cataclysms and tragedies: deep global economic recessions, business bankruptcies, nuclear explosions, renewed global warfare, widespread ecological disasters, violent crime, or large-scale fatal epidemics. At the lower end are trivial events that are annoying or painful, but which even at their worst, generate little negative impact. Examples would include mild recession, small operating losses, verbal conflict, mild disease, and actions with limited, localized environmental damage.

This scale of potential harm will need to be adjusted for the probability of the risk occurring, in order to generate the full calculus of risk eventuation.

Likelihood of Occurrence

Where precise risk analysis is available, probability can be expressed as a percentage, sometimes even to within a decimal fraction of a percentage. In the financial world, for example, components of risk probabilities in some derivative instruments are very carefully disaggregated, analyzed, weighted, and then reintegrated into a single risk factor which captures issuer risk, interest-rate risk, market risk, currency risk, counterparty risk, and other risk elements. In the absence of such refined (and expensive) analysis, cruder scales of probability, with broad categories of high, medium, and low, can act as reasonable surrogates for quantitative (but not always accurate) analyses of the likelihood of certain events transpiring.

The probability of the harm actually occurring may be difficult to pinpoint in many areas. There is no easy reference table or formula to set an accurate percentage on the likelihood of some risks occurring. But, history and a detailed analysis of present variables, which could influence the realization of the risk event, are often useful proxies for a more precise predictor.

Composite and Comparative Risk

The combination of the two elements, scale of potential harm and likelihood of occurrence, will yield a result that is significant as an absolute figure and as a basis for comparative risk analysis.

On the comparative side, it is obvious that an event of potentially great harm with a high likelihood of occurrence poses a greater risk than an event of little potential harm with a low likelihood of occurrence. Similarly, it is obviously easier to make comparisons within a single system or between similar systems than across dissimilar systems. For example, the potential harm of a major natural disaster or global epidemic could exceed that of a single nuclear blast many times over. Yet the probability of either event occurring at any given time is very difficult to predict. Cross-category risk equations are complex and less than perfect, but can provide a broad guideline for assessment, and for preventive or responsive action where appropriate.

Broad analytical techniques can be applied to yield useful, if not perfect, comparisons, where necessary. During the Cold War, chilling terms such as mega-deaths, blast vectors (adjusted for topographical configuration and weather patterns), ground zero, and other scientific elements of damage and likelihood were calculated precisely and integrated into strategic models and scenario planning. These horrifying calculations led to risk-adjusted valuations of potential damage and relative performance assessments of varying warhead and delivery system configurations. Within this type of highly analyzed system, it is easy to calculate composite and relative risk under different scenarios, since the elements of the calculus are, to a greater or lesser extent, the same. The major differences are found within common categories rather than between dissimilar categories.

A cyber-criminal planting a computer virus that can crash the global capital system or defuse control systems in the defense industry, creates a new type of risk where both scale and probability are difficult to predict. For such areas of high uncertainty, it may be difficult to justify investments in the development of risk management systems on a quantified basis. An overall contextual approach based on past or present general policies—varying from *laissez faire* inertia to heavy 'no regrets' investment—will tend to drive the investment decision on response capabilities, almost as much as a rough independent assessment of risk.

Capability to Respond

The second half of the risk calculus is the capability to respond to risk once realised. Response can be defined as actions taken to confine or limit the damage caused or to repair damage at low cost.

The capability to respond is often a difficult concept to capture in a single figure, or even in a complex equation. It is a concept that requires an understanding of both allocated and available resources—capabilities that are ready for immediate deployment and those that can be assembled from prepared or unprepared sources, which are not part of frontline response mechanisms. These secondary and tertiary resources, which could be made available, are particularly difficult to assess, but are critical elements in civil defense, civil disaster and disease response systems. Primary response mechanisms—the police against crime, national central banks and the IMF against destabilization of currencies or even the international monetary system, local health care authorities against epidemics, the nation state, the UN and World Bank against hunger and refugee flight—are the most significant components in our overall global architecture. Back-up institutions, such as the US Federal Reserve Board, the US Department of Treasury, and the World Bank in the global monetary system, and Atlanta's CDC in the health system, will need to be included in a full calculus as well.

The calculation of capability to respond to risk is most accurate where there is a proven and documented track record of success or failure by available resources. Tests or drills performed in the real world are second best; intelligent computer simulations are also valuable. Rough assessments of capability are of the lowest precision, but may be necessary in secondary and tertiary areas.

Response capability will also depend in part on the nature of the risk event. Within the same category, the response capability may vary based on the precise nature of the risk event. For example, the FBI may be well equipped and successful to date at limiting or responding to foreign-terrorist risk in the US. But that ability may be far less effective in the next wave of risk of terrorist-generated harm arising from cyber-attacks (e.g. redirecting military satellites, stealing computer codes or planting a dangerous computer virus) or the deployment of biological or nuclear weapons of mass destruction. Accurate calculation of response capability may require disaggregation and recategorization of risk events to assess the differential response capability.

The calculation of response capability does not stop at cataloging institutions, listing back-ups, and measuring secondary and tertiary resource levels. Ultimately, it is the impact of the response that is critical just as it is the true impact of the harm inherent in the risk event. The capability of the relevant institutions and response mechanisms to deploy adequate resources in an effective manner drives the real content of the calculation.

In many areas, as we shall see throughout this book, the true capabilities to respond effectively to major risk events are surprisingly inadequate.

Probability of Capability being Effectively Deployed

The probability of response capability being deployed effectively and on a timely basis is the second element in the calculation of potential response impact. Powerful fire engines and sophisticated hydrants are of little value if the trucks remain parked in the station house or cut off from a supply of water or chemicals in the event of a fire. Excessive delay in the deployment of response resources can also reduce the impact and results of response initiatives. Delayed deployment may be as damaging as non-deployment of resources in a time-sensitive situation. If firemen are delayed at the start or on their way to a fire scene, they may only find a smoldering ruin upon arrival. This would be true of delayed response to a fatal viral outbreak, or irreporable environmental damage.

The element of human skill and intention may have a decisive influence on the likelihood of deployment. The impact of individual and political will can thus play a major role in the overall risk calculus.

The total response capability is thus a combination of two main elements—the capability to respond at primary, secondary, and tertiary levels adjusted for the probability of timely deployment of that capability.

Net Risk Assessment

A calculation of net risk can be assessed—based on the full risk eventuation calculation net of the total risk response calculation. The function of the four elements can be operated to determine the overall net risk inherent in a complex system. Net risk assessment will vary as a result of different inputs on scale of potential harm, probability of that harm occurring, ability to respond, and probability of effective deployment of that capability. Overall assessment of net systemic risk will be critical to decisions on strategy resource allocation, deployment planning, and on risk management.

At a higher level, the combination of independent systems risk indicators can even create input to a total systemic risk calculation, i.e. a consolidated indicator of the effective status of our world relative to the harm that could be realized. In the 1960s and 1970s, the cover of the

Journal of the Atomic Scientist operated to distill an enormous amount of complex information into a single indicator. A clock face with a minute hand nearing midnight indicated how close we were to a nuclear holocaust. The closer the hand was to 12, the greater the risk of a catastrophic nuclear war. Such simple indicators can play a valuable role in capturing and communicating the content of complex risk systems, and in motivating effective response.

Opportunity Calculus

Similar to the risk calculus, net opportunity can be divided into four interdependent parts. The first two—value of the opportunity and likelihood of occurrence—make up the element of content. The last two—capability to capture the opportunity and probability of effective deployment—make up the organizational, or capability element. The combination of the two yields a net opportunity calculus—an adjusted value of an opportunity that allows it to be compared to other opportunities and even to net risk assessments in order to set priorities on strategic action.

Value of Opportunity

The value of the opportunity is a pure value of the opportunity regardless of the likelihood of outcome. External systems and situations do not always create opportunity, unlike risk. Opportunity may be presented through response to external developments, or created by unrelated thoughts or by development programs. It can be proactive as well as reactive in its genesis. Some opportunities are straightforward and are "pure" positive initiatives, for example, launching a new product category, writing a new novel, or rolling out a new business model. Some are offsets to risk; opportunities may exist to reduce the potential scale of harm or likelihood of occurrence of that harm. Other opportunities may allow individual or collective organizations to build capabilities to respond to risk or improve the probability of effective deployment of that capability.

Likelihood of the Opportunity Arising

Just as for risk, the value of the opportunity needs to be adjusted for the likelihood of occurrence. A highly valuable opportunity with a low likelihood of occurrence may be less valuable than a lesser opportunity with a higher likelihood of occurrence.

Combination of the Two

A combination of the two yields an initial assessment of the adjusted value of the opportunity. Yet that value cannot exist in a vacuum. The adjusted value of the opportunity on a stand-alone basis needs to be further clarified by the capability of seizing the opportunity, and the probability of that capability actually being deployed.

Capability to Capture Opportunity

Many apparent opportunities of value have, in the real world, a nil value due to an individual's or an organization's inability to convert the opportunity into real value. A gap in the market is of no value to a company without the marketing or distribution skills to fill it. Synergies between two companies may never be realized if neither has the funds or management resources to make the acquisition or integrate the two businesses effectively. Major investment opportunities or other initiatives may not be captured if an organization lacks resources or other requisite capabilities. Many shortfalls in capability can be addressed and are a key part of strategy in a more people- and capability-dependent world.

Probability of Capability being Effectively Deployed

Even the most capable of organizations and individuals will not be able to capture opportunities if the capability is, voluntarily or involuntarily, not deployed. For reasons of prioritization, regulation, distraction or limitation, attractive net opportunities, which an organization is capable of capturing, may be passed and the net opportunity calculus is reduced to zero.

Net Opportunity Assessment

Just as for risk, the four opportunity elements, once combined, create a single net opportunity assessment which sums up the fully adjusted value of the opportunity. Based on this calculus, relative values and priorities can be set among opportunities. In addition, comparative values can be set on fully analyzed net risks and net opportunities to drive investment polices and programs.

It is an obvious truth of any function which operates as the risk and opportunity calculus, that a nil value at any stage—content, capability, or probability—reduces the entire calculus to zero automatically. In the absence of a zero variable, the equations can generate useful results for comparison, prioritization and a formulation of response. The two calculations—net risk and net opportunity assessment—are two of the key elements in a well-analyzed and well-documented strategy.

Comprehensive Strategy

Although the two equations of risk and opportunity are necessary for the determination of strategy, they are, however, not sufficient on their own. A comprehensive strategy will also require a visionary element, a structural element that adds systems understanding to the risk and opportunity assessment, and an element of motivation and leadership. Each element will need to be fully elaborated on its own. The overall approach to strategy will need to be thorough and effective if these individual elements are to be fully diagnosed and integrated into a best practice strategic model that combines vision, strategic content, organizational capability, and the strategy process into a unified whole.

The Limits of Predictive Strategy

It is obvious that no strategic analysis or risk calculus can forecast all changes. The modern world is too complex, too dynamic, and to an extent, too unpredictable. The best strategic models are those that not only assess the value and implications of future risks and opportunities to the best level possible, but also build an enhanced capability and effective approach to respond to unpredicted risks and opportunities.

Modern strategy is more flexible, more adaptable and more vision-driven than its antecedents. An appropriate understanding of the implications of this dynamic nature of the content and process of strategy will underpin the correct use of each constituent element in a comprehensive strategic program.

Recurring Patterns and Paradigm Principles

As we examine the full range and flow of complex global systems, we also observe a set of recurring patterns and a large number of common principles of evolution and behavior. Whether the pattern is seen in technologically driven systems, systems of human behavior, the evolution of a disease, the spread of criminal organizations, the rise of transnational companies, the contagion of capital crises affecting the emerging markets, or the pollution of the environment, the common systemic pattern can often be characterized by a number of shared paradigm principles. Business strategy has had to change as a result.

Transnational businesses and organizations, like other dynamic systems, have a life of their own. Increasingly, they share a common set of defining characteristics. Systemic understanding in the business world is evolving from a more limited structural perspective, once characterized by the language of strategic architecture, design principles, and foundation elements. Business and economic scholars are becoming more aware of the fact that corporate business systems are evolving into "biological" entities with a dynamic interconnected nature that can only be addressed on a holistic and "living" basis. Modern authors use the language of the "corporate ecosystems," where all processes within a business are seen to be interrelated in a dynamic and living system. Data flows, product or manufacturing chains, social systems and cultures, value-added chains, and all other moving components of the modern organization are similarly and validly described in the complementary language of architecture and of systemic dynamism, interconnectedness, and interdependent evolution.

For each salient systemic characteristic, there is an implied strategic imperative that takes priority in the implementation stage. Mastery of systemic behavior thus requires a view of the dynamic whole—a view of the principles and rules pertaining to the organism as a whole as well as to its constituent elements. Many of the risks and opportunities inherent in systems devolve from this "living" nature of dynamic systems, from the interplay of evolving elements in the overall "ecosystem" of the whole.

Ten Recurring Patterns

There are 10 recurring pattern elements that define the nature of an archetypal system. These elements also provide a conceptual foundation for the development of an effective strategic approach that takes into account a full understanding of systemic behavior. In this new paradigm, the systems under analysis are both distributive (which drives the globalizing nature of many of the challenges we face) and substantive, thereby combining the content of those distributive channels into a seamless pattern of global systemic behavior.

1.   *Globalization*:   Globalization redefines many of the major sources of risk and opportunity we face today. Voice messages, data and information, products, people, capital, images, ideas, hazardous waste, pollution, drugs, and almost anything else you can think of, can now be transported between the major centers of the world with increasing efficiency. Ships, aircraft, trains, automobiles, trucks, telephones, faxes, satellite relays, modern banking and interbank systems, express delivery companies, the Internet, and intranets provide delivery and distribution systems that efficiently span the world. This globalization, perhaps the most commonly cited element in the evolution of complex businesses and economic systems, creates a whole new set of management and human challenges.

Businesses and trading systems work around the clock, seeking out opportunities, and managing risk and opportunities in over 200 countries spanning different time zones with different histories, languages, cultures, communication standards, regulatory systems, and economic structures. Money moves freely between destinations, seeking out the highest available returns. The microeconomic laws of supply and demand now apply at a global level as goods, services, money, people, jobs and other elements of global business mix and flow from one country to another with little interference, interdiction, or control.

Globalization is the easiest of the trends to identify in transnational business systems. The highly visible signs of McDonald's, Burger King, Domino's Pizza, and other fast-food franchises are transforming eating habits around the world. Other brands are establishing new standards of global social status and aspirations—Rolex watches from Switzerland, Mercedes-Benz cars from Germany, Louis Vuitton briefcases from France, Gucci handbags from Italy, Ralph Lauren sports apparel from America—reflecting the growing global nature of brands, trade, and information. At a less visible level, combined companies like Air Liquide and British Oxygen Company (BOC) serve the world's industrial gas markets. International airlines have gone from operators of national hubs and spokes, to vast networks of international routes, sharing routes, building international alliances, and operating powerful computer-driven global reservation systems. Bechtel and Asea Brown Boveri win engineering contracts from Albania to Zimbabwe. Even in businesses once considered or regulated to be local in nature, the world over is opening up as never before. Financial services businesses like Citigroup, ABN Amro, and GE Capital, law firms and even once sleepy local utilities are spreading their wings across the globe in new models of international expansion.

In a systemic environment, where globalization is the salient characteristic, the imperative for management is for consolidation and focus of response at a global level. National responses are bound to be ineffective. Fragmentation of effort will be fatal. Only a concerted global response of sufficient magnitude can reduce risk or capture opportunity for change.

2. *Complexity*:   The complexity of dynamic global systems is increasing rapidly. The business world provides many examples of the striking complexity of modern business, as companies become multinational and transnational, as products, variations, and services proliferate, and as logistics and manufacturing systems flex and evolve globally. Competitors, suppliers, distributors, owners, and managers are all in a state of perpetual change and increasing complexity.

The challenge of this complexity is both practical and theoretical. The more complex a system, the more opportunities there are for positive growth and also for individual element failure. The more dynamic variables there are, the greater the chance for a catastrophe—in both the mathematical and real-world sense. This catastrophe would appear as an unexpected event or a series of related events—an apparent discontinuity in the operating system, which will not be anticipated by most of the players in that system. The recent emerging market crises would fall into this category, as would the 1987 Black Tuesday, Marlboro Friday, and other capital-market headaches.

On a product level, global vehicle manufacturer BMW famously suggested that there is more computing power in its 7 series automobile in 1999 than in the rocket which put a man on the moon thirty years earlier. Deutsche Bank spends DM 600 million a year on information technology alone to support its universal banking model. The Internet can now link up 30 million personal and mainframe computers around the world. The Star Alliance, which links some of the world's leading airlines, now flies thousands of flights every day from most of the world's major cities. Its reservation system books seats for millions of passengers per year from hundreds of countries with countless variations and special instructions. The number of countries within which companies compete, the wide range of products and brands they provide, and the needs of managing a global network of suppliers, operators, and customers inject a note of increased complexity at all stages of the business system.

Response to a highly complex system will require full engagement of individual effort at all levels of complexity in a common structure of engagement and a common vision of the desired outcome. Yet in complexity, perhaps the most important element of effective response is to not lose sight of the simple priorities—to set out a clear and compelling vision to guide the organization through the complexity, and pursue it through a limited set of highly effective priority actions. Constant assessment, communication, and uninterrupted effort at all levels will be required to bring about constructive change in a complex system.

3. Turbulence: Turbulence creates or reflects greater than average discontinuity in a system. It occurs where there is dramatic change in the environment, critical variables or functions within a system. It can occur periodically or irregularly during the evolution of any system.

In many cases, turbulence erupts at the point of intersection of two dissimilar or non-identical systems. Air flows, liquid movements, weather patterns, populations and social systems all reflect a level of turbulence at points of intersection as well as at internally generated points of convection and catastrophe. Not all turbulence is predictable. But mastery of turbulence and volatility, to the extent possible, is one of the key factors that contributes to transnational business success. The result of turbulence is great volatility in the relative position and performance of elements within the system. This volatility obviously creates significant threats as well as opportunities for participants in the system.

Turbulence in business is typically characterized by rapid changes in the regulatory or competitive order, fundamental changes in business definition, or dramatic change in the nature of products, services or business systems. The majority of the world's industries now consider themselves to be in a period of turbulence. Destabilizing turbulence has become the new normal environment for modern businesses. The computer, financial services, automotive, steel, retail, food, cigarettes, defense and airline industries, to name but a few, are all in a period of destabilizing change and turbulent transition.

New leadership within an organization can also create internal turbulence in even the most stable of external environments. Recent analyses have shown that arrival of new leadership is often associated with significant changes and visible increase in value to shareholders in an enterprise. Necessary change can be made without the constraints of past association and old politics.

According to a Bain & Company survey on turbulence that spanned 8,000 companies in 17 industries sectors over more than a decade, turbulence and catastrophe created significant competitive volatility and opportunity for change. New leaders emerged in two-thirds of the sectors surveyed. Returns to shareholders of winners were over 20 per cent per year. Losers in these same sectors showed returns of less than 5 per cent per year. Former leaders, saddled with the high operating costs, but not the benefits, of industry leadership, dropped to less than half the return levels (measured in total shareholder return) of their replacements at the top of the industry league tables.

As turbulence primarily occurs around changed circumstances, catastrophic events and at points of systemic intersection, the strategic management imperative is to predict and respond to the causes as well as the effects of turbulence. For a catastrophic event (in the mathematical and real-world sense of the term), deployment of a response capability can be well prepared and quickly launched to manage or to benefit from inevitable change. New capabilities will need to be built to profit from destabilization of the old order. In some cases of systemic risk and harmful turbulence, avoiding the catastrophic intersection of conflicting systems or providing a stablizing influence may be the best solution of all.

4. *Dynamism:* One thing is sure in the modern world—the current paradigm will change. Dynamic systems, by definition, do not stand still. The implication for participants in the system, willing or unwilling, is to understand, anticipate, influence, and take advantage of the inevitable movement and change as much as possible. The implication at a systems level is an increase in the potential for catastrophes: more movement, more variables in play, more opportunities for linear patterns to intersect, and more chances for discontinuities to generate further discontinuity. The path toward chaos has been well spelled out by numerous commentators, and is supported by the notion of complex, dynamic systems intersecting and influencing each other in ways we cannot yet begin to contemplate.

In the business world, constant progressive development is the order of the day in financial services, telecommunications, consumer goods, manufacturing enterprises, and in the service sector. In some cases, the accelerated pace of change has been due to a lifting of restraints on the evolution of natural systems. This is the case in areas impacted by deregulation, such as the removal of Regulation Y in the US financial services business, which capped passbook savings rates; its removal triggered a process of dynamic development which has already spanned two decades. The trend, started in the 1980s, of privatization and the removal of trade and capital barriers also initiated major change processes. These liberating events released pent-up forces for change. A second factor in dynamic change and evolution is the impact of new enabling systems, in many cases driven by technology and telecommunications. A third driver of dramatic change is the removal of conceptual inhibitions to business definition or development, as new business models reset industry standards of excellence.

The key to the management of a dynamic system is rapid and effective response. There is a heightened need for constant monitoring of the system and setting pre-established trigger points to activate prepared responses. Advanced scenario planning, deployment drills, and agreed conditions for deployment will avoid delays and allow effective responses to be deployed in a timely manner.

5. *Acceleration*:   The pace of change is accelerating in virtually every dynamic global system. Complexity, globalization, the intersection of systems, and the unprecedented pace of technological change and its spreading influence only serve to accelerate change in an already rapidly evolving set of systems. In some cases, great investments are made in the business and military world to deliberately speed up the pace of change—competing to develop new products, new channels, new weapons systems and new delivery capabilities ahead of competition. "Time to market" is a critical success factor in today's competitive battlefield—the shorter, the better. Due to deliberate actions and the following of trends derived from natural evolution, the pace of change is accelerating and shows no sign of relenting. Not keeping pace with accelerating change may create a dangerous gap between a monitoring response capability and the underlying system it is meant to control.

In the business world, time is increasingly a key success factor in competition. Toyota Motors recently announced that it could make a car in five days from the time of order to delivery, a dramatic reduction from the previous average of 30 to 60 days. Product development, logistic chains, and other elements of competition are now driven by accelerating change. In many cases, technology and adoption of global best practices are key factors in the process of acceleration.

The Internet, for example, and real-time response to ever more demanding customers is only one of the rapidly evolving sources of technological change and successful new business models. The Internet is an accelerating cyberworld of interconnected networks of individuals, content providers, distributors, and manufacturers. There are many views of the future evolution of the Internet, but all of them share the expectation that the system will change radically and quickly, and in ways that will stretch the capabilities of even the most seasoned and intelligent Internet experts.

John Chambers, Cisco's fast talking chief executive officer, has admitted that "this industry is moving so fast that it is almost impossible to keep up with it." In addition to the organic development of his business, Chambers and his team executed 24 separate acquisitions over a five-year period, quickly developing into one of the leading Silicon Valley success stories.

Going further back in time, the early study of time and motion spawned the industry of consulting, whose genesis lay in the value of accelerating task execution. Accelerating task time on a fixed-cost base created lower unit costs, greater profits, and relative competitive advantage. During World War II, production experts noticed that the efficiency of producing finished bomber aircraft was accelerating, and that each accumulated unit of experience produced a predictable decline in the time and cost required to assemble an individual aircraft. The experience curve was born, setting out a normative trend of declining unit cost as an organization gained scale, accumulated experience, and built its internal knowledge base. As individual and organizational knowledge rose up the learning curve, costs and time to produce slid down the experience curve.

More recently, the competitive value of superior time management has been rediscovered and "time to market" has joined "time to produce" as a critical success factor in the modern business world.

As systems accelerate and gain momentum, it is important for managers to project forward to see the logical outcome and impact of this salient systemic trend. Change programs will need to take into account the nature of the system, the impact of acceleration, and the history of successful initiatives to manage or profit from the accelerating pace of change. Rates of acceleration are often predictable and that predictability can lay the groundwork for beneficial action. Initiatives focused on the root of the system as well as its accelerating branches will be critical to manage risks and opportunities effectively.

6. *Continuous Obsolescence and Reinvention*:   The very nature, as well as the elements and order, of a system can change over time. Non-linear or fundamental changes are now a common element in the archetype, creating a need to discard old models, as well as to adapt to change within an existing paradigm. Understanding historical rules is therefore a necessary, but no longer sufficient, knowledge base from which effective systemic action can be taken. New paradigms have redefined the nature of competition and reset challenges for modern managers. Within a dynamic and complex system characterized by the 10 paradigm principles set out here, it is obvious that learning must keep pace with change and even anticipate or create non-linear change for advantageous purpose. No static model or approach can capture the full complexity of dynamic systems behavior. Perhaps the most famous characterization of a misguided adherence to outdated perceptions and strategies is the military adage that "today's generals are always fully prepared to win yesterday's wars." The same is true of many failed strategies in the business world. Companies and leaders of systemic organizations playing by yesterday's rules may find themselves making decisions today that will cost them dearly in tomorrow's markets.

The nature of competition is fundamentally changing and companies that fail to adapt to new standards and paradigms are often condemned to highly visible failures. IBM missed the market shift to PCs and eventually lost a reported $1 billion trying to catch up in a market that eluded its strategic grasp. American car-makers, driven by outdated concepts valuing design and size, were decimated by Japanese competitors more in tune with the new market need for smaller, cheaper, and more efficient vehicles with higher build quality and greater reliability.

Ironically, much of the success of Japanese penetration in the US market with superior products was underpinned by their adherence to the quality concepts of American statistician W Edwards Deming. Deming's integrated understanding of manufacturing, quality, cost, and statistical control created a new paradigm that enabled a whole new generation of leaders, many of them Japanese, to rise to the top of some of the world's largest industrial sectors.

By the same token, the unbundling of formerly integrated value chains in the airline business led to a new, more focused model of competition for leading airlines of the world. The sale of non-core catering operations and ground handling units, the outsourcing of jet engine and airframe maintenance, and the sharing of costs in expensive reservations systems have allowed the more advanced airlines to focus greater resources on customer service and network management. The impact on customers and on profitability has been remarkable. Successful competitors have adopted a whole new approach to competition and their business systems. The best have reinvented themselves as lean, focused international players with as little asset exposure as possible. Airline industry consolidation, driven by sequential waves of mergers, acquisitions, and alliances has further contributed to the redefined nature of the entire industry.

Where a system is constantly changing and redefining its content and its boundaries, the imperative is to develop a highly flexible capability to respond to situations that evolve in new and unexpected patterns. Constant monitoring, extrapolation, and interpretation of risk factors are required, placing a high value on planning exercises and simulations. Core objectives need to be continually reassessed.

The content and capability of the response mechanism need to be constantly renewed and old practices specifically discarded as soon as they are obsolete. Deployment of inappropriate or outdated responses may be worse than no deployment at all in the face of a redefined challenge—well-intentioned initiatives can become part of the problem rather than part of the solution.

7. *Connectivity*: The new state of interconnectedness has been neatly summarized by one of the leading experts on the effect of technology on modern business: "We're talking about connecting everything in the world to everything else. That means that every artifact that we make will be embedded with some chip, some little sliver of dim intelligence, maybe only as smart as a bee or an ant. But all of those pieces, some of them moving around and some stationary, will be connected, and will be communicating with each other. So, the graph of the number of things that we make, and the graph of the numbers of things that are connected, will in the near future converge and meet, and everything we make will be connected to everything else. And that is the network. That is the Net, in the large sense that we talk about."

Connectivity is not just about computerization and the global Net. It is a phenomenon of the weather, trading systems, cultural norms and behavior within old and new systems. With the push of technological advance, the interconnected nature of the world is becoming more visible and linkages more subject to deliberate understanding and management. Even the remote Himalayan Buddhist kingdom of Bhutan is now wired up to the Internet and receives satellite television after thousands of years of isolation and cultural independence.

The development of new Value Managed Relationships, which integrate supplier and customer economics in a new win-win recombination, has broken down barriers between formerly separate stages of the value chain and connected previously competitive enterprises.

A corollary to connectivity and interconnectedness is interdependence. As all things are more visibly interconnected, they also will depend more on each other than ever before. The holistic nature of individual systems and the "system of systems" is an inevitable construct that emerges from an understanding of the full nature of accelerated connectivity.

Cisco's view of the next phase of development of the Internet is broken down into seven related stages, which capture a vision of consolidation, connection, and convergence of activities in a leading edge industry. The seven stages of industry evolution are:

- consolidation of data networking companies
- all-in-one data/voice/video networks
- consolidation of phone companies
- availability of free voice services over data network
- consolidation of data/voice companies
- optical inter networking; broad band available everywhere for the cost of pots (plain old telephone service)
- ultimate interconnection of systems—getting everything connected is everything

In systems where interconnection is a salient characteristic, it is essential to first understand all of the present and future connections, linkages, and interactions. All opportunities and risks presented by connectivity need to be identified and exploited. In addition, back-up systems should be prepared in case of a systemic collapse. Firewalls, circuit breakers, and pressure values should be built in where possible. A constant monitor for risks to systemic integrity should be put in place and compliance procedures developed and implemented. Key participants in the system should be given roles in the back-up system in order to expedite implementation if necessary.

8. *Convergence***:** Convergence occurs when two non-identical systems move toward a common end point or pattern without merging or fully consolidating into one entity. The borders between systems will break down over time as incentives and influences drive systems with similar objectives and technologies toward a similar set of operating characteristics. Although systems can diverge as well as converge, the majority of systems relevant to the leaders of businesses, countries, and global institutions are more likely to be on a converging path toward a greater sharing of characteristics and patterns in the future.

In the telecommunications and technology sector in particular, the major strategic and investment decisions facing the leaders of these businesses are dominated by a dynamic set of changes related to globalization, complexity, accelerated change, and convergence. Communication companies like traditional telecom operators are spreading into data information and entertainment. Bell Atlantic now offers high-speed (ADSL) Internet access with America On Line (AOL). AT&T purchased TCI. US Regional Bell Operating Companies (RBOCs) buy and run cable companies in Europe. From the other direction, traditional entertainment companies like cable operators now offer Internet access (@Home, Roadrunner) and even offer upgraded telephony over upgraded Hybrid Fiber Coaxial (HFC) networks. And the traditional providers of data and information, Internet service providers (ISPs) and software companies are spreading out in both directions. ISPs become Internet Telephony Service Providers (ITSPs) offering low cost Internet telephony. Microsoft buys into cable companies and Web TV.

Convergence can also be seen in the areas of financial services. Banks, insurance companies, stock brokers, investment and private banks are converging on competitive service offers to the high-net-worth individual, offering to take over his or her lucrative "wealth management" functions. The manufacture and distribution of asset management products is a common hunting ground for all of these players, with bewildered customers facing a dizzying world of choice that deregulation and globalization have recently thrust upon them.

In an interesting convergence of customer behavior, the consumption of beer, wine, and spirits in different countries with differing traditions are now converging toward a common global pattern. Over the past 50 years, wine-drinking countries like France and Italy have demonstrated a long-term decline in the liters of pure alcohol (LPA) consumed in wine; beer and spirits consumption have been on the increase in these countries. Traditional beer-drinking countries like Germany and Austria have been consuming relatively less beer and more wine and spirits. Similarly, spirits-led countries are heading toward a higher consumption of the softer alcoholic beverages of wine and beer. Eventually there will be a roughly even mix of drinks in most countries as measured by LPA, unless taxes or other artificial interventions disrupt the natural convergence of the markets.

As patterns and systems converge, the critical factor for management success will be to develop a consolidated response to both the end state toward which the systems are converging and the process of convergence along the way. If that end state carries with it high costs or risks, the convergence must be redirected or converging systems partitioned if possible. In both cases, the effort will require a consolidated effort in the environment surrounding the converging systems—geographic, national, commercial or other—in order for an impact to be made. Even if the end state is undesirable, the convergence may be so advanced that redirection or partition may not be practical. In this situation, a consolidated and common effort to address the full set of problems inherent in the end state should be undertaken. Best practices should be replicated and ineffective approaches quickly discarded before the undesirable end state itself becomes entrenched, institutionalized, and even more difficult to transform.

9. *Consolidation*:   In many systems, there is a visible trend toward consolidation of subsystems and formerly independent entities into larger unified blocks. This can be seen within the business system and at a corporate level as mergers and acquisitions combine ever larger players into single units. At the end of this last century, we saw the first $100-billion merger and the proposed combination of three banks in Japan to create the first $1-trillion (in assets) financial institution. In the political sphere as well, there is a trend toward amalgamation, which has been visible for over two centuries. Even in the religious world, mergers and alliances have also restructured the landscape of traditional establishments. In the US, the individualistic Congregational Church in the USA—the church of the pilgrim fathers—has successfully merged with the Evangelical Synod of North America and the Reformed Church in the US to create The United Church of Christ, whose name alone suggests corporate-like consolidation. Where industrial consolidation is not evolving quickly enough for some national leaders, the pace can be suitably accelerated. Malaysia's announcement in August 1999 of the proposed consolidation of 21 commercial banks, 25 finance companies, and 12 merchant banks into 6 large banking groups reflects the government's sense of urgency and importance of consolidation of fragmented financial services players in that fast-growth economy.

This phenomenon of consolidation is not new. When Henry Ford launched his enterprise in Detroit, there were over 100 independent automobile manufacturers. A cottage industry at the time, many new businesses were started to take advantage of the coming wave of horseless transportation. Foundering on the increasing costs of competition, challenged by the increasing demands of technological evolution, and unable to survive the passing of the founding entrepreneurs, or the absorption by General Motors (GM) and other giants, many small companies have gradually consolidated to become a few (and increasingly fewer) large ones. Technology, opportunity, cyclicality, globalization, complexity, and a host of factors drove this pattern of consolidation from entrepreneurial fragmentation to a massive efficient scale. This applies to non-automotive businesses as well. Banks, insurance companies, brokerage houses, investment banks, asset managers, custody services, airlines, utilities, telecommunications companies, supermarkets, department stores, luxury goods companies, manufacturers of beer, spirits and soft drinks, advertising companies, law firms, accountants, energy companies, airframe and engine manufacturers, defense equipment manufacturers, building suppliers, hotel chains, and other industries all reflect a process of consolidation across recent years which continues today.

Where systems are consolidating, response imperatives for strategic change are twofold: either to match the size of the newly consolidated entity or to enforce deconsolidation if possible. Participation, or even leadership is usually the best response in the commercial world. In areas where consolidation creates unacceptable societal risk, deconsolidation or containment may be the best response. Deconsolidation will require the exploitation of the weakest links—breaking down the whole through effective efforts focused on a single link or limited set of links in the chain. An effective approach for containment or redirection may also require the development of a matching, or even superior, capability to offset the strength of the consolidated entity on a full and direct basis, and perhaps even at every component level of the system as well if possible.

10. *Rationalization:* Over time, systems will tend toward a more efficient relation of means to ends. Forces will seek paths of least resistance. Energy efficient behavior consistent with the achievement of a prescribed goal will be visible—with human behavior no exception to the rule. One of the critical aspects of systems management will be to understand and redefine the end goal that drives the rational behavior of the system and its constituent elements. That goal or vision is the end point that gives a dynamic system its *raison d'être*.

The process of rationalization can be seen in learning curves and in the experience curves of price and cost in the business world, and in countless small decisions driving individual and collective behavior toward a defined end point—whether articulated or implicit. A key element of success in driving positive systemic behavior is to assure that the perceived end, from each individual's personal perspective, is the same as that of the collective. Multiple agendas and dissimilar objectives can create discordant systems behavior due to a conflict of end-point objectives.

The objective of every business enterprise is to achieve the most efficient means to the desired end. Customer needs should be met at lowest cost and maximum extraction of available revenue. Efficient and effective operations are complementary objectives pursued by large and small companies. Over time, costs normally track down a predictive trend, profitability matches relative market share and industry economics replicate themselves in a consistent manner. The art and science of resource allocation is a constant process of optimization— allocating capital, staff, and other assets to pursue the highest available return consistent with the creation of substantial competitive advantage and long-term shareholder value. The result is a system in constant evolution toward a desired end state on the most efficient and effective basis possible.

Rational systems behavior can be guided by constructive intervention at the level of means, the actions undertaken to achieve the ultimate goal, or of the end itself. Intervention at the level of individual action driving toward the end state may be expensive (in terms of force expended to drive change) and, unless sustained and focused, often ineffective as well as inefficient. Intervention and guidance aimed at changing the emerging end state of a system, the goal toward which the means are directed, may prove to be a better use of resources. By resetting the ultimate goal, the means will be forced to adjust, with or without assistance, to meet the demands of the new direction. The exercise of leadership is as much about the setting or resetting of the ultimate goal—redefining the end of the system—as about the alignment of systemic rewards, punishments, and feedback to change the process to achieve that end most effectively.

Other Common Principles

Other common principles of systemic evolution appear in some, but not all, complex global systems. Although not common to all systems, one of the many contributions made by R Buckminster Fuller to our collective understanding of systems behavior is his observation that systems, over time, progressively ephemeralize and become less substantial in their manifestation. The tracked becomes trackless. The wired becomes wireless. The fixed becomes mobile. The large becomes small. The drawn out becomes instant. The assisted becomes unassisted. The present becomes remote. The visible becomes invisible. The physical becomes virtual. Ephemeralization is an unending process in multiple dimensions.

This process can be seen in system after system, including the development of modern telecommunications (with mobile, wireless, small, virtually instantaneously operating handsets without operators), robotics (with accelerating miniaturization), finance (who goes to a bank branch any more), retail (with online shopping and the impending arrival of virtual supermarkets) and computers (where Massachusetts Institute of Technology (MIT) specialists are designing wearable computers). One expert even describes the latter phenomenon in the technology area as computers "dissolving into the environment." Although ephemeralization is not a universal principle, its relevance indicates that other trends as well as those highlighted above contribute to common patterns of change and progressive evolution.

Feedback and Control

Although feedback loops and other internal communications mechanisms are a characteristic of every dynamic system, some systems are driven, at their core, by the need for feedback of a particular type. Feedback-driven systems can be positive or negative. Should the risk or negative content of a system become dangerous, the imperative is to cut the feedback loop. By starving the total system of its necessary sustenance, harm or risk can be mitigated and the system neutralized.

Systemic Behavior in the Business World

Each of these 10 pattern characteristics of systemic evolution in the business sphere could, by itself, provide rich material for further study. To pick but one, consolidation can provide an example of the depth of the impact that just one trend has had on modern industry.

During the first half of 1999, $570 billion of industry consolidating transactions was completed in America and $346 billion in Europe. Both were visibly higher than in 1998. This acceleration in the pace of global consolidation is a continuing trend that has been gathering momentum over decades. The phenomenon is not linked to any one sector or country. Although financial services is leading the way, others are not far behind.

Consolidation in Finance Services

In 1990, there were four banking transactions exceeding $1 billion; in 1997, there were 25. Virtually every month there is a major merger or acquisition redefining the financial services landscape, further consolidating the sector and creating ever larger enterprises. Citicorp and Travelers, each with a market capitalization of around $80 billion, merged as a step toward the creation of a business capable of reaching a billion customers worldwide. Upon the announcement of their merger, the value of their combined shares rose $30 billion, creating shareholder value equal to the full equity market capitalization of Merrill Lynch. In Europe, the top five banks now exceed $400 billion in assets each.

At the end of the 20th century, the proposed consolidation of Industrial Bank of Japan, Fuji Bank, and Dai-Ichi Kangyo Bank into a single entity opened the door to the world's first bank with assets exceeding $1 trillion. Although a major step forward in the race to prove that size does matter, the milestone of $1 trillion will no doubt be just one of many checkpoints on a long journey of continuing consolidation —which is still a long way from the finish line.

The mergers of UBS and Swiss Banking Corporation (UBS/SBC), Chase/Chemical, Bank of Tokyo/Mitsubishi Bank, Citicorp/Travelers, Banc One Corp/First Chicago NBD, and Bank of America/Nations Bank have created a new generation of leaders in many of the world's pre-eminent banking markets. Many further deals are under discussion or being implemented around the world, promising even greater consolidation in the future.

Different Visions, Same Result

There are different reasons underlying consolidation initiatives, but the overall result is the same. Domestic consolidation of retail banks is the major factor driving consolidation of the global financial services today. Seventy per cent of banking acquisitions over $1 billion between 1990 and 1997 were retail banks acquiring other retail banks. Half of these transactions were in the US, with the other half being international. All of the cross-border deals were driven by non-US competitors. The 1998 crop of transactions in the main continued these trends.

The rationale for consolidation has been consistent—reduce fixed costs, increase distribution scale while eliminating duplication, increase cross-selling opportunities (primarily in the retail and commercial sectors), provide a larger customer base across which brand spend can be amortized, and reap the benefits of technology spend. The last two points will be increasingly important in the future as well.

The information technology (IT) spend of the top five banks over the last decade has reached $17 billion. Four US branded retail businesses alone—American Express, Visa, Citicorp and Chase—spend a combined $500 million per year just on advertising. It has been estimated that any retail mutual fund in the US needs to spend $50 million per year on media to make a meaningful impact on the national market.

Despite a high failure rate for acquisitions generally, many of these domestic consolidation deals, if properly managed, carry the potential for success. They consolidate overlapping market share positions. They are driven by "hard" cost synergies. They combine similar businesses that are more likely to be integrated effectively.

A minority of the large transactions between 1990 and 1997— around 30 per cent—were driven by a logic of combining "manufacturing assets" with "distribution assets." This was the logic behind Lloyds Bank's acquisition of Cheltenham & Gloucester in the UK. It is the stated logic driving the creation of Citigroup, the recently announced merger of Citicorp and Travelers. New distribution channels—software companies, Internet service providers, card system operators (and attendant loyalty programs), supermarkets, direct banks, utilities, retail distribution, and other new avenues to access the customer—will increase the range of potential targets and strategic alliance partners to fuel the growth of this class of strategic competition.

It should be noted that the past record of development of the cross-selling model has been patchy, at best. Professor Rowland Moriarty of the Harvard Business School once described cross-selling in financial services as "Doggie doo doo!" The UK, US, German, and French businesses, which have attempted to be all things to all people in all places, have found this to be an expensive and difficult path to pursue. The goal of delivering a full set of global quality products and services has proven elusive to banks such as Barclays and NatWest.

Many past proponents of cross-sell strategies or cross-market acquisitions are refocusing their efforts on a more limited set of products and markets, in which valuable leadership positions can be developed and maintained. The track record of "soft" synergy mergers, driven by expected cross-sell opportunities, is poor. However, new and larger combinations are emerging to test the negative presumption. These new combinations may yet set the pace for consolidation in the future.

No End in Sight

Neither of the two major acquisition trends highlighted above—domestic consolidation and combination of manufacturing and distribution assets—are trends that contain a natural limitation on growth.

Domestic consolidations are unlikely to stop growing at national borders. Contiguous markets and high-value customer segments will lure acquirers across borders when the marginal return on attacking an adjacent customer segment is higher than the marginal yield on a low-value segment in the home market.

Eventually, regulators will limit acquisition-led growth within the boundaries of a defined market for antitrust reasons. This will push consolidating companies with a high-growth imperative into adjacent or remote markets, and contribute to the global nature of competition and accelerating pace of consolidation.

The global trend toward consolidation for financial service providers and their customers is also encountering less administrative obstacles than in the past. Regulatory barriers to entry and to competition are eroding or disappearing sharply in the aftermath of a series of "Big Bangs" in financial services markets around the world. WTO, Afta, Nafta, GATT, and other facilitators of the global development of trade in goods and services will accelerate the process of internationalization and consolidation in the financial services sector, just as they will in almost every other area of manufacturing and service.

Automotive Consolidation

The financial services industry is not the only one driven by consolidating companies. The British automobile sector, at one time the pillar of the global industry, effectively has no more independent vehicle manufacturers. The Rolls Royce and Bentley marques are in the hands of BMW and Volkswagen. Jaguar and Aston Martin are now part of Ford. British Leyland, itself an agglomeration of great motoring names, has been swallowed (with some indigestion) by BMW. Outside the UK, Saab and Volvo have seen part of their businesses also absorbed by GM and Ford. Daimler-Benz, the parent corporation of Mercedes-Benz, has merged with Chrysler. Renault and Nissan are exploring the opportunities to create value from their combined operations. Ferrari is part of Fiat. The long list of recent consolidations goes on at an accelerating pace.

The same is true for the suppliers. The old approach to the supply of automotive components has also long been rejected in favor of larger and more consolidated supply systems. No longer do individual companies supply headliners or seat upholstery directly to original equipment manufacturers (OEMs), i.e. the vehicle manufacturers such as Ford, Fiat, BMW or Mercedes-Benz. Instead, suppliers contribute to the creation of a highly specified interior system, which is delivered to the OEM for last-minute assembly as a package. The same is true for headlights and lighting systems, batteries and electrical systems, and shock absorbers and suspension systems. The impact of the automotive suppliers on the giant vehicle manufacturers has been striking. One Ford vice president summarized the impact when he said: "We used to deal with 1,500 suppliers. Now we deal with 200. In the future, we are aiming at 50 key suppliers only. Those companies which cannot keep pace with these changing demands will not survive."

A Resilient Phenomenon

The strength of this pattern is particularly striking since, on average, a merger or acquisition fails to create value for shareholders. Some acquisitions, for example, the acquisition of Snapple by Quaker or NCR by AT&T, were spectacular failures which cost shareholders billions of dollars. Although there is a proven approach to effective mergers and acquisitions, most companies, particularly those unfamiliar with the skills necessary to make mergers or acquisitions work, fail to learn or apply best practice approaches. The result is a destruction of shareholder value in the majority of transactions and a large group of disgruntled acquirers. In one study, 91 per cent of CEOs who had recently acquired a business were disappointed by the first year's results.

Despite this dismal record, the consolidation wave rolls on, realizing unprecedented heights at the end of the 1990s and continuing apace into the 21st century.

Winners and Losers in the Search for Strategic Excellence

As we step back from this pattern of consolidation and other common systemic characteristics, and even from the empirical models of systems, risk and opportunity set out earlier, we see that there are clear winners and losers in the development and application of strategy in the complex modern environment.

In contemplating the challenges, both business and societal, which share many of these same elements, it is valuable to understand what creates winners and losers. It is instructive to document and analyze the approaches and actions of these few enterprises that have most successfully mastered the global challenges of this volatile era. A small subset of companies has broken out of the box of satisfactory underperformance on a consistent and reliable basis. They are the winners in the search for strategic excellence.

Visions have been realized. Superior operating performance has been demonstrated time and time again. Crises have been mastered. Strong platforms of capability and flexibility have been built to respond to risks and opportunities—expected and unexpected. Resources have been allocated to generate higher returns. Individuals and teams have been inspired to higher levels of achievement and reward.

The lessons to be drawn from the winners and losers in the search for strategic excellence can be extracted, examined, and articulated in order to understand the state-of-the-art approach to global strategy. That approach, which combines the best approach at each stage of strategy provides the most effective guide for leaders and participants in any global initiative or enterprise.

In every industry, no matter how difficult or turbulent, there are winners and losers. In the shoe industry there are hundreds of defunct manufacturers in Europe and the US at one end of the scale, and a triumphant Nike at the other. For every McDonnell Douglas, there is a Boeing. For every RCA or Bull, a Dell or Microsoft. New business models replace the old. New winners emerge and reap the benefits of their success. Old leaders and lagging followers decline, may be taken over, broken up, or pass into insolvency. Most of the independent survivors drag along at a level of operating performance and financial return well below the leaders—contributing to industrial underperformance and taking up much of the space in the global industrial landscape.

The list of companies who have proven a sustained ability to generate superior results is small. Less than one in 10 large companies in Europe and the US has consistently earned its cost of capital every year over the 10-year period, 1989–1999. Yet these few and a select group of new companies have broken out of old limitations to reach new heights of operating performance and strategic excellence. In the coffee industry, which is growing at 1 per cent a year at best, Starbucks has shot up 65 per cent per year with a better formula for success. For the shoe industry, which is experiencing GDP growth, Nike grew at four times that rate for a decade. A short list of winning stories highlights the tangible benefits of strategic success.

Cisco

Cisco is the fastest growing company in the history of the computer industry and is the 10th largest company in the world in terms of market capitalization. It is the acknowledged worldwide networking leader, with more than 80 per cent of the Internet built on Cisco equipment.

Cisco handled one-third of the world's electronic commerce in 1997, with over 72 per cent of the company's orders transacted over the Internet. Group turnover has reached $8.458 billion, and it employed 10,900 staff worldwide at the end of 1999.

By exploiting the convergence and consolidation opportunities of modern software systems through effective acquisition and growth, Cisco has emerged as a leader in the areas of software and applications. Its share price rose from $3 to $70 over a five-year period; market capitalization increased from $9 billion to $220 billion. By mastering the critical factors of consolidation, convergence, and accelerating change in the dynamic world of operating systems and applications, Cisco has driven to extraordinary levels of value growth and shareholder return.

3M

Once a narrowly focused manufacturer of overhead projectors and lenses, 3M has become one of the world's most creative and exciting companies. Admired globally for its innovative products and commercial success, 3M provides a classic example of economic benefit from fostering human creativity.

British Airways

The former state-owned and fully integrated airline was once a problem-ridden state-owned flag carrier beset with service problems, trade union conflict, and poor financial performance. Now British Airways (BA) is a dynamic global competitor operating an efficient network of flights and operations around the world. It became an industry leader in service and profitable growth during the 1990s.

By "unbundling the value chain" and restructuring the content of the business system to focus on core expertise, BA was able to offload and outsource engineering, catering, and other areas that were not critical to customer and network needs. Following its privatization in 1987, BA became a fully privatized airline, leading the European industry in profitability, service, and reputation amongst its peer industry group and achieving global recognition as a leader in innovative customer and loyalty programme management. BA's success has made it an attractive partner as well—a key factor since acquisition and international alliances are at the heart of a strategy to add BA's assets to a winning set of global operating relationships that includes American, Australian, and other selected airline and non-airline partners around the world.

Microsoft

No one has ridden (or even driven) the dynamic and complex world of technology and software as well as Microsoft. Dominating the screens of millions of PC users, Microsoft has occupied a key space in the new cyberworld, which provides a convenient access window for experienced users and beginners alike. By providing a common reference point for other software developers, Microsoft has exploited opportunities to drive convergence, consolidation, commonality and rationalization for its own benefit. Its enormous market capitalization of $475 billion in 1999 and the elevation of founder Bill Gates to the status of the world's wealthiest individual are only a few of the rewards generated by this company's remarkable ability to master the full set of systemic challenges in the software world—technological, distributive, financial, and competitive.

Intel

Along with Microsoft, chip-maker Intel has ridden the rising wave of computerization and accelerating power of PCs in particular. In some ways, the success of Intel can be seen as an example of ephemeralization, packing greater and greater amounts of processing power onto smaller and smaller chips. As the capabilities of processors grew exponentially (and predictably) from the early limited range to the full capacity of the Pentium III and MMX chips, Intel has demonstrated its ability to continue to lead the process of innovation, design, and integration.

Dell

By pursuing the vision of a new direct business model, Dell created a new integrated business system that linked manufacturer directly to customer, thus eliminating the costs, delays and problems of middlemen. Dell was able to supply a better product at lower cost with superior service. Customers and shareholders alike reaped the rewards.

General Electric

Living proof that manufacturing conglomerates can also be leaders in strategy and operations, General Electric (GE) has achieved strategic leadership in its 10 divisions while setting new standards and operating excellence along the way. With sales of $100 billion, profits of $10 billion and a market capitalization of $400 billion in 1999, GE is universally cited as one of the world's most admired companies.

Singapore, Inc.

One surprising entry in the area of corporate winners is the consolidated set of enterprises that make up Singapore, Inc. From a small, swampy Malayan trading outpost to today's bustling international and multi-cultural city, Singapore's growth and increasing prosperity can be seen to exhibit many of the characteristics of an effective corporate enterprise.

The Development Bank of Singapore (now known as DBS and merged with the local POSBank in 1998), Singapore Airlines, Singapore Power, the Port of Singapore Authority (PSA), Singapore Technologies, and Singapore Telecom have all risen to the list of top companies across many areas of the Asian business landscape. The Singapore stock exchange, as a result, has risen in value to $200 billion in 1999, almost exceeding that of its three adjacent neighbors (Indonesia, Thailand, and Malaysia) combined.

Although many of Singapore's companies are facing new challenges in their markets, the overall network of companies has been run exceptionally well and has weathered economic storms better than their neighbors in emerging markets. Singapore, Inc. demonstrates, at government level, many of the characteristics of Next Generation Strategy in an advanced form. There is a proven demonstration of the value of a coherent and cohering vision, the politics of alignment, and a system characterized by an effective set of rapid and capable decision-makers. In addition to showing the benefit of integrated management of strategic content and capability, Singapore stands as a clear and winning example of the applicability of business principles to areas outside of the commercial sphere as well.

The Man from Del Monte

The dramatically successful turnaround of the business of Del Monte Royal Foods in recent years provides a good case study of a winning strategic program driven by effective diagnosis, design, and implementation. As a direct result of the program, operating results doubled and the parent company's share price rose more than 200 per cent in a 12-month period.

The turnaround story is particularly striking since the vision and leadership for the change program came from an existing leadership and senior management team. Usually, dramatic change occurs only when there is a change of leadership at the top. In this case, although there were some changes at an operating level, revolution was led by the monarch. The story of the turnaround and the leadership of Vivian Imerman, the colorful chairman and chief executive officer, provides an example of how a comprehensive strategic approach can yield breakthrough results in a long-established enterprise.

Background

The Del Monte businesses, formerly part of an integrated global operation, were broken up and sold separately following the KKR take-over of RJR-Nabisco. The Anglo-American Corporation of South Africa teamed up with entrepreneur Imerman in a complex structure to win an auction for the Del Monte Foods business at the end of 1993.

The collection of assets acquired included a minority share of a Philippines pineapple plantation, a fully owned pineapple production unit in Kenya, a South African deciduous fruit operation, 50 per cent of the Nabisco operations in South Africa and a full set of manufacturing and distribution operations in major European countries. Soon after the original acquisition of Del Monte Royal Foods (DMRF), further production and distribution assets were added in Italy through the acquisition of Confruit, a strong local juice and nectar business.

Tying all of the businesses together was the Del Monte brand and experienced operating management team.

An Asian-style Crisis

Soon after the acquisition was completed, unexpected troubles emerged, which required radical action. Many of the problems faced by Del Monte during 1995 and 1996 were identical to crisis-related challenges faced by managers in the Asia-Pacific region in subsequent years. Asian currencies moved adversely, as did all relevant European currencies. A weakening of the selling-countries' currencies and a strengthening of the producing-countries' currencies created intense margin pressure across all business units. The external environment became increasingly hostile as large distribution chains in Europe continued their relentless pace of consolidation. Pressure on all food manufacturers heated up as the "balance of terror" increasingly moved in favor of the trade.

Product proliferation fragmented management attention and diffused brand spend. Scarce resources were invested across a range of high growth but low margin opportunities in new-era drinks and other diversified areas. Operating management, schooled in a traditional environment of strong brands and operations, were unable to respond effectively to a complex and distressed situation, which promised to get worse before it got better. To top it off, a fragmented shareholder structure at Del Monte Pacific Resources, the Philippines productions and marketing arm, proved incapable of achieving the full potential of the business.

During 1996, the share price continued to slide. An incremental response to fundamental problems continued to highlight the need for a radical and comprehensive response to the problems facing the group. A significant personal ownership stake held by Imerman only increased the importance and urgency of a program to address the problems.

Comprehensive Strategic Program

The turnaround of the Del Monte business began with an exhaustive diagnosis of the business—internally and externally. All elements of the business systems were analyzed in detail and tough decisions taken. The senior management team specifically requested that no stone remained unturned. No issue was off limits. By the end of the six-month review, a weary group finance director quipped that "at the beginning of this, we stated that there were to be no sacred cows in the review process. Well, there are none left—they all were shot in the last six months."

The Del Monte restructuring program addressed all elements of the problem in a co-ordinated multi-pronged approach.

1. *A new vision*:   Following an intensive review of the business and its dynamic environment, a new vision was developed to focus on core capabilities, the venerable Del Monte brand, and opportunities for profitable growth in the production, distribution and sale of well-known pineapple, fruit, and vegetable products. Each country and operating unit was assigned a role in the new vision, and strategies set in place to achieve the vision. A task force approach was taken at the top level to oversee the program to realize the vision.

2. *A new organizational model and enhanced capabilities*: Imerman realized that his team needed a new set of skills to deal with the crisis. Greater personal incentives were required. A new and more entrepreneurial culture was needed to address current and future trade challenges. Within 18 months, 11 of the top 15 management positions were filled with new faces. The organization structure was simplified. Duplicating or unnecessary positions were eliminated. In all, 500 staff positions were targeted for reduction around the world.

A core team comprising the chairman and his three senior operating and finance executives—Jacques Fragis, Francois de Lavallette, and Andrew Hawkins—set out to reverse the decline.

3. *A comprehensive restructuring*:   A change of ownership and legal structures took place to solidify the business position including a new shareholding structure in the Philippines. Following the break-up and sale of Del Monte, all the new owners of the branded businesses around the world had taken a participation in the ownership of the main source of the product. With their ownership stakes came matching board representation. The resulting complexity created a difficult and even unmanageable situation. Del Monte Royal Foods (Europe), Del Monte Corporation (USA), Kikkoman (Japan and parts of Asia), the Macondray Group (Philippines), and others restructured the ownership of the operation, with only Del Monte Royal Foods and the Macondray Group remaining. Only two equal partners shared ownership and control of the business. Rapid and effective change became possible and a full transformation program was successfully implemented.

Jointly led by Imerman and the Lorenzo family, the new streamlined business was able to build on complementary strengths to increase revenues, product categories, productive yields, quality, and profits at the same time.

In Europe, an equally dramatic transformation program was put in place at an operational level.

Improved operating results also needed to be restored. Faced with a secular decline in volume, compounded by a currency and trade-driven margin squeeze, Del Monte attacked operating costs across the board. Country operations were consolidated or closed. New distributors were appointed. IT systems were simplified. Unprofitable customers were cut, which saw the reduction of the Italian customer list from 9,000 to 2,700 in less than one year. Ineffective marketing spend was terminated. Unprofitable product lines were trimmed. Organizations were simplified. A new set of incentives kept the operating management team fixed on realizing the ambitious new vision. "We had the legacy of global-scale operating systems and only a regional business," Imerman said. "The costs were killing us."

The cash costs alone of the European restructuring program were estimated to exceed US$60 million. A portfolio of non-Del Monte branded products provided a priority list of candidates for divestiture. Property and plant left over after a consolidation of assets in Italy were also put on the block. During the restructuring phase, an auction of an Italian tea business was successfully concluded to help pay for the restructuring.

4. *New standards*:   New standards were implemented and a more conservative approach to accounting taken by the management team— "rebasing" the accounts. Characterized by a complex history of acquisition-related charges, multiple reporting entities, and changes in accounting policy, Del Monte's controlling shareholders were appropriately concerned about a complexity discount on the share price. Executives at Del Monte and Anglo-American Corp agreed that the reporting approach should be simplified as much as possible and "all of the bad news" incorporated into a single restructuring adjustment. Over a billion rand (US$200 million) was written off in an adjustment of the brand value carried on the balance sheet. A further 300 million rand was taken as a provision for current and future restructuring costs. The year end was moved to December from November. New product development charges and the depreciation schedule were shifted to conform to international accounting standards. A new group finance director was appointed. Debt covenants were re-negotiated or adjusted to reflect the new approach. All lenders were supportive and many positively applauded the changes.

Although the vast majority of management effort was focused on the existing business, selected new opportunities were pursued which would accelerate future growth at low capital cost. Joint ventures were successfully negotiated in Russia and India. A high quality Thai plantation, the Siam Agro Industrial Company, was acquired and its operations restarted. New line extensions and packaging concepts were developed. Advertising spend was refocused on core brands and well-established premium brand values. A bolt-on acquisition of complementary Just Juice in the UK added volume and market share to a strong Del Monte branded presence in the market.

July 1997—End of the Crisis

Ironically, just as Asia was entering a period of prolonged crisis, the Del Monte management team was turning the corner for the first time in four years. The dramatic news of the turnaround program was announced in July 1997. The share price, which had dropped to below two rand, began a steady climb. Earnings for 1997 stabilized at 30 cents per share, helped by favorable results from the Philippines. Results for 1998 reflected a 70 per cent increase in earnings, to 50 cents per share. The share price more than tripled following the announcements and the proven delivery of forecast results.

At the time, Imerman was quoted as saying: "We had our backs to the wall and no choice but to undertake a radical approach. It took an extraordinary effort for more than a year, but we are now back on track. A year ago, things looked grim. Now we have a stronger, leaner business, a new and energized management team and a range of interesting strategic options for the business. Without the intensive turnaround program we would still be facing far more difficulties than opportunities. Now the opposite is true. Only a comprehensive effort could have changed the situation and gotten us to where we are today."

Volatility and Turbulence Return

After two years, the period of linear, stable progress came to an unexpected end for the company. A new shareholder, having replaced Anglo-American as a leading investor in Del Monte, created unpredicted turbulence at board level through litigation and public airing of alleged disputes between shareholders and management. Unexpected change and difficult challenges became the ordinary state of the business. The apparently stable and progressive future of the company was again at risk. Linear models rapidly became outdated and a new approach had to take into account the continuing flow of change and turbulence in the commercial environment—internal as well as external. The positive results that continued were a testament to the newly strengthened capabilities of the organization.

The Derived Model

These examples of winners, along with other successful companies often share a common set of strategic characteristics and a high degree of pattern integrity in their approach to winning strategy, although the precise content of their strategies may differ dramatically.

Based upon the examples of winning companies, a number of common elements to their strategic approach can be derived and analyzed. The seven common elements of successful strategy are spelt out below.

1.   *Clear and Correct Vision*:   It is not enough to state a bold strategy and to communicate it effectively. A vision has to be right, not just aspirational. The Allegis concept, linking hotels, airlines, and other assets together, was not based on sufficient sharing of costs, assets, or operations. The team responsible for an overly inclusive vision soon left and the once integrated businesses were swiftly unbundled.

One of the chief characteristics of an effective visionary strategy is that it motivates managers and leaders to clarify operating decisions, and to set a higher standard of excellence and to motivate their own organizations to achieve higher and more aspirational goals.

In today's risk environment, there are few low-risk, high-return strategies. Neither are status quo strategies any longer effective. The old ambition of acting as a good steward of a company's businesses is no longer enough. Winning businesses need a guiding star above the horizon and a captain to chart a course toward the goal. The failure of many groups to grow profitably and to take advantage of the opportunities presented by evolution or turbulence can be attributed to the fact that, as one frustrated executive bemoaned, "we got a steward when we needed a captain…"

2. *Structural Optimization*:   Cisco and Microsoft are pursuing ambitions to restructure their external environment through strategies of alliance and acquisition as well as organic growth. BA and Dell have built new business models which redefined their value chains and allowed them to outperform traditional rivals. GE is constantly reviewing its portfolio for divestitures, acquisitions, or alliances to strengthen competitive position and financial performance.

Many businesses continue to operate with a fully integrated value chain, while competitors have slimmed down and focused. Others have attempted to restructure their industry through mergers and acquisitions mergers, but failed to create shareholder value. Highly visible failures in the mergers area would include a series of aerospace transactions by conglomerates or diversification by unfocused industrial competitors. The net cost to shareholders from these failures may be counted in hundreds of billions of dollars, even based on extremely conservative estimates of cost and lost shareholder value.

3. *Operating Excellence*:   By definition, none of the winners listed above qualify as businesses that have fallen into the trap of satisfactory underperformance. Dell's market leading product and service performance, Microsoft's increasingly capable software packages, and Singapore's effective response to the recent crisis all reflect the achievement of a goal of excellence in operation as well as strategy. GE's culture of operating excellence and firm benchmark performance hurdles sets an industry standard for clarity and effectiveness.

4. *Right Organizational Model*:   BA and other operators of global businesses have driven their businesses from a new network concept since the late 1980s, empowering individuals in the field as standards are set and monitored at the center.

Complex and cumbersome models of organizational structure can only inhibit the achievement of full potential. At IBM, "Big Blue" lost leadership opportunities in PCs and software, in part due to an overwhelming bureaucratic culture that valued conformity over creativity.

New models and approaches are needed to respond to more dynamic and challenging environments. The task force is one of the more effective organizational approaches to gain favor in advanced management systems. Fast, flexible, not tied to the past, cross-disciplinary and easy to focus, task forces have become a key weapon of every senior manager's arsenal of useful approaches. A pre-set end to their existence only serves to intensify the sense of urgency and effectiveness, and to accelerate the achievement of results.

In a fast-evolving world, responses which require the establishment of new institutions or a redirection of the old may be far too cumbersome amd time consuming. The creation of new institutions can be an enduring source of change, but may also be a time-consuming, expensive, and ultimately unrewarding initiative.

5.   *Enhanced Capabilities*:   Skills building, high-quality teams, and gifted individuals are the hallmark of successful growth companies. Microsoft's stated goal of purchasing "high bandwidth" individuals and the exceptional success of high growth professional service firms, which reward profitable growth with specific growth incentives and training spend, reflect the value of investment in individuals, skills, resources and development programs. GE has proved to be so successful in its management programs that it has been the source of many CEOs of other companies as well as its own large divisions.

The skills and capabilities required to compete, especially in small or service sector enterprises, are increasingly the only real sources of competitive advantage. Failure to develop and retain key staff, as many failed acquisitions demonstrate, will have a high cost in the short, medium and long term. Incentives also need to be aligned—of those companies reflecting superior profitable growth, over 90 per cent had compensation packages with a specific growth element. Of the remainder of the Standard and Poor's (S&P) 500, less than a quarter had a profitable growth objective in their compensation system.

6.   *Integrated and Aligned Strategic Design*:   The integrated elements of strategy are assessed before action at each of these, and other, winning companies. Failure to pull all of the components together at Microsoft or Cisco, for example, would have undercut the value of their acquisition programs as well as the strong and profitable growth patterns of their existing business.

Assurance that all elements of the system are aligned to optimize performance is the hallmark of a winning enterprise, and Singapore, Inc. is a master of this process. Religion and racial politics, education, training, compensation, investment, planning, communication, monitoring, military service, and a national communications program all form part of a strategy of a country that pulls strongly in the same direction with a shared sense of purpose and a visible pride in common achievement. Yet for every Singapore, there is a Russia. In the wake of Gorbachev's *perestroika* and Yeltsin's ascendancy in the Russian Federation, enormous opportunities were lost through an ineffective and chaotic tax system and criminalized business hierarchy. With little help from the West relative to true needs and a frittering away of what scarce resources were made available, Russia's fragmented and misaligned structures have kept it from approaching anything like its full national potential.

The stage of integration, alignment, and implementation is where many strategies become unstuck. Many companies with capable analysts are incapable of translating insight into action. The whole, in the end, is worth much less than the sum of the parts. Obstacles—cultural, political, strategic or operational—surface to prevent the enterprise from achieving its full potential. The capabilities of the individuals involved are not fully engaged with solutions—collective potential is not realized and individuals become discouraged, disaffected, and, ultimately, disengaged from the effort altogether.

7. *Detailed Implementation Plans*:   Clear plans of action are required to conclude the design phase and lead smoothly to the execution phase, where effective planning procedures and organizational characteristics make clear progress in the actual marketplace. The value of the implementation plans can be seen in the quality of results, which placed all of these companies into the winners' circle.

Creativity, Intuition, and Understanding

In many cases, a balance of linear and non-linear approaches drove the content of winning strategies for these businesses. A visionary approach linked a projection of stable elements from the past (the linear component) with "discontinuous" or paradigm-changing elements (the non-linear component) in a coherent approach to breakthrough strategies. These new visionary approaches required not just a new process, but also new levels of creativity, a greater respect of intuition and an acceptance of alternatives to past models of business success.

Linear analysis provided the disciplined foundation for creative thought and essential input to strategies to redefine the patterns and trends whose exploitation yielded exceptional results. Only a combination of linear and non-linear inputs could achieve the full potential of these complex businesses.

It is important to underscore that discontinuous strategies did not allow leaders or managers to opt out of the hard graft of linear analysis. On the contrary, they required more data-driven analysis than past models. All of the expanded dimensions of linear strategy as set out in the traditional models of business analysis were required *plus* an overlay of creative thought to drive out the best strategy for a given situation.

Creativity required a willingness to discard old models and to start the process of understanding and action unencumbered by past patterns of thought and past prejudices on what can or cannot be done. It was and is a liberating, rather than limiting, approach.

Learning from the successes, creativity also requires a high level of receptivity to allow new external information or internal intuition to penetrate into conscious thought patterns without attempting to limit or control these new thoughts with old models of understanding. The reception and processing of thoughts, ideas, hunches, concerns and flashes of inspiration form the building blocks of creativity. This ability to be open to receive new ideas and unexpected inspiration is an essential capability. We must improve our ability to capture valuable perceptions on the margins of our consciousness and at the frontiers of our process of thought. Our sixth sense, so often correct, requires a receptive capability to receive inspiration from the outside and to capture emerging thoughts from within. Often imperfectly formed, these faint flashes of intuitive insight are often the most valuable insights from the deepest regions of our capacity. This capability is often associated with the feminine and the right brain, although it is by no means a gender-specific characteristic. Sir Muhammad Iqbal, philosophical leader of the Muslims in India early in the 20th century, even associated the exercise of creativity with the divine: "In order to realize their own unique nature, all human beings must become more like God. That means that each must become more individual, more creative, and must express that creativity in action."

Because these linear and discontinuous changes are often systemic, complex, and multivariable, new approaches will be required; new "mental models" will have to be developed and new levels of understanding and creativity in the definition of solutions demanded.

Much of the insight required to define and execute complex strategies operating at a systemic level come from identifying, understanding, and managing patterns of behavior at a very high level. Perceptive identification of these patterns often works at a high level of abstraction, which is best pursed through intuitive, rather than linear logical, processes. The sheer complexity of problems and opportunities may make a full linear analysis either too time-consuming or too expensive. Winners in the business world now work at "Internet speed," and with a new level of understanding and insight. The identification of patterns in the data describing complex systems can be critical to the definition of an effective response. The perception of common patterns in dissimilar environments can generate beneficial cross-comparison and insight. The extraction of lessons learned from observation and practice in one system can lead to useful insight and action in another.

The Value of a (Correct) Systemic Perspective

Much of the content of George Soros' book, *The Crisis of Global Capitalism,* focuses on the transformation of his perspective on the global capital system. His original view was that the capitalist system was, like the movement of the planets, an absolute, independent system that could only be understood, predicted from selected data input and profited from (or not) as those predictions unfolded in the capital markets around the world.

Predictable inefficiencies were arbitraged, inevitable consequences anticipated, and risky investment rewarded by exceptional returns as systems unfolded in new patterns during dramatic periods of adjustment. His billion pound profit made on the back of the collapse of sterling in 1987 was only one of the many grand coups which yielded superordinate returns for investors in his appropriately named Quantum Fund.

He later recanted these early views and now espouses a doctrine of greater central control and intervention in economic markets. This surprising turnaround was inspired by a new view on the global capital system, now seen to fall into the category of reflexive systems—those capable of being influenced by collective human action. In addition, the risk of a global economic meltdown, so close to reality in 1997, caused him to rethink the nature and value of a more reflexive view of the capitalist system.

Collective behavior can, he now believes, change the nature and direction of the capitalist system, creating a need for a more thoughtful set of interactions and a more comprehensive set of monitoring and managing institutions. This understanding recategorizes aggressive investment behavior from benign self interest to a potentially more problematic type of action—converting apparently neutral investment funds into purveyors of risk, crisis, and even direct personal harm to millions of individuals. The hopeful side of this more reflexive view is the implied perspective that global systems of distribution and content can be usefully analyzed, understood, and managed toward more positive outcomes.

Consciousness of the systemic nature of the risks we have created and the reflexive nature of those systems can drive us toward a different set of collective (systemic) behaviors aimed at creating much more positive results.

The same insight into the nature of systems can also drive positive change in behavior with regard to other systems, such as those underlying the environment, disease, terrorism, crime and other reflexive global systems. Past myopic perspectives, mistakenly categorizing reflexive systems as absolute, have frequently led to missed opportunities and unnecessarily increased the risk of unmanaged negative outcomes. The lack of understanding and missing positive intervention from miscategorization has unconsciously created mounting risks which, from a more informed systemic perspective, could have been predicted and avoided.

A Unique Source of Insight

R Buckminster Fuller was a unique source of exceptionally creative thought on the nature and behavior of systems. Interestingly, he arrived at his capacity for trenchant systemic observation from an unusual visual handicap. Unable to see anything but colors, patterns, and broadly defined images (being extremely far-sighted) until the age of four due to a rare eye affliction, his mind developed in a manner more attuned to holistic, patterned perspectives than the usual atomistic approach learned through the observation of a collection of individual, clearly delineated objects. As a result, he was more capable than most of his colleagues to see patterns driven by underlying systemic behavior, to see the waves and patterns where others saw only drops and molecules. The process of ephemeralization is only one of the trends in universal systemic behavior he discerned and built on in a career that was notable by significant contributions to science, architecture, design, and literature. In each discipline, he used common systemic concepts to drive creative insights and applications across a number of historically disparate disciplines.

The Fifth Discipline

The value of a systemic perspective to drive new levels of creative understanding and informed action also provided the foundation for Peter Senge's famous Fifth Discipline. That discipline—of developing a learning organization capable of effective systemic understanding and action—underpinned a new approach to management and organizational behavior. Organizations and individuals that have mastered the challenge of understanding and managing complex systems have a real ability to influence the content and direction of those systems to their advantage. Systemic knowledge, according to Senge, requires different thought processes, paradigms of conceptualization (the mental models mentioned earlier), and behavior.

Like other intellectual disciplines, systemic mastery can be learned and applied. The resulting mastery of complex systems can create enormous advantage—relative and absolute—for the knowledge corporation. That same mastery can create enormous benefits for all of us living in a world characterized by complex and interconnecting systems.

Because systems operate as a function of a larger number of interrelated variables, it may be impossible to develop a sufficiently robust and dynamic linear model to describe the full set of behavioral characteristics of non-linear systemic behavior. We have yet to design, for example, a computer model capable of predicting the weather. It is difficult to design and update continually a complex model which may drive off more than a dozen key inputs, and where changes in the weightings may occur on a frequent basis. Although a number of software packages are available to capture and process inputs in multivariable models, most are essentially mechanical formulae to list, weigh, and integrate these inputs. Some advanced packages attempt to describe interconnectedness and highlight cultural and other soft factors, but none can process the full set of inputs as swiftly, and as creatively, as the human brain.

A Continuous Culture of Creativity

There is no end to a culture of creativity—as organizational goals are achieved, new ones will arise to replace them in the pursuit of the overall vision of the enterprise. Creativity, like success, is a journey not a destination. There is no end to improvement, growth, and greater reward. There are opportunities available in every direction. Pursuing the most valuable of these creative opportunities in the most effective and efficient manner is a defining characteristic of the winning creative organization.

At the same time that there is no end to the process of vision realization through the application of a creative approach, it would be a folly to assume that there is any model or approach that can lead to perfect understanding. There is always an element of the unknown and the unexpected. It is essential to leave an open space in the thought process to allow applicable new information to come forward and for inspiration to flourish. Remaining open to further inspiration, renewed creativity, fresh change, and insight is a kind of built-in protection against a closed mind.

The Gates of Wisdom

Bill Gates, the world's richest man, and a master of quantitative analysis and systems understanding, summed it up well when he stated his simple but profound conclusion that "often, you have to reply on intuition."

Creativity and Intellectual Capital

The foundation for creative initiatives resides in the intellectual capital of an organization. Like other asset categories, intellectual capital can be unbundled for further analysis and targeted development. Stewart Thomas in *Intellectual Capital* has outlined some of the elements of the constitution of highly valuable intellectual capital. Based in part on the approach taken by Swedish financial services group Skandia, one EIU report further breaks down the content of intellectual capital in the business world into three interrelated categories: human, structural, and customer.

Human capital resides in the staff of an enterprise and is itself made up of sub-elements of innovation, attitude, tenure, turnover, experience, and learning. Employee surveys, new product success records, human resource records, research experience, know-how, and other "hard" elements of human capital can serve to flesh out analyses and set targets for development in this area.

Structural capital resides in the documented sources and registers of data existing in a company, customer information, financial data banks, operating manuals, patents, intellectual property, and other encoded knowledge. The gap between the use of this structural capital and full potential usage can provide a rich vein of value for data mining and commercial exploitation.

Customer capital actually embraces downstream relations with customers and upstream relations with suppliers as well. Past studies have shown that 80 per cent of organizational learning takes place at the customer interface. Since each enterprise is a customer itself, as well as a provider of products and services to its own customers, the opportunity to learn exponentially exists at both ends of the business system. Erosion in the customer base thus carries both hard and soft costs of lost value.

Pioneering work on customer acquisition retention and penetration by Fed Reichheld is only one of the sources of new measures that support improved understanding and more effective action in this area.

The wealth generating capability of any organization now resides as much in its capability to capture, measure, and manage intellectual and human assets as its capability to manage traditional balance sheet assets such as plant, property, and equipment.

3M's Ten Commandments of Creativity

3M—the former Minnesota Mining and Manufacturing Company—is the acknowledged master of the game of creativity in development, application, and extension of intellectual capital. From an uninspiring base of expertize in overhead projector lens technology 35 years ago, 3M has grown to global leadership in refractive technology, adhesives, and other exciting areas of high growth and profitability.

A brief summary of the 3M approach, led by long-term veteran Livio DeSimone can provide a framework for companies and groups looking to move forward in their quest to optimize the development of their own intellectual capital. As summarised aptly by the *Sunday Times*, the 10 commandments of creativity are:

1. *Downplay Management*:   Senior managers are expected to lead, not to direct. Barriers to performance are to be removed, not institutionalized.

2. *Smile on Chaos and Lack of Discipline*: Particularly during the early stages of conceptualization, a high degree of freedom is tolerated in the creative process: "Control consciousness kills initiative."

3. *Make Nerds Network*: Internal learning benefits from contact, just as extended learning is best developed at points of contact with customers and suppliers. In the technology area in particular, networking is vital. 3M's Annual Technology Forum brings together 6,850 individuals from various disciplines to meet, share ideas, and develop relationships to share future ideas and initiatives. There is always a potential for greater transfer of ideas and knowledge where there is greater contact.

4. *Thou Shalt Follow Through*: Ideas and initiatives with no immediate application are not expunged from the repositories of corporate intellectual capital. PostIt pads was a concept that took a decade to gestate. Tambacer, a cardiac drug, took two years longer. At the right time, each made a significant impact on its market.

5. *Blur Job Distinctions*: Eliminating rigid boundaries is a key element of a process to enable the creative thought process to work. Each employee has a right and an obligation to contribute to the overall success of the division, and ultimately the company.

6. *Divide and Grow*: 3M expressly avoids what could be called the IBM syndrome of enormous, monolithic similarity in dress, behavior, and thought processes. In order to maintain a feeling of intimacy and to foster a culture which is "lean and mean," 3M has divided itself into 50 small business units with separate responsibility for products, research, development, and financial results. Where small departmental budgets are not sufficient to drive new technological ideas, the company's internal venture capital fund—the Genesis Grant—steps in to distribute $1 million each year in supportive development funds.

7. *Hear Everyone Out Once*: All members of staff at all levels are encouraged to speak out at meetings. There is no monopoly on good ideas by the most experienced or the most vocal. The strategic process, particularly at meetings, is set to reflect this understanding.

8. *Practice 360-degree Performance Reviews*:   In order to break down barriers between elements of the hierarchy and to maximize the development of intellectual capital, supervisors, direct reports, and colleagues of the same level are canvassed for performance review input. A more holistic view of contribution of strengths and weaknesses can be extracted to confirm decisions on compensation, recognition, reward, and also to provide a comprehensive view for development priorities.

9. *Warm and Fuzzy Things Matter*:   Celebrating victories, attributing success, and personalizing products through an institutional memory extending back over decades gives employees a feeling of personal engagement in their enterprise. Even Scotch's cellophane tape, developed in 1930, is often mentioned as the product idea of Mr John Borders, a Chicago-based sales manager, who has long since left the company.

10. *Hire Good People and Leave Them Alone*:   Pursuing the best talent available and giving them room to develop is a foundation element at 3M. Employees are encouraged to spend 15 per cent of their time on unstructured experimentation and development. These unstructured experiments often are more valuable than the carefully designed and traditionally structured approaches to product innovation and service enhancement.

This 10-point approach to the encouragement and enablement of creativity has been enormously successful, as attested by the fact that 3M is now the leader in many fields of technology and application. 3M's leadership in commercial areas owes much of its success to their leadership in the process and content of innovation within the borders of their own enterprise.

The Losers

For every success story like 3M in the business world, there are many more stories of failure or underperformance. For every Boeing, there is a McDonnell Douglas. For every GE, there is a Westinghouse. For every British Airways, an Air France or Alitalia. For every Ford, a GM or even a Kaiser. The list of companies that have lost strategic or performance leadership extends across industry sectors and national borders. The specific reasons vary, but can often be attributed to failure along one of the key elements of the diagnostic, design, or implementation phases of strategy, or to a critical loss of creativity and flexibility in a dynamic environment.

Lessons Learned

From the contrasting stories of success and failure emerge a number of valuable lessons, which can inform the development of a best practice model of strategy. The first insight is that there is no one element of strategy that is dispositive—all elements need to be in place in order to generate superior results at operating and strategic levels. Strategic diagnosis, design, implementation, and capabilities all need to be fully aligned and optimised to realize an aspirational vision for the firm.

A vision is essential, but cannot be developed in a vacuum. A thorough understanding of the history and current state of a business is essential to create a meaningful vision that is capable of being realized through implemented strategy. A thorough and transparent process of diagnosis and design is essential to ensure that systemic characteristics are understood, relevant net risks and opportunities are quantified, and that full consideration of an organization's capabilities are appropriately built into strategy.

In all of the winning examples set out in this chapter, a shared approach integrating diagnosis, design, and implementation supported successful initiatives. Only those strategies that are effectively executed in the workplace can create superior results and establish leading strategic positions. From these winning approaches, a best demonstrated example at each stage of the strategic process can be extracted, refined, and integrated into an overall model of collective best practice. That advanced model, set to provide a guideline to the most valuable strategic programs of change, now and in the future, is here labeled Next Generation Strategy.

3 Next Generation Strategy—A "How To" Guide

Next Generation Strategy is a new state-of-the-art model of global business strategy. It is essentially a hybrid concept assembled from the best practices of a range of proven superior performers in the business world. Resulting from the cross-fertilization of proven principles of historical best practice in strategy, it adds a set of principles and insights from an understanding of complex systemic challenges and the need for more creative breakthrough strategies and more capable organizations. Next Generation Strategy thus contains elements that are both linear and non-linear, combining them through a fresh approach that is both comprehensive and creative. Through the careful application of the content and process of Next Generation Strategy, organizations and individuals will be far more able to achieve their vision of a more successful future.

The Past as Prologue

Most business strategies are based upon linear models of analysis. Most corporate strategies are designed and executed in an approach that is essentially mechanistic. The traditional approach is occasionally formulaic and often tedious. The essential problem with the models most often employed in this approach to strategy is that they are simplistic, reductive, and most critically, rarely lead to sustaining an acceptable level of return. They rarely lead to an engaging vision for the individuals who make up the modern organization. The traditional linear models—3Cs, 5 Forces, 7Ss, and all of the other odd and even numbered approaches to the unbundling of strategy—can provide useful checklists for review, and can stimulate useful strategies and tactical ideas. Infrequently, however, they do lead to exceptional or breakthrough strategy. These foundation constructs of traditional business strategy do provide useful building blocks in the formulation of a more valuable Next Generation Strategy. The thought and learning they represent should not be lost. Yet the limitations on the approach they suggest should also not be overlooked and their true contribution properly measured.

Business Definition

Much of the strategic thinking of the 1970s and 1980s was driven off a simple model of business definition. Following the expansionary period of the 1960s and in the wake of the 1973 oil shock, many businesses had evolved to a point where they needed to redefine their businesses, make bold strategic decisions on their portfolios, cut cost levels, and restructure investments.

Many senior managers of large businesses had seen the business world as they knew it disappear forever. The strategic ground under their feet had changed dramatically and the clocks could not be turned back. Competitors were now global. Old business practices and historically acceptable levels of cost and service performance led to failure and bankruptcy. Customers, faced with wider choices, became more demanding. Comfortable relationships and established procedures respected for decades vanished forever. Senior managers needed to understand the shifting business borders in this new world in order to redefine the businesses they were in, as a first step in determining how to respond to the seemingly endless flow of performance pressure and need for comprehensive change.

Capital had become more expensive in the inflationary period following the oil shock, and business performance was stressed further in the adverse operating conditions of the 1981 recession. Deregulation and privatization in Europe and the US removed some of the artificial borders on business definition and behavior. As a result, complex and international businesses stepped quickly into an entirely new order of industrial and intracompany competition. In this new order, many discovered that they needed focus, restructuring, and redirection at a fundamental level. In some countries, notably the US, the competitive dynamic had intensified under pressure from a Japanese onslaught in steel, automobiles, machine tools, construction and farming equipment, and other core industrial sectors. A more selective market put pressure on cost levels, product quality, service levels, design quality and customer understanding, which were all being pushed to new levels by the invading Asians.

The 3Cs Model

The most commonly used model to define or redefine the borders of a business was the 3Cs: costs, customers, and competitors. An analysis of these three elements would properly define the borders of a business, and identify the relevant set of competitors and customer groups that are central to strategy in a particular business system. A high degree of sharing in all three categories meant that apparently divergent businesses could be considered to be one strategic unit and managed accordingly. A lack of sharing in all or many of the categories meant that the businesses should be managed as separate entities. Airlines and hotels, for example, are different businesses (different costs and competitors) despite a high degree of sharing of customers, as Allegis discovered to its great cost. Business definition is as much an art as a science, and there are many gray areas where business judgement and the consideration of other factors are required to arrive at the right answer.

With a clear definition of the businesses he or she was competing in, the strategic manager could begin a process of strategic design based on a clear understanding of the competitive arena and the resulting rules of the game. In many cases, old business barriers were breaking down, business portfolios becoming far more complex to manage, and business definition a necessary step in the allocation of staff, capital, and other corporate resources.

Although business definition sounds extremely basic and slightly academic, its application can drive significant change in a business portfolio where the elements of the business are insufficiently differentiated. This lack of clear definition often arises in businesses whose development was primarily driven by geography, a founder's personal capabilities, or built around a particular set of customer relationships or core skill areas.

A major manufacturing business in Europe, for example, had developed a long list of apparently related businesses built around a historical competence in metal forming, cutting, and molding. It had grouped together all of the businesses with these characteristics into a core manufacturing business. Upon application of the 3Cs model, it became apparent that these were, in fact, 22 separate businesses rather than one. Some were competitive and profitable; others were not. Following a set of 22 separate strategic reviews, over half of the businesses were closed, thus freeing capital and management resource to develop the more promising units in a focused manner. Application of the 3Cs model had transformed an apparent cost and profit challenge into a portfolio challenge. Had the insight of business definition not been brought to bear, years of painful and expensive effort would have been invested without any hope of creating sustainable order, focus, or profitability.

Business definition, even in its most classical form, is a dynamic exercise. Failure to understand the evolution of business definition has spelt disaster for many businesses and the careers of many businessmen. Lucas Industries is a world-famous British engineering firm based in the heart of the UK. For over a century, it developed and manufactured many world-leading products in lighting, aviation, engine components, electronics, and in other technology-related engineering sectors. Now part of a global engineering firm following its merger with Verity of the US, Lucas Industries participated in many of the changes driving the globalization of the engineering industry. But not all of the changes had been well mastered. One senior manager at Lucas Industries, having started as a shop floor apprentice and risen to divisional managing director, oversaw a business with nearly half a billion pounds in annual sales. In a discussion of the use of business definition in the determination of strategy, he ruefully concluded that he had seen the definition of his business change fundamentally along all 3Cs in less than a decade. He succinctly summarized his perspectives of the preceding decade of accelerated change as a lesson in changing business definition.

"When I took this job, we were a dominant British components business. After a while, we were a middle-sized European supplier of components and subsystems. By the end of the decade, we were a subscale global systems, subsystems, and components supplier. In the beginning, we were the leading and, often, only supplier to successful British OEMs. By the end, we were supplying European, Japanese, and American customers in a highly competitive arena. Our costs and quality levels, which were essentially component driven in the early days, became uncompetitive and absorbed into larger systems assemblies. The margin in our business was increasingly taken over by the bigger systems designers and assemblers. As the borders of our business changed, our returns dropped. So we went from being a highly profitable British supplier of components to an unprofitable global supplier of components and systems. To be honest, it took us too long to realize what was happening, and by the time we did, it was too late for a lot of our product groups."

Lucas Industries went on to streamline its operations, refocusing on a sustainable set of businesses in the new order. It now continues to produce many global leading products and technologies as part of a consolidated global entity. As for the senior manager, despite his admirable work ethic, his devotion to the company that spanned 40 successful years in various operating units and a detailed knowledge of every product in his division, he had been unable to foresee the fundamental changes or adapt quickly enough to the new world of competition. He opted for early retirement and left behind a much diminished, but much wiser, set of colleagues and operating business units.

The Five Forces Model

In his best-selling book *Competitive Strategy*, Michael Porter outlined a set of five forces that drive competitive strategies within a properly defined industry—domestic or international. An understanding of these forces and an enlightened management approach reflecting that understanding could lead to superior competitive performance in the market. It could also lead to higher and more sustainable financial returns to stakeholders in the enterprise. With its roots in industrial economics, the 5-Force model combines elements of structure and conduct into a view on rules of competition and the forces for change (and therefore opportunity) in an industry.

The five competitive forces can be summarized as follows:

1. *The Entry of New Competitors*:   New competitors in an industry are destabilizing and costly. They require a competitive response that will absorb scarce resources and reduce returns. A critical element in effective strategy is to dissuade competitors from entry, provided the cost/benefit calculation justifies the investment. The full costs of competitive entry, over the long term, will usually justify a significant investment in competitor contra-strategy in order to pre-empt entry.

2. *The Threat of Substitutes*:   Pricing, and therefore profitability, will be influenced by actual and potential substitutes. Buyers face a range of choices and the cost/value balance, the other side of the threat of substitutes, will have a significant impact on decisions. Competitive gaming will thus be driven by an understanding of a full external set of

products available to buyers, not just an internal perspective on production and value delivery.

3.   *The Bargaining Power of Buyers*:   The ability of customers to drive supplier behavior, primarily through pricing and terms which affect the supplier's cost base, will have a significant impact on the economics of all firms in an industry. The relative power of supplier and buyer can make some industries more attractive and others far less interesting. Differences can appear in the same industry across different geographies. In some industries, this force is clearly the dominant driver of industry profitability and attractiveness.

In the "balance of terror" between grocery retailers and suppliers, the balance differs dramatically between northern Europe and the US. In north European countries, the top five retailers dominate the grocery retail distribution market in every major country. Own label sales are high. Retailers are increasingly setting price and delivery terms, deciding on new products and packages, and setting inventory requirements, delivery schedules, credit terms, take-backs, and other microeconomic policies. The dominance of a small set of retailers is increasing, developing a set of retail chains whose relative size far outweighs the strength of almost all of their more fragmented suppliers. Even mighty Nestle, Unilever, and other international food giants struggle in Europe against Tesco, Aldi, and Carrefour, testing the limits of the increasing bargaining power of buyers. The same is true of emerging US giants like Wal-Mart who are now also expanding into Europe.

In the US, on the other hand, suppliers are more consolidated than the distributors. Category management, i.e. the management of an entire section of the supermarket on an integrated basis to maximize profit per square foot, is more heavily influenced by forward-thinking suppliers than by fragmented regional supermarket chains in most parts of the country. Future margins and opportunities for food companies, as a result, are much brighter in the US than in Europe. The relative profitability and strategic future for many players in these industries will be driven by their ability to understand and exploit the power they have in this fundamental area of scale, strength, and exploitation of the forces of competitive advantage.

4.   *The Bargaining Power of Suppliers*:   Just as buyers will use their influence to drive supplier behavior, suppliers will do the same—

exploiting the benefits of their position and the choices they have. Microsoft, Intel, and other tough-minded suppliers can often dictate individual terms and even influence the overall development of an industry. Differing concentration of the supplier base, scarcity of supply, substitutability, and other factors can drive a competitive dynamic to very different outcomes.

5.   *The Rivalry Among the Existing Competitors*:   Competitive rules of the game will drive investment and return patterns across an industry. Investments in capacity, technology, new product development, price reductions, capital plant, marketing, research and development, and all other elements of the business value chain will be influenced by the nature and intensity of competition between existing firms in an industry.

These five forces, which shape an industry's fundamental economic performance and attractiveness, can also contribute significantly to the development of individual firm strategy within the borders of an industry. Originally seen as primarily descriptive and indicative of industry potential to earn returns above the cost of capital, understanding and mastering these industry forces are increasingly indispensable in determining a winning competitive strategy for individual firms within the industry.

Although Porter did not specifically set out the link between the five forces and individual firm strategy, he did map out three generic strategies for successful competitive strategy. They are differentiation, cost-based leadership, and focus. Differentiation is a strategy driven by superior value added to customers. Cost-based strategies offer superior value to customers through low costs and prices. Focusing on a limited set of objectives to create a superior business model is the final generic approach. According to Porter, being caught outside these three generic models is being "caught in the middle" and likely to generate substandard returns.

The 7Ss Model

The 7Ss model is a fusion of insights from the worlds of academia and industry. The model emerged from a set of working sessions between strategic consultants and academics. Each brought a set of experiences, ideas, and draft models for consideration. The final 7Ss—strategy, structure, systems, staff, skill, style, and shared values—have been a staple of most strategic diets for a long time, and still inform many approaches to organizational design and strategic review. The content of each S can be described in summary terms as follows:

1. *Strategy*: The set of coherent decisions and actions to create relative advantage against competitors and improved relations with customers. Resource allocation is a key part of this process.

2. *Structure*: The organizational structure and operating approach which clarifies tasks, responsibilities, and roles in the corporate hierarchy.

3. *Systems*: The procedures, processes, and flows of activity that allow an organization to operate on a daily basis. Some of the systems are common to all businesses and include information systems, capital allocation procedures, control systems, compensation and promotional systems, and other elements of the operating business mix.

4. *Style*: The behavior of the leadership, and therefore usually the body of an organization. The decisions, priorities, behaviors, and symbolic aspects of an organization's culture frame the way in which a business acts under different circumstances.

5. *Staff*: The people—individually and collectively—who make up the organization.

6. *Skills*: The capacities and capabilities of an organization as a whole, i.e. the ability of an organization, through the individual within it, to get things done.

7. *Shared Values*: A mixture of explicit and implied values and goals of the organization. Not confined to mission or value statements, shared values are those which have been effectively internalized within a business and guide its actual behavior.

Low Standards and Satisfactory Underperformance

Throughout the period of application of these classical models, most businesses in Europe and the US could be described as underperforming, generating results well below their potential and often below their cost of capital. In a recent survey of major corporations in Europe and the US, less than 10 per cent of companies surveyed earned their cost of capital every year over a 10-year period. For the US, the number was only 7 per cent, in the UK 4 per cent, and in Germany 5 per cent.

Taking a step back and looking at the 10-year returns of companies on a collective basis, the picture gets more complex. The average company from a sampling of S&P 500 companies would demonstrate an annual growth of 5 per cent in sales and a financial performance of a full 1 per cent below the cost of capital. Value added and profit patterns are objectively unacceptable, but, over time, have become accepted. From a systemic perspective then, the constellation of the largest complex business organizations often earn a return on their capital that is less than its cost. The long-term consequences of this established under-performance call into question the strategy, systems of management, and even compensation across many business entities.

It is clear that a new approach to strategy is needed where past approaches have led to so many unacceptable outcomes. Past strategic approaches need dramatic improvement, and the game is getting even more challenging as business and economic systems evolve, and become more global, more complex, and more dynamic over time.

Super Models of the 1990s

As the business world tested and shaped the traditional strategic models, a number have evolved into more sophisticated forms, providing more comprehensive diagnostic structures and requiring a more thorough approach to strategy development and execution. Derived from the classic models, extra dimensions allowed old models to be kept more up to date, and to move toward a more modern functional or prescriptive form.

The 7Cs Model

The 7Cs model of strategy is an enhanced version of the core 3Cs model of business definition. In addition to defining the borders of a business, the 7Cs model provides an expanded list of many of the constituent elements of strategy. The additional categories can also be used as a prompt to identify potential trends or discontinuities that, if properly exploited, can provide the leading content of a breakthrough strategy. The brief summary of the new Cs, in addition to the original three of costs, customers, and competitors, are:

4. *Context*: The contextual description of a business relates to the regulatory structure, licensing regime, political influences, technological environment, trade and quota arrangements, patent limitations, and other factors of the industrial environment that surround a business. Active management of the key elements of the environmental structure and regulation is one of the new challenges in transnational business environments. In some of the most dynamic and complex industries like telecommunications, financial services, and utilities, the regulatory and other contextual elements are often the primary focus of senior management and can be major sources of value creation.

5. *Capabilities*:   The relative skills and capabilities of individuals and the organization as a whole are increasingly the critical source of incremental revenue, profits, and competitive advantage. This is true for both manufacturing and service businesses. In particular, as the depopulation of the US and European manufacturing sector follows a depopulation of the agricultural sector earlier in the century, the rise of the service sector increases the strategic importance of the capability of individuals and of the overall organization.

6. *Channels*:   As businesses develop rapidly in e-commerce, retail formats, logistics, and other areas of distribution, the role of channels and channel evolution increases in significance. Increasingly, the ability to dominate delivery and distribution allows competitors to control the customer and restructure the value chain to decrease the time and cost of service to customers. The ability to bypass intermediaries and go directly to the market, thus shortening the distance between producer and customer, creates enormous advantages over competitors encumbered with older and less flexible channel structures and systems. Channels and customers are often tightly linked, with new channels providing access to a different set of customers as well as reducing costs and improving service.

7. *Capital*:   Even before the Asian crisis decapitalized many Asian corporates and set off a competition for scarce equity capital, the use of capital and the integration of corporate and operating strategies with capital-market initiatives was a growing area of interest for advanced CEOs. No longer seen as merely a sourcing of funds at market prices, the effective management of capital (or lack thereof) and capital markets have also become a source of competitive advantage and shareholder wealth creation.

The list of Cs relevant to the formulation or execution of strategy could be even further extended. Other Cs that have cropped up in the past include compensation, core technologies, communications, and co-operation, along with the other variations on the theme that could not be neatly forced into the "C" format.

Eight Strategic Laws of Gravity

Following the development of more sophisticated models of competition in complex international markets, a number of strategic laws of gravity surfaced from the application of a set of diagnostic models from the 1970s and 1980s. Driven by experience curves, growth-share matrices, brand-portfolio analyses, ROS/RMS (Return on Sales, Relative Market Share) modeling, and other analytical templates, the eight strategic laws of gravity went further than their predecessor models in specifying the precise content of strategy, rather than just listing categories of content. Adapting these laws of gravity to individual business situations still takes significant effort, but the direction in which they are leading is clear and informative.

1.   *The Primacy of Correct Business Definition*:   Understanding the true borders of a business—now and in the future—is a critical step in setting a strategy for business. As business definition evolves, strategy will need to follow or lead the process of change.

2.   *The Economics of Market Control and Leadership*:   When properly defined, a market-leading position can drive shareholder value to the highest possible levels. Niche or scale leadership can each provide an avenue to superior financial performance.

3.   *The Value of Incremental Share to the Leader*:   Reinforcing leadership, building market power and influence, and contributing to the financial strength of the leader will build on the advantages of leadership and drive the economics of followers. Given an industry-leading cost base and greater range of potential synergies, market share has a particularly high value to market leaders.

4.   *The Importance of Relative Competitive Position, Performance, Investment*:   Historical analyses from the early Personal Information Manager Systems (PIMS) database to more modern studies of industrial economics underscore that relative performance in the market drives financial return. A revenue share of 30 per cent of a market will have fundamentally different characteristics if the second largest is only 1 per cent, or if a larger competitor has the other 70 per cent. The importance of relative performance is also critical in investment and strategic initiatives. Key adjusted models that show correlation between relative market share and return on sales or equity reflect the value and implications of this perspective.

5.   *The Inevitability of Declining "Experience Curve" Costs and Prices*:   Originally uncovered in the analysis of cost and input efficiencies in the production of bomber aircraft during World War II, the normative trend of a predictable decline in real unit costs, and hence prices, over time has proved to be a universal microeconomic truth. From oil prices to crushed and broken limestone to pencils to computing power, the same phenomenon is consistently visible across industries, countries, and over time. Although the roots of this insight are old, understanding and management of this rule continues to be a critical element of modern strategy.

6.   *The Objective of Discouraging Competitor Investment*:   Through cost management, investment, service excellence, brand and channel power, customer management, and technological applications, competitors may be dissuaded from costly entry into core markets and market segments. The cost of dissuasion is usually far lower than the future costs of intensified competition.

7.   *The Role of the Broader Industry Value Chain and Profit Pool*:   The internal and external business systems, and location of profits and losses throughout these systems is a critical element in the determination of effective strategy. Originally set out in a pair of articles in the *Harvard Business Review* by Orit Gadiesh and James Gilbert, the concept of the profit pool has already become a core concept in modern strategy.

8.   *The Value of Organizational Investment*:   All of the preceding laws of gravity can only be pursued to the advantage of one competitor through a superior set of individual capabilities, organizational structures, and established operating systems. A failure to compensate individuals and teams for profitable growth, effective operation, and motivation of colleagues will ensure underperformance in critical areas.

The 9Ss Model

The two extensions to the 7Ss model added by Japanese strategic consultant Shintaro Hori are steering pattern and syndication. The additional element of a steering pattern—a set pattern of management leadership and principles of direction, which together send out a powerful message of how leadership can expect to achieve results within a business—contributes significantly to the nature of the systems and shared values of an organization. Derived from years of observation of failed multinational strategies in Japan, Hori's extra element reflects the universal need to develop and implement a consistent and integrated model of leadership and operating culture at all levels of the organization in all geographies.

The second additional S is syndication—the sharing of risk, redefining of the value chain, and creative combination and recombination of business assets and processes. It reflects the new shared nature of competitive initiatives in many areas. Even complex cross-competitor alliances in the airline and software sectors are now commonplace, as are more traditional cross-border joint ventures, franchises, dual branding, outsourcing, and other forms of sharing of risk, costs, brands, asset categories, capital burdens, and other essential activities. In particular the evolution of technology and new channels has brought together businesses in horizontal and vertical syndications, which otherwise would not even have been considered in the past.

Modern companies are constantly searching for new avenues to create competitive advantage, reduce costs, improve return on capital, and share burdens where individual scale will not allow any one company to shoulder the entire responsibility for an operation or investment. Adding the element of syndication captures this new area of shared initiatives, which did not fit neatly into the existing category of either structure or systems.

Limitations of Single-Shot "Strategies"

Reengineering. Time to Market. TQM. ISO 9000. These standards and buzzwords are, to a greater or lesser degree, old wine in a new bottle. They describe valuable initiatives, focus operating plans, and may lead to significant improvements in business performance. However, they are not full strategies, nor do they provide visionary leadership to the organization. Most are focused solely on internal operations. Too often, these internally focused tools or techniques push real strategy off the agenda. They can inadvertently sacrifice long-term growth, ignore competitive threats and opportunities, and miss opportunities for industry structural optimization. The full development of organizational capabilities can be lost in favor of an all-consuming set of short-term internally focused initiatives. In some cases, overzealous pursuit of a limited set of objectives can even damage the fabric of the organization and demotivate key staff within it and put future profits and growth at risk.

A major error repeatedly seen in unsophisticated businesses is pursuit of a standard, across-the-board pre-set return on capital for all units. One large Asian conglomerate recently announced the appointment of a new CEO who fell into this trap quite publicly. The company, well respected for its technical competence in many fields, had fallen into low levels of performance for almost a decade. Having had a long history with the company, which has operations ranging from banks to metal forming engineering subsidiaries, the new CEO announced boldly that his new strategy was to achieve an 8 per cent return on capital in every business. Unfortunately, the portfolio was diversified and complex, and the organization was so unschooled in strategic management that the implementation of this "strategy" proved disastrous.

Businesses in dreadful competitive positions that should have been divested became the target for investment capital to raise operating performance. New targets for cost reduction and revenue enhancement were set (unrealistically) to justify the new investments which were, in fact, doomed to an eternally low return. On the other hand, some efficient businesses that were already operating at a 12–15 per cent return on capital should have been able to step up to a 5 per cent increase.

The drive to achieve the 8 per cent target also obscured a deeper truth about some elements of the portfolio. Some businesses that had been operating on an integrated basis were, in fact, multiple businesses. In one engineering business, for example, a major business unit was actually composed of two separate businesses. One was a capital-intensive, low-return manufacturing enterprise, while the other was a high-growth, high-margin service business with decreasing links to the core manufacturing operations. The single goal of 8 per cent return on shareholders' funds made it less likely that the divisional manager would agree to spin off the attractive business, which would have created significant levels of shareholder value, due to his desire to achieve his one-dimensional 8 per cent "strategic" target.

The somewhat brutish CEO, in attempting to drive his organization toward higher levels of performance, unfortunately chose a dangerously blunt instrument. By confusing an operating target (and a rather unambitious one at that) with a truly insightful strategy, he set his organization from the outset on a path toward sub-optimal shareholder wealth creation and further operating underperformance.

Structure, Content, and Process of Next Generation Strategy

It is time to take stock of the role and value of strategy. Past results have been, on average, unacceptable. Global systems have grown, evolved, and become more complex. Accelerated change has occurred in all aspects of the business system. Many old models, strategies, and capabilities have failed to keep pace, falling into levels of satisfactory underperformance that have failed to create real value, to engage increasingly demanding employees, or to secure and retain the most attractive customer segments. The net result has frequently been a failure of strategy to realize the vision of its leaders or to achieve the full potential of existing business positions.

In the future, businesses will need to select and implement the best practices from the past, while simultaneously advancing strategies to meet the new challenges of the future. A new approach to strategy will need to integrate past, present, and future insights into a single workable whole.

A Synthetic Approach

Next Generation Strategy, which is set to represent the best of that new approach, has its roots in two separate disciplines. On the one hand, it is derived from traditional models of strategy. It is consistent with many of the fundamental strategic laws of gravity and incorporates many of the insights captured by thought leaders such as Michael Porter, Peter Drucker, C. K. Prahalad, Gary Hamel, and Shintaro Hori. On the other hand, it is an extension of dynamic systems theory as applied to complex global systems. It is both linear (from its traditional roots) and non-linear (from its systems foundation). A synthesis of these two apparently contradictory or antithetical elements will change fundamentally the content, process, and characteristics of best practice strategy.

Next Generation Strategy demands an eminently practical approach. It was derived from application, observation, and testing for more than a decade in the real business world as well as from a solid grounding in the most recent academic research.

As the practical content of this chapter implies, Next Generation Strategy leads to action, not just reflection, and the value of any strategy is seen only in the results it brings and the capabilities it builds. This hybrid approach to strategy will be valuable only insofar as it leads to a new set of actions that achieves a higher standard of operating excellence in the field.

Unlike older strategic models, which culminate in a single theme or prescriptive plan, Next Generation Strategy will embrace all of the basic elements of linear strategy plus an enhanced focus on complex systemic modeling and specific development of the capabilities of an organization. At all three phases—diagnostic, design, and implementation—a dynamic model demands a higher degree of intuition, creative thought and greater freedom to innovate along the way than old mechanistic approaches.

Next Generation Strategy will have some of the look and feel of a computer operating system. It will be characterized more by a robust strategic architecture than by a strict single strategic prescription. It will rest on a base of sound engineering principles—the strategic laws of gravity—but will also enable an organization to respond quickly to unexpected changes in the environment. It will be flexible in local application and will be enabling, rather than limiting, from an organizational perspective. Strategies are not forever, but like a software release, each Next Generation Strategy will carry with it much of the genetic code for its own progeny. Like an operating system, the Next Generation Strategy architecture will also need to be comprehensive and aligned, with all elements of the system operating in harmony and working toward the realization of a common vision, the implementation of supporting strategies, and the achievement of the full potential of a business enterprise.

Linear and Non-Linear Content

The context and the content of strategy change over time in a dynamic and often unpredictable pattern. At all stages of its development, state-of-the-art strategy contains two fundamental, and sometimes conflicting, elements. One of these elements is linear and operates in a deterministic way to surface apparently predictable elements of strategy. The second element is non-linear in nature, or at least non-linear when seen from a narrow two-dimensional perspective.

An example of a component of linear strategy is activity-based costing and extrapolation into the future. This exercise is a key input to re-engineering (which is an approach, not a strategy) and other building blocks of strategy. A second linear example is the forecasting of customer demand given past patterns of consumption and forecast macroeconomic growth. Segmentation of that forecast demand can provide direction to the development of marketing spend allocation and can identify useful tactical initiatives to build the business. This linear approach provides necessary inputs to the determination of strategy, but is insufficient to fund a comprehensive approach to the achievement of full potential.

Every strategy will need to consider these linear elements. Similarly, every strategy may either drive non-linear change or be significantly affected by "discontinuities" in traditional operating systems. In every opportunity to craft a strategy, there are opportunities to consider the design and implementation of a non-linear strategy that redefines the borders of a business, resets the parameters of performance, and sets new standards of excellence in a situation of conflict, challenge, and change. Brilliant breakthrough strategies are those which are usually driven by this latter element of strategy, by non-linear change in the traditional manner of thinking and operating. Examples of non-linear breakthroughs in recent years would include Japanese automobile manufacturing techniques, portable music and telecommunications devices, direct business models, Internet applications, biotechnology and genetic manipulation/enhancement, value chain unbundling, rewards and points programs, technological gateway management, and a long list of other new approaches to business.

In the systems parlance of chaos and catastrophe theories, non-linear strategies are those that create a discontinuity or, more accurately, an apparent discontinuity in a linear system. By anticipating the impact of the evolution of a complex system, or by even creating beneficial discontinuity, exceptional strategies can be designed and implemented in a business, military or political environment to create a new level of performance and reward for those leading the changed paradigm.

"Discontinuous," "non-linear," and "breakthrough" strategies, which characterize Next Generation Strategy, are not, in fact, truly discontinuities. They are continuities at a deeper, more complex and more multivariable level of understanding. Strategies which can appear as discontinuities are, in fact, continuities, extrapolations, applications, and intersections when seen from a more comprehensive systemic perspective.

The result of the derivation and application of Next Generation Strategy will be the achievement of the true full potential of an operating system and the full realization of the aspirational vision of its leaders.

The Three Phases of Next Generation Strategy

A fully elaborated Next Generation Strategy is best developed through three sequential phases—diagnostic, design, and implementation. The first phase sets out clearly the current and past state of the business from all relevant perspectives, and describes the range of options available for the future. The second phase begins with a vision of what the business can become and defines a clear strategic path forward, including a detailed implementation plan. The third phase implements the strategy in the market place, monitoring progress, correcting and adapting along the way, and ensures that the maximum value is captured from the design and implementation of the strategy.

The elaboration and execution of strategy is not a one-off event. It is a dynamic process that will require constant attention, updating, and change. Our environment will always produce surprises—discontinuities by their very nature are not all predictable—and the result of those changes will require strategic change and redirection on both an ad hoc and a regular basis. The structure, operating principles, and capabilities of the organization will need to be reset to be able to complement and adapt strategy in a dynamic environment.

State-of-the-art strategy will make the best of what we do know, and establish an effective process to respond to the unexpected. The three phases of Next Generation Strategy will both maximize the benefits of the learning and information available in the context of the expected, and prepare as much as possible to profit from the unexpected.

Diagnostic Phase

Before setting out on any strategic direction, it is essential to learn the lessons of the past—lessons gleaned directly from a particular business history and the immediate competitive environment. It will also help us to understand the lessons learnt from adjacent, similar, or relevant sources of learning and knowledge. A full diagnostic looks outward as well as inward to understand the full range of options for the future.

1. *Point of Departure*: The first element in a Next Generation Strategy diagnostic phase is a description of the point of departure, the current state of the business in absolute terms and, in the business world, in relation to competitors. This will include a snapshot of past and present visions, assets, results, organizational structures, products and processes, the context in which the business operates, and any constraints on operation and strategy. The expanded version of traditional models of business analysis, i.e. the 7Cs or 9Ss, may prove a useful checklist for description. Past aspirations as well as events will need to be captured, as they are equally a part of the fabric of the organization and the net risks and opportunities inherent in the enterprise. The point of departure analysis should also identify the relevant systems influencing, directly and indirectly, the current and future success or failure of the business.

2. *External Dynamic*: Each business sits in the middle of a constant flow of external systems which, to a greater or lesser extent, directly affect its performance and influence its activities. These systems are related to economic growth, consumer spending patterns, capital markets, interest rates, labor markets, competitive investment and initiatives, supplier dynamics, product substitution, pricing, regulatory and tax system rules and changes, channel and technology evolution, and other environmental and contextual systems specific to an industry, business, or organization. The industry profit pool and structural trends in particular will require thoughtful analysis and interpretation. Each of these external systems will need to be understood on a stand-alone basis and as part of a dynamic whole. In particular, the three core behavioral attributes of large systems will need to be understood as they unfold in new and changing patterns of globalization, complexity, and dynamism.

The external profit pool is an extremely useful tool for analysis here—an approach which takes the entire industrial system, from raw materials through to after sales service, and adds up sales and profit at each stage of the business system. The resulting industrial "profit pool map" will illustrate where the risks and opportunities reside. A current and future industrial—or external—profit pool map will be critical to include in this analysis of directly relevant external systems.

The relevance of different elements of the mix will vary by individual external systems, as will the priority placed on each for analysis. In the retail grocery trade in the US, supplier and customer systems are of the greatest importance. In telecommunications and financial services, the regulatory environment and changing global competitive map are in the top rung of key concerns. For a software company, technology, and competitor and customer evolution are of equal importance.

The systemic trends in areas directly linked to the industry or the enterprise in question need to be listed, documented, and analyzed. Channels of distribution, competitive strategies, changes in customer behavior, the impact of technology, and other elements of structural evolution will need to be understood at all levels. Future directions and implications will need to be modeled and debated. The structure of the industry and the rules of the competition, valuation, and co-operation will need to be clarified.

3. *Internal Dynamic*:   Just as a comprehensive and dynamic view is necessary to understand the strategic context of an organization, the same approach is necessary to fully apprehend the full internal nature of an enterprise within its existing borders. Costs, capital, core processes, revenues, profits (by customer channel and product in a business setting), capabilities, technology, value chains and the complex cultural systems operating to drive behavior will need to be documented and analyzed. The full set of enabling resources—financial, physical, intellectual, and others—will need to be reviewed. The hard and soft elements will need to be thought through separately and on a combined basis.

Linear tools will be useful here, from venerable experience curves to modern business process diagnostics. But the traditional models of cost, pricing, working capital management, and organization may need to be seen as static points in an evolving system with more potential for improvement than calcified applications would suggest.

Just as there are external profit pools in an industry, the flows of revenues and costs create internal profit pools at different stages of the value chain. Some elevator companies make no money on new installations any more. The future service and repair contract may represent over 100 per cent of the full profit in the transaction. In the hotel business, operating profit from hotel property ownership is low compared to the management side of the business. Property ownership profits are far more likely to come from capital gains and losses—driven by local market supply and demand—than by profits related to international management practices. A clear distinction in this industry between the two distinct profit pools has allowed operators and owners alike to focus better on their strengths, and to avoid diffusion of effort in less familiar waters.

4.   *External Influences*:   Limiting a strategic diagnostic to those elements that are currently and directly related to a single enterprise is a guaranteed recipe for future underperformance. External trends and changes will have a critical impact upon operating achievement and financial performance. It is valuable for senior managers to extract the lessons learned in other spheres of activity in order to manage best the challenges and opportunities in their own. Standards of excellence can be redefined from a new set of winners in other unrelated industries. New business models, emerging channels, new lifestyle trends, technologies, demographics, best practices, new concepts, new competitors, changes in the risk or opportunity calculus could all trigger fundamental change. In the future, technology, the Internet, and e-commerce, for example, will trigger fundamental change in almost all aspects of business.

A new combination of external hard and soft factors may well come together in the future to both drive linear change and contribute to non-linear discontinuities that create new risks and opportunities. Much of state-of-the-art strategy is about seeing new connections, links, and patterns between apparently unrelated systems and events, and maximizing the benefits of these insights in creative new ways.

Often, significant value can be created by summary comparison to apparently unrelated systems and best practices. Channel evolution in the personal computer business can contain valuable lessons for vendors of mobile telephones or high fidelity audio equipment. Online e-commerce best practices for women's clothing can have beneficial learning for sporting goods suppliers. Customer management systems, for example, as seen in the rise of powerful loyalty programs, can be imported to supermarkets or financial services from airline leaders. Category killers like Toys R Us, Starbucks, Staples, and others can inform the strategies of retailers in more fragmented industy sectors. Japanese management practices shook up the entire manufacturing world through the systematic application of Deming's statistical models of quality control.

Be Tough on Sources of Data

It is important to be tough minded about the sources of comparative external data. Chemical subsidiaries of oil majors in the US fell into the trap of easy complacency years ago when they often selected subsidiaries of similar large oil majors as the only relevant source of comparative cost and performance data. By excluding the leaner, more flexible independents, they did not see the impending erosion of their sources of competitive advantage. The result of inadequate sampling in the diagnostic base condemned many of these companies to a future of divestiture, dismemberment or painful cost reduction and difficult reorientation of cultures which had lost touch with the basic flows of their industry once understood in the proper full context.

On a more positive note, the hotel and soft drinks industries have learned valuable lessons from an understanding of the unbundling of the value chain in the airline industry. They have learned to refocus on customer segmentation, loyalization, and subsequent expansion of frequent flyer points programs into sophisticated communications channels, customer data centers, and even virtual second currencies.

Many of the external influences which are critical to strategic success may be long term, even generational, in their application.

As a result of new attitudes toward work by younger employees, the managers at all levels of the business will need to challenge the way they interact with employees. This next generation of employees in particular, will have a different attitude toward their jobs, their work styles and their life objectives. More independent and demanding, less loyal and respectful, this new generation will not respond to old models of discipline and obligation. Tony Chew Leong Chee, the insightful executive chairman of Asia Resource Corporation, recently summed up the whole issue concisely and accurately when he stated that "the new generation needs to be engaged, not employed."

5. *Internal Influences*:   Some of the elements of externally influencing systems can also be seen to have a profound impact on internal operations as well—technology can drive telecommunications, new business models or lifestyle trends can change the shape and nature of an organization's structure or operating principles. Best internal practices from analogous industries can set new standards of operating excellence. New concepts and success stories can prompt creative thinking. A fresh way of viewing the past and present data can shed an entirely new light on the systems internal to the enterprise in question.

New Optics and Systemic Analytics

In the customer field, the value of loyalty and the economics of loyalization as a new view of internal business economics were clearly documented for the first time in 1988 with the publication of *The Loyalty Effect* by Frederick Reichheld. This classic work demonstrates the enormous leverage available in the customer system through segmentation and loyalization through the penetration and retention of key customers. The internal advantages of superior retention of the most attractive customer segments are enormous. Acquisition costs are non-existent, incremental product sales easier, pricing less constrained, operating costs lower and profits much higher for loyal customers than for "promiscuous customers" who switch suppliers for price, promotions, or other reasons. Most businesses, Reichheld discovered, suffered from a leaky bucket problem, i.e. focusing expensive efforts on acquiring new customers while ignoring the outflow of valuable customers. Businesses which had "cracked the code" on the retention system opportunity had levels of profitability double that of lagging firms still fighting yesterday's battle on the customer acquisition front.

In the cost area as well, there are new approaches to the diagnosis of complex cost behaviors which go well beyond traditional profit and loss categories. Normative unit cost trends are still important, as are static relative cost analyses. But new conceptual approaches such as activity-based costing, cost of quality, cost of complexity, cycle time analysis, just in time (JIT) inventory systems, integration with supplier and customer economics (blurring the boundaries of external and internal systems), Total Quality Management (TQM), and other models are opening up new areas for insight and action. The opportunities for outsourcing (and insourcing) have also allowed cost and profit center managers to re-cut their costs and redesign their organizations on a new basis.

6. *New Global Paradigm*:   A consolidation of the previous five elements of diagnosis into an integrated and holistic view of past and present will allow leaders to see a fuller future view of an enterprise, its environment, and the true platform for the development of future strategy. New patterns can be seen. New systems of risk and opportunity will emerge. New rules of the game can be understood and exploited. New organizational challenges will be clear. A deeper view—into the past and into the future—will be possible.

Actual performance can be contrasted with true full potential in a changed paradigm. Sources of underperformance can be identified and alternative standards of excellence contrasted.

7. *Range of Options*:   The final stage in the diagnostic phase involves identifying the range of options available and spelling out the strategic implications, implied actions, and the pros and cons of each. Although there is a large number of potential options in any complex decision set, most real options can be captured in a more limited array. A disciplined approach will usually limit the number to six or fewer options. One option is always status quo—where little change is recommended due to limited forecast change, internal and external, and a currently satisfactory level of performance. In today's dynamic world, this is rarely the option of choice. One of the characteristics of winning companies in turbulence is a constant dissatisfaction with the status quo, signaling the low likelihood of this option in all but the rarest of instances.

At the other end of the spectrum is a breakthrough (or breakout) option—exploiting all high priority opportunities and actively pursuing a dramatic program of change and transformation to achieve business success. This more radical option is easy to choose, but difficult to implement. According to one Harvard Business School study, major transformation programs failed in over half of the cases studied. If a breakout program is alliance- or acquisition-led, then it is equally important to remember that over half of these high profile initiatives fail as well.

Options of radical change may well, in theory, create the highest value for shareholders or key constituencies. But the proven difficulties of their execution will need to inform the choice and the care with which implementation plans and resources are set to realize that choice once made.

Between the unsatisfactory status quo and challenging breakthrough options of dramatic and fundamental change are a limited set of intermediate options that can serve either as alternative end goals or as steps along a path toward eventual achievement of a more radical set of changes. Driven by the notion that many institutions, encumbered by past structures, cultures and practices may need to learn to walk (or to walk faster) before breaking into a full and sustainable run, leaders of some organizations will need to match change in strategy with change in capability.

The Design Phase

Once the diagnostic foundation is in place, the design phase of Next Generation Strategy can proceed. In order to be effective, the full complement of architectural elements will need to be put in place, creating a new set of imperatives with regard to the process and content of strategy.

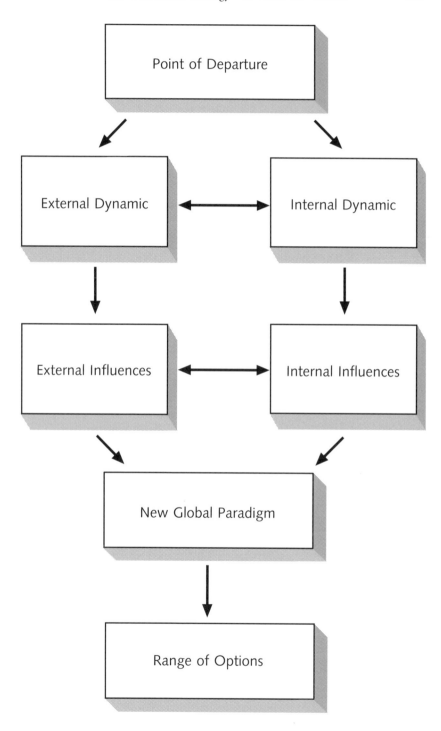

Figure 3.1: Diagnostic Phase

The seven new imperatives relevant to a large, transnational or multinational enterprise are:

1. *New Vision*: Perhaps the most important element in any strategy is the overarching goal of the enterprise. What is the purpose of an organization? What is it trying to achieve? What is the guiding star to which decisions can be oriented to drive an organization consistently toward a common goal? What is the aspirational goal that will motivate employees, guide investment decision, and inspire shareholders? A true vision will answer all of these questions in a simple, clear statement of collective ambition. A vision can be absolute, and independent of any other entity, or can be relative to a competitor, customer group, technology, process, or other defined systemic element.

A vision is not strategy. Military history neatly sums up the difference: A vision is to conquer Europe. Strategy is to do it through a series of alliances and overwhelming encounters on the ground. Tactics are to do it quickly, at night, with tanks.

In order to be successful, a vision must be able to be translated into strategies that in turn can be translated into defined actions with measurable results. A vision will guide many strategies. A strategy will guide many tactics. Tactics, traditionally narrowly defined within the military context as actions taken in the face of the enemy, need to be fully informed by an understanding of the overall objective and the strategic framework which will determine the best set of decisions going forward. Without a clear and cohering vision, even well-defined and well-executed strategies will have no clear purpose and provide little aspirational leadership to the members of the group looking for a sense of greater purpose in their efforts.

2. *Structural Optimization*: As the borders of business dissolve and evolve, a new strategy is required to build a winning approach at the right stage of the value chain. This will require a co-ordinated effort to optimize the internal and external structural configuration of assets and entities. As a first step, clear strategies in this area require a fresh look at the entire system of value added and a redefinition of business. Classical models of business definition will need to be dusted off, updated, and refined to take into account the full complexities and dynamic evolution of international business. Once properly defined, businesses will need to address the risks and opportunities of restructuring, both internally and externally.

Restructuring can lead to an entirely new business system created by spinning off processes, outsourcing, acquiring or merging, combining and re-engineering, and pursuing corporate transformation programs. The era of businesses attempting to be all things to all people in all places at all times is over. Diffuse strategies have proven too expensive to pursue and yielded poor results to shareholders and managers alike. Some of the most successful strategies in recent years have been characterized by radical new approaches to business definition. Winning companies have shed assets once considered necessary parts of an integrated business chain, and have fought successfully for valuable leadership positions on a narrower field of competition. A key element of success in modern strategy is focus—applying resources differentially to achieve new standards of excellence in narrowly defined fields of priority action.

The internal component of structural optimization drives toward an optimization of the internal structures and workings of a business system. In the past, most businesses operated in a similar, traditional manner. They required a fully integrated approach to manufacturing a set of products and servicing a set of customers through a fully owned business system. Management was general in nature and the leadership of an organization expected to provide sufficient expertise at each stage of the value chain to manage the system effectively. As the world became more complex, the fully integrated model fell away, leading to the more sophisticated approach to business system design which led to the unbundling of the value chain. Non-core assets and activities were discarded, leaving management with an ability to specialize in a more limited range of activity and expertise, focusing on what they knew best and deriving competitive advantage through relatively higher investment and focus on selected elements of the value chain.

The internal structural component of Next Generation Strategy takes this concept one step further. Instead of merely unbundling the value chain in order to focus more effectively on a limited set of activities and assets, Next Generation Strategy requires managers to seek a new approach to optimize the structural components of an enterprise. Taking into account the full system within which an enterprise competes to create value for customers and shareholders, Next Generation Strategy principles require the consideration of old borders of business definition being discarded and a new range of possibilities explored. Inventory costs can be shared with suppliers. Customer and supplier economics can be integrated in a new form of value managed relations. Competitors can become allies. System and subsystem provision can be outsourced, but controlled through highly defined design specifications. Franchises, joint ventures, strategic alliances, shared technology ventures, new channel development on a shared basis, multiple associations, loyalty program affiliations, dual branding, and a whole new set of approaches to efficiency and effectiveness in the internal system need to be explored and assessed. Optimization of the internal processes and structures is the first design element in the creation of a full Next Generation Strategy.

At the same time, external restructuring will redefine the industrial landscape within which the firm completes. This may require a decision on participation in industry redefining mergers, acquisitions, alliances, co-operations and major external structural initiatives. Regulatory change may be required. Industrywide solutions may be the best path forward. Winning in the redefined businesses of tomorrow will require a constant review of changing sources of market power and influence at the cutting edge of strategy.

Reaching cyclical peaks in the late 1980s and 1990s, consolidation is one step in the direction of a more efficient set of industrial economics. The next phase of macroeconomic efficiency will be to move beyond simple consolidation into the creation of an optimal industrial configuration, including regulatory structure, supplier and customer dynamics, capital markets, taxes and industrial combinations. Just as the internal options are greatly expanded through a more systemic understanding and consideration of a larger set of options, the list of macroeconomic options as well is far longer than in the past. Alliances, mergers, minority investments, consolidations of part of the value chain, creation of information sharing or buying consortia, research and development co-operations, distribution alliances, and other complex variations on the theme of simple consolidation can create new levels of efficiency and effectiveness for all of the participants in an industry.

3. *Best Organizational Model*: Over the past 20 years, a number of industrial sectors have developed to the point where businesses needed to display both a differentiated and rapid response to demands at the local level and a need to respond collectively at a global level. The reasons for global activities are twofold: to manage systems, initiatives and investment that transcend borders and where global scale carries with it important benefits, and to facilitate increased sharing of information between markets for concerted action against small and large competitors. Freedom and capability to respond effectively at a local level and realization of the benefits of global scale are two complementary goals that will have to be achieved simultaneously in the years ahead. These demands may well create a need to redesign both the structure and operating principles of the organization.

The past few years have seen trends accelerating that will impact the strategies, and therefore the organization, of the next millennium. The first is a broadening of boundaries to embrace global as well as local or regional markets (and competitors). The second, which is related to the first, is recognition of the possible need to develop an acquisition or "inorganic" growth program, often crossing national boundaries or existing product groupings. The third trend, which will pose great challenges, is the increasing number of strategic alliances being forged across borders and markets. The final trend is toward still higher levels of performance—toward the need to extract full potential from assets deployed.

The old model of command and control is poorly adapted to work in a complex and dynamic international business environment. The associated bureaucracy is too slow, the center too remote from fast-moving markets, and the internal environment often considered stifling for young, ambitious managers. Decentralized organizations, which have swung in and out of fashion over the past 30 years, are also poorly suited to focus the full weight of institutional expertise and resource on high priority international problems and opportunities. Transnational businesses need to optimize the performance of global scale assets and processes *and* remain fast and flexible in local markets, often against more focused local players. A new approach to organization, which in many ways resembles a distributed information network, can often optimize the value added from the center, while enabling individual business units to respond swiftly and effectively to local market demands. As businesses refocus on a limited set of priority actions, organizations must bring to bear their full capabilities in these areas—intensifying local efforts and operating more effectively on a co-ordinated global basis.

A Network Model

One model that meets the full range of new strategic challenges might well be described as a network model, since it closely resembles the physical configuration and operating approach of a modern distributed information system. First described in a 1989 article entitled "The Webs

We Weave" in *Management Today*, the network model has become a new source of value and advantage in a transnational enterprise. Every business unit serves local demand, communicates extensively with other units; and is guided by a shared vision, operating protocols, central priorities, and investment decisions laid down at the center. The center provides a more limited range of value added services, and also acts as an intelligent switch to deploy resources around the business. The network is truly inter-dependent, drawing on the capabilities of each unit to strengthen their collective performance

Organizations that adopt this model can expect a radical shift in the structure and functioning of the organization. Costs at center can be reduced. Information will be more thoroughly processed and more widely available. Hierarchies will break down. Key problems will be studied by managers, often from different disciplines, on a task force basis. The transparency of business units will increase the exchange of performance-related information. Travel and communication will increase as well. And the range of skills demanded of management will broaden to include the process and communication skills needed to run an interdependent organization.

On a standard organization chart, a network model will reassemble the classic matrix organization. Yet, although the organizational chart may look familiar, some of the operating features of the model may be new. The corporate center of a network model will be able to clarify its role in adding value. It will manage those issues that are best handled by a corporate office—tax, legal, accounting, collective purchasing (if appropriate), shareholder relations, corporate communications, major group initiatives (acquisitions, divestitures, etc.)—and those issues that are better handled by a single central body than by a combination of smaller bodies. But it will, as the manager of global systems and assets, in addition function as a "switch" in delegating responsibility to individuals and teams closer to the markets.

A key unit of analysis and execution of specific initiatives in the network model will be the task force—a multidisciplinary team with a focused objective, a pre-set timeframe for its existence, and a high degree of freedom and autonomy in responding swiftly, effectively, and creatively to a challenging situation.

One of the greatest challenge in the years ahead will be to get closer to the customer while fending off global and regional competitors, or to put it the other way round, pursue a common global vision while adapting to local market needs. The achievement of both of these complex goals demands a new organizational model, as well as improved operating and corporate strategies.

A network organization may allow these complex yet flexible strategies to be developed and executed effectively; and can create new levels of personal reward for both employees and shareholders.

4.   *Operating Excellence*:   The second of the two principal elements in the structural side of strategic architecture is the setting of new standards and goals—redefining success at a higher and more aspirational level for all the participants in enterprise. The roots of most performance goals and measurement systems lie in the annual report categories of revenues, costs, profits, assets, and liabilities. A second generation of analysis has led to a new set of goals based upon a deeper understanding of how a business operates and how it creates value for its stakeholders. Relative cost position, share of profit pool, retention economics, cost of complexity, cost of quality, and other concepts have emerged, which led to an improvement in the management of the components and systems of costs. Recent best practice has moved further forward, looking at the more complex sources of value creation in an organization. Intellectual capital, balanced scorecards, EVA^{TM} and brand equity concepts are now more fully recognized for their contribution to the overall value growth of an organization. Industry specific measures, such as delivery service standards (e.g. FedEx, UPS, and DHL), time to next generation product (e.g. Intel), share of wallet (e.g. American Express, Citibank), and share of total food spend (e.g. Unilever, Asda) capture the true operating objectives of each company.

As the structural content of strategy advances, and as these new sources of value can be clarified and developed to the advantage of the organization, the target level for these organizational standards and goals can also increase. One of the characteristics of extraordinary companies as described in the book, *Built to Last*, is a culture that sets (and then achieves) BHAGs—Big Hairy Audacious Goals. In Next Generation Strategy, new standards of excellence and stretch goals are commonplace, not extraordinary elements of strategy.

It is, however, pointless to set industry leading performance measures for a lagging business if the industry structure operates in a way to penalize competitors below a certain scale. The standards and goals must be set to capture the full potential of a business position, but not to force an organization into the commitment to unrealistic goals or impossible objectives. Next Generation Strategy will allow businesses to set and achieve new standards of excellence and avoid the trap of satisfactory underperformance. But no proper strategic approach will countenance the setting of short-term goals that cannot be achieved by the organization, for the inevitable result is failure, demotivation, and disengagement.

Results and Rewards

In the future we will see a new, more comprehensive and more valuable set of measures and systems linking results, value and reward. We will also see an increasing hurdle for acceptable performance—as new and clearer standards of excellence for individual companies and for industries alike are set by markets, owners, and managers of business. The performance of the whole interconnected system will need to improve. A new and shared approach to business valuation and business standards will need to be set. Carefully measured targets will need to be achieved.

Many of the more useful modern texts on strategy have addressed the need to look afresh at the sources of shareholder value creation and the sources of operating improvement. Not all sources of advantage and performance fall neatly into profit centers or traditional balance sheet categories. A broader notion of contribution is required if investment decisions are to be properly made by enlightened managers. Much of past underperformance has been driven by a passive acceptance of prior low standards. The most successful corporation set stretch goals and achieve them—goals of efficiency, effectiveness, profitability, and market performance. Implementing new measures and systems of value and reward will need to be reflected in the full set of standards and measures adopted to develop an enterprise.

Internal standards of recognition, reward, promotion, and compensation may need to be reset to align effort behind the most valuable initiatives. An escalating increase in variable compensation that is linked to performance is often the way to encourage higher levels of focus and accomplishment.

5. *Enhanced Organizational Capabilities*: Perhaps the most difficult internal system to analyze and understand surrounds the soft issues captured in the human area of organizational behavior and capability. People issues such as hiring and firing, employee retention,

job specification, capability, teamwork, culture, skills development, organization, performance measurements, incentives, motivation, recognition, and reward are now clearly at the heart of modern strategy. The dynamics of the human resource systems are inevitably a combination of objective information and subjective judgement. These internal systems and issues require careful thought, sophisticated analysis and the application of significant amounts of management judgement. Only through an effective organization can full change programs take place and can modern enterprises achieve their full potential. It is easy to aspire to the creation and management of a highly capable organization that is characterized by widely acknowledged values and behaviors, has access to (and uses) state-of-the-art business information and practices, is populated by outstanding people with leading industry skills, is run through rapid and effective decision-making processes, and is overseen by a corporate center that supports and adds high value. But a precise plan for each component will be difficult to specify and can be even harder to implement.

The development of an effective network model of organization or a new approach to objective setting will force management to rethink the past and readdress the integrated issues of strategy, structure, style, capabilities, operating principles, incentives, and culture. Implicit in each organizational model is an approach to assessing and developing a set of skills and addressing the quality of individuals within the organization. A network model, for example, will require a more enabling use of technology and increased interactive skills on the part of its members. A second major component is a new set of linkages between clear objectives and the system of rewards within the organization. Results and rewards need to find a higher level of integration in order for a fully fledged strategic architecture to operate effectively.

6. *Integration and Alignment*: It is essential to pull together all aspects of strategy—vision, content, and capability—into a coherent whole. From a defining vision through to an implementation plan, all elements of the strategy need to be checked for potential contradictions, inefficiencies, and even beneficial synergies that may have been missed when the component parts were developed separately. An overlay of intuition and analysis will be required to make sure that the plan is realistic and achievable. A common communications program can be built in to ensure that progress is reported to key constituencies against pre-set targets, ensuring the continuing and co-ordinated commitment of all stakeholders. The integration process will need to be interactive—to review the top-down and bottom-up perspectives repeatedly and in ever finer detail—to confirm that all wrinkles are ironed out. The strategy is then fully tested—logically and practically—and the supporting strategies then combined into a coherent and integrated single design.

It is also essential to align all aspects of the strategic business system. To implement the chosen strategies will require that all barriers and inconsistencies be removed and all organizational forces applied in the same direction. Too often, ambitious visions fail to materialize because there is insufficient organizational alignment to implement the supporting strategies. Like a freight train leaving a station, one misaligned element can reduce the overall effort dramatically. An extended 7Cs model to business systems analysis can be useful here. In addition to a fully aligned set of objectives and capabilities in costs, customers, competitive strategy, channel strategy, capital funding and allocation, organizational capabilities (including research and development), regulatory or other context, further alignment of compensation (rewards and recognition), culture and communication will be required. And the role of core technologies cannot be overemphasized in almost all business strategies. To be effective in implementing strategy, the entire business system and the full capabilities of an organization need to be properly aligned to benefit fully from the power of their application.

Reward and Recognition

Just as the content of strategy and structure of organizational paradigms are changing, the systems of reward and recognition will need to change in order to align fully individual behavior and group objectives. Particularly in western economies where manufacturing is eroding as a source of employment and the service sector is taking up the lead role in job and wealth creation, the traditional system of compensation and other incentives will need to adapt. From a wages-for-unit-of-work mentality to salary plus bonus based on objectives plus share participation schemes, the standard system of compensation has become increasingly individualized and aligned with a model of specific employee activity, perceived value added and shared capital market upside.

The next generation of compensation systems will evolve further in two directions, increasing in complexity but moving even further into relevant behaviors and value systems. First, the new linkages will align results and rewards in a manner that will cover greater time periods and embrace a broader array of measures of value. Second, new systems of reward will go beyond pure cash and share incentives into the elements of value to employees that affect lifestyle as much as pure economic interests. We will see more and more creative elements in the mix of "non-taxable benefits" or so-called "psychic income." Flexible work hours, flexible work locations, telecomunicating, child care, paternity leave, sabbaticals, internal universities, funded further education, transfer options, spousal benefits, job sharing, and other options to the standard work week will be built into the compensation structures as valuable components of the full package of benefits weighed by employees.

Longer-term objectives may be necessary due to deepening understanding of the dynamic nature of strategy and the need for time to pass to assess the full contribution of isolated activities. More creative compensation schemes and their link to performance will be required to address individuals within a system who are no longer content with being employed in a safe job structure. Next Generation Strategy employers will need to engage their colleagues through a more sustaining set of rewards and environmental characteristics of a business. Through both of these new compensation variables, there will be opportunities to create a new linkage between results and rewards, as well as creating a more valuable compensation currency for increasingly valuable individuals.

Fostering Intellectual Capital

As an interesting aside, in addition to linking more clearly with the creation of long-term assets, longer-term rewards can effectively contribute to the protection of highly valuable intellectual capital within a company. The vesting concept, which matches compensation with the time-frame of fully measurable value creation, can create exit barriers to employees benefiting from expensive investments in personal skill development and training. Increasingly, employees have become the well-funded repositories of the (intellectual) capital of an organization. Particularly for young employees unmotivated by the late stages of vesting pension plans or impending retirement, the personal value of transferring that capital to a new employer is tempting. More complex compensation schemes can drive incentives and disincentives from the perspective of a strategic balance sheet that rewards and punishes changes in the soft capital of a business.

It would not be surprising to see an exit barrier erected in the future which requires departing employees (or their new employers) to reimburse the cost of past training and development and to pay for the intellectual capital removed from the organization or transferred to another. Establishing a market price for intellectual capital could lead to an improvement in employee retention, and thus protect the intellectual capital that has been so expensive to develop. A more complex set of compensation schemes could create and underpin a real market in intellectual capital and reflect the true flows of value and investment in a service economy or technology business.

7. *Detailed Implementation Plan*:   Too often, the process of strategy stalls on the threshold of implementation. Many well-designed strategies never have an impact in the marketplace. Many visions are never realized because the demands and challenges of the implementation phase are ignored or execution presumed to be the province of operating personnel far from the lofty heights of a strategically minded CEO or leader of a change program. The devil is often in the detail, and the risks and opportunities resident in the implementation phase of strategy are often overlooked or underestimated.

A final output of a Next Generation Strategy design is a detailed effective implementation plan. Specific targets, controls, measures, and checkpoints will need to be set and policed to ensure that the full implementation value of a strategy is realized. Throughout the process, strategies need to be designed for implementation. Theoretical approaches are only valuable insofar as they lead to plans that contain specific and measurable actions. Strategies which are not implemented have little value to any of the stakeholders in an enterprise—owners, partners, suppliers, distributors, and employees alike. In fact, strategies that are not implemented carry significant negative value—high opportunity cost on the management time invested, alienation of the most capable employees, organizational cynicism and loss of faith in leadership, and lost opportunity in the marketplace. A guiding principle of strategic formulation is that strategies are not fully defined unless you know what you will do differently on Monday morning at 8am, and then to actually do it on a consistent, measurable basis.

One optional element of many Next Generation Strategies is a set of beta tests and pilots to assess the workability in the real world of new approaches. Beta testing, or testing of a developed model in a real

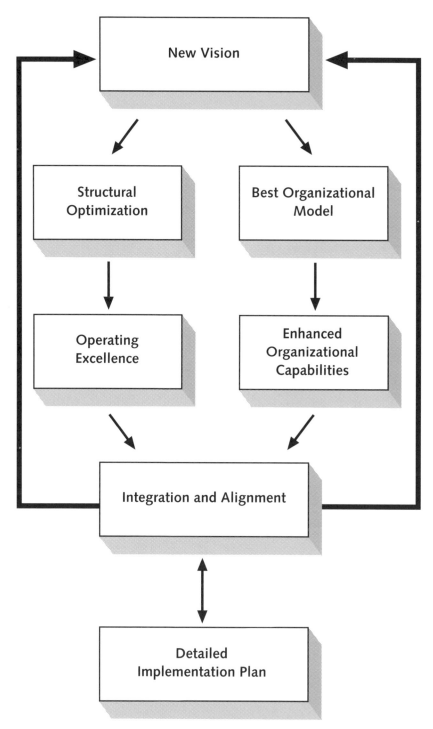

Figure 3.2 Design Phase

operating environment, can be a particularly important element in the implementation of a risky new approach. Changes which threaten (or promise) to disrupt a long established way of doing business may need detailed testing and a phased roll-out to ensure that the risk of change is properly managed and the new model improved through development in the real world.

All too often, traditional strategies are documented rather than implemented. Clever titles or code names are dreamed up for strategic initiatives. Glossy charts or PC-based presentations are rolled out in front of boards, management groups, and external audiences. General statements of direction and commitment are made. Detailed and expensive reports are drafted, edited, and bound for future reference. But little happens. Checkpoints are missed, with little effect. Limited results soon dwindle even further. Satisfactory underperformance reigns, and in a few years, another sub-optimal strategy and approach is launched and results again fail to meet expectations and potential. Strategies designed for implementation have a far better chance of generating results and creating value for the businesses that generate them.

The elaboration of a detailed implementation plan should be a natural consequence of strategic design, the culmination of an inexorable flow of logic from insight to action. Good strategies are always designed for implementation and the process of detailed elaboration seen as a value adding exercise in its own right. A proper implementation plan will translate vision, strategies, and tactics into a meaningful set of actions to drive change in the marketplace. It will specify actions, responsibilities, and time lines. It will identify (in advance) required support, interlinked initiatives and organizational dependencies. Authority and required authorizations will need to be clearly spelled out. On the organizational side, management rights and responsibilities can be documented.

Specific attention will need to be paid to each of the seven elements of the execution phase—core team constitution, resource inventory and allocation, resource acquisition, standards and measures, leadership and motivation, corrective management, and full value capture—and allowances made for the demands of daily operations of the business.

Implementation Phase

Next Generation Strategy requires all three phases of strategy—diagnosis, design, and execution—to be given equal structure and attention in the process of elaboration. As for the other two interrelated phases (diagnosis and design), seven key elements of effective execution are essential for the implementation of strategy.

1. ***Core Team Constitution***: Some breakthrough strategies will require the constitution of a separate project team dedicated to the diagnosis, design, and implementation of the strategic plans. Others will require operating and functional staff to reallocate their time to accommodate a broader set of activities. In either case, careful allocation will be required to create the most efficient and effective mix of resources on the core team. For individuals within the organization, skills, development needs, career prospects and planning, succession, enthusiasm for participation, and opportunity cost of the assignment will play a role in the allocation of individuals—full- or part-time—to the strategy program.

In many modern organizations, the core team operates as a task force comprising members from different disciplines and working toward a common goal on a highly focused basis. Given the holistic nature of advanced strategy, the task force should be cross-functional and should include members who have a range of interests and expertise. That core team, or strategic task force, may be able to implement and monitor a broad program of creative change most efficiently and effectively.

2. ***Resource Inventory and Allocation***: A need to take stock of the resource demands of the strategy follows the elaboration of the implementation plan. For each key initiative, the skills and other assets required would need to be specified: financial, technical, technological, and intellectual. Against each need, a realistic assessment of the status of current resource is required. Needs and availability can be compared, leading to an identification of gaps and areas where excess resources may be currently available. This inventory will enable leaders to allocate available resources efficiently and to plan to acquire resources and skills that are lacking.

External resources such as outside experts or sub-contractors may also require allocation to a program of change if they can supplement the skills of an organization. Market research firms may play a role in the diagnostic phase. Systems providers may play a role in the implementation phase, as could brokers, investment banks or other capital-market intermediaries. Strategic consultants can play a supporting role in all three phases of a Next Generation Strategy program, and may even have experience and insight to initiate, support, and guide the entire process.

3. *Resource Acquisition*:   Where there are resource gaps, insufficient skills or a limited timeframe, a specific program of resource acquisition will be required. There are, in general, three approaches for rapid acquisition of needed resources. The first is a program of training for existing staff. Upgrading skills through special training programs is one way of both achieving strategic project goals and strengthening the organization for the longer term. A second approach is to recruit and integrate new individuals to increase the skills base, and to strengthen the overall capability of the organization. A third approach is to acquire resources on a project basis for the duration of part or the entire strategy program. Especially since the painful downsizing experiences of the 1980s and 1990s, many senior management teams have resisted investment in large staff teams to drive strategy in the operating units. Outsourcing practices have led to selective purchasing of state-of-the-art capabilities from strategic planning consultants, systems design houses, tax planners, executive search firms, and other providers of essential components of the implementation program. Outsourcing can provide fully capable resources as and when needed without incurring the costs, and potential long-term liabilities, of additional in-house capacity.

4. *Standards and Measures*:   One of the many reasons why business systems do not operate according to the visionary exhortations of their leadership is that feedback systems, usually in the form of management information systems, are incomplete or tuned in to the wrong station. Too often there is data overload and insufficient usable information. A business system may have decided to focus on profit pool targeting, customer segmentation and retention, and other strategy-specific objectives. Unfortunately, the feedback system often is driven by traditional profit and loss measures of cost and revenue, depriving the executives of information necessary to steer toward a more useful set of goals. Successful intervention in the direction and even the purpose of an organization will require a new set of feedback mechanisms and business measures to navigate effectively toward a different and more profitable future. Successful strategies can best be driven by managers with a new "strategic dashboard" indicating the performance of a simplified list of critical strategic variables against target on a regular basis.

New measures of value and new standards of excellence in performance are the common foundation for the achievement of operating excellence. Measures of external performance can include relative service performance, relative cost position, market power and influence, industry P/E ratio, share of industry profit pool, share of key customer segment or share of wallet (percentage of total consumer spend), or even the unappetizing "share of stomach" (share of total spend on food—including supermarket, restaurant and convenience). Measures of internal performance can include contributions to research progress, new product development, additions to group intellectual capital, sales, profits, and other measures of achievement that contribute to the realization of full potential.

5. *Leadership and Motivation*:   Effective leadership throughout the execution phase will require the full complement of leadership skills—setting an example of dedication, demonstrating proper corporate values, communicating effectively, setting targets, interfacing with internal and external constituencies, and providing central guidance to the process. It is worth highlighting that strategic programs require both visible leadership—action-oriented leadership from the front—and supportive leadership from behind the scenes to ensure full implementation of the strategy. A network model of organization will require leaders both to guide and empower individuals and teams working on critical elements of strategy.

It is a hard truth that, often, individuals or teams at the top need to change to provide new direction and effective leadership to an organization. Revolution rarely begins with the monarch, and significant increases in shareholder value are often associated with the arrival of new, change-oriented management teams free from association with past practices and prior levels of satisfactory underperformance.

Resource allocation, acquisition, and overall leadership are necessary, but not sufficient, components of an execution program. To create truly superior results, individuals and teams must be inspired to give the best of themselves, to set and achieve new standards of excellence in their thinking, their actions and in their overall contribution. That high level of performance is only possible with the wholehearted support of the individual and team—a level of commitment that is only possible if hearts and minds are captured by the vision, the strategy, and the plan of action. This level of commitment cannot be presumed and will require faith in the leadership, belief in the plan and a clear understanding in the personal benefit—economic and non-economic—to those who choose to participate in the program.

6. *Corrective Management*: At an oversight or steering committee level, effective systems of feedback and control are required to ensure the effective management of programs of strategic change and redirection. Regular reviews will need to be scheduled and a mechanism established to track progress and redirect as necessary. Often, rules of engagement are set against a prescribed set of critical performance indicators—the strategic dashboard—to ensure timely and effective response to shortfalls or problems in the execution phase. Initiatives which are on track or ahead of schedule can be highlighted and those responsible commended. Those which are slightly behind or lagging for the first time can be reviewed by strategic controllers and swiftly corrected without absorbing scarce senior management time. Those initiatives which are significantly off-track or repeatedly failing to meet deadlines will require the attention of senior management and appropriate corrective action taken: resources can be reallocated; sanctions for underperformance meted out or a better approach thrashed out and new objectives and deadlines set.

7. *Full Value Capture*: Ironically, many strategies, even when well designed and executed, fail to yield full benefits due to a lack of explicit effort to capture the full value—internal and external—of the strategy. Internal value is lost when valuable learning is not captured, best practices not documented, and organizational heroics not sufficiently rewarded. Hard and soft benefits can be frittered away if no one asks how the full benefits of a strategy can be exploited within the organization. External benefits as well may be lost if there is no explicit effort made to capture the full value of strategic advances. Capital markets, customers, potential customers, potential recruits, lenders, and other stakeholders in an enterprise could all represent sources of value through a specific and comprehensive stage of value capture.

Full value capture is one of the most important, and least understood, variables of strategy. As a strategy unfolds, there are a large number of opportunities to increase the value created by the strategy. Each component piece needs to be investigated separately and as part of the whole. A summary list of some of the elements of value that could be captured through a more comprehensive opportunity screen are:

Content Value: The full content of a strategy needs to be reviewed to ensure that the full benefits of structural optimization and new operating standards are achieved. The potential for increased revenue and decreased

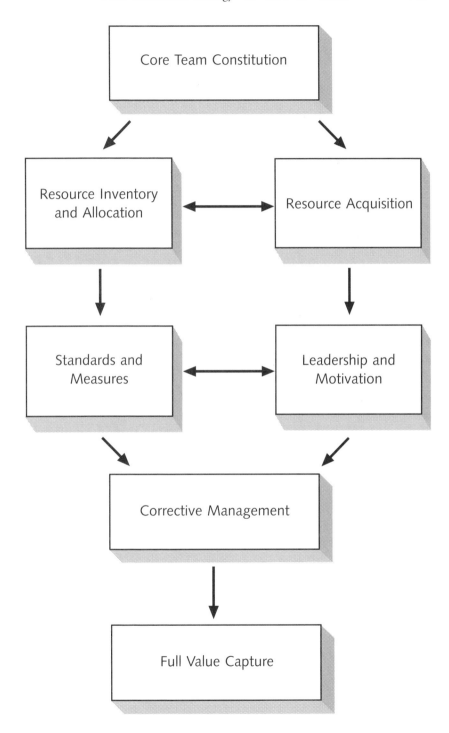

Figure 3.3: Implementation Phase

costs, in aggregate and on a unit basis, is important. New levels of product or service performance can create higher value and may be able to justify higher prices. Share gain strategies may carry related scale opportunities to lower costs, as would strategies to improve processes or reduce yield loss.

Capability Value: Lessons learned, best practices, parallel applications and other benefits which accrue from a strategy may strengthen the organization directly and indirectly. Capturing and codifying, packaging and distributing opportunities for capability development should be an essential part of every strategy.

Capital Value: Shareholder value may not be sufficiently captured if the full value of a strategy is not played through to its logical conclusion in the capital markets. Dividend policies, separate flotations, mergers, spin-offs refinancing or even just better communication to analysts may improve the market value of an enterprise and increase shareholder wealth.

Option Value: Each successful strategy, by its nature, reduces risk and captures opportunity. Each strategy, properly executed, lays the groundwork for further strategies in a dynamic process of evolution and progress. A new strategy will also open up a broader range of options which can be drawn upon as part of a future vision or detailed strategy for the enterprise in its next generation of development.

Full Potential Value: In the end, it is often instructive to return to the beginning, and compare the result with the early assessment of full potential in the diagnostic and design phases. Gaps between actual result and performance potential need to be highlighted and corrective actions taken to maximize the benefit of action taken.

This comparative analysis can also form part of the next diagnostic phase, reflecting the constant, flowing nature of strategy in a world of complex global systems.

Organization Implications of Next Generation Strategy

Next Generation Strategy differs in content and process from earlier models of strategy. Only through change at all levels can a new approach to strategy unlock the full future potential for a business enterprise. Next

Generation Strategy is comprehensive in its view rather than limited in focus. It embraces an approach of optimizing the capabilities of an organization as well as resetting the structural or institutional content of strategy. The output, rather than a specific plan or single theme, is a combination of specific actions, coupled with the development of a robust architecture—a set of principles, approaches, and strengths that can be adapted quickly to respond to unanticipated changes in a dynamic external environment or in the internal business system.

The Soft Issues

The organizational and human element, the so-called soft side of strategy, is increasingly the focus of thoughtful strategists and managers. Intellectual capital, the learning organization, the knowledge corporation and their conceptual brethren are the watchwords of many books on strategy appearing over the past few years.

Although the soft side of strategy is agreed to be of fundamental and increasing importance many senior manages are still struggling to develop the right approach to build the best possible system of response and rewards. In particular, the issues of culture, teamwork, and motivation are consistently noted by respected business leaders to be sources of great value addition. All of these issues also carry a high degree of difficulty to analyze and change effectively. As one enlightened CEO quipped: "Perhaps we should not call this the 'soft' stuff any longer—perhaps we should call it the 'even harder' stuff."

Organizational Characteristics of Winners and Losers

Although each particular strategy will vary, a thorough analysis of 4,000 companies in turbulence showed that 80 per cent of outcome—positive or negative—was driven by conscious management actions. Successful programs of change varied widely due to differing industrial challenges and performance pressures, but all winning companies demonstrated the same organizational characteristics.

1. *Focus: External vs Internal*:   Winners were universally focused on the external factors surrounding their business—customers, competitors, channels, influencing systems, and economic drivers. Constant attention to the outside world kept them focused on the priorities that made the biggest difference in the marketplace.

A leading danger signal of excessive internal focus is strategic plans made without reference to competitors, customers by segment or changing business context. Losers are often preoccupied with their own internal issues, with energies and attention distracted from more valuable external issues in the marketplace. A failure to focus on the external risks and opportunities inherent in a business will ensure that they are not properly managed and full potential not realized.

2. *Horizon: Long Term vs Short Term*: A second shared characteristic of winners was an ability to navigate toward long-term success. During periods of crisis and prosperity, the most successful companies proved their capacity to "navigate by the horizons, not the headlines." The clear articulation of a long-term vision was one common characteristic of most of the winning companies.

Organizations with a history of underperformance often have an excessive amount of energy and interest tied up in short-term financial results. As a result, critical initiatives with a longer-term payback are deferred or inadequately funded, and operating results are often oversold to match external expectations. Short-term results are important, but not at the expense of sustaining investments and initiatives that are required to underpin the long-term health of the organization.

3. *Organization: Fast and Flexible vs Slow and Bureaucratic*: In today's dynamic and accelerating world of global competition, it is not surprising that a consistent characteristic of winners was a response capability that was fast and flexible. Leading organizations were not only fast and flexible in response, but also in the pursuit of proactive goals to create competitive advantage and high levels of financial return.

An inability to make swift and effective decisions in today's dynamic and rapidly changing world will ensure that opportunities are missed or risks realized through lack of a timely response. In fact, a critical element in net risk assessment is the probability of timely deployment of effective response. A slow and bureaucratic organization will not only miss opportunities, but will also increase its inherent risk.

4. *Attitude: Dissatisfied vs Satisfied with the Status Quo*: Surprisingly, leading companies were never satisfied with their achievements. The status quo, no matter how admired, was only seen as a stage on the path to realize better opportunities or to reduce critical risks in the strategic development of the enterprise.

Change and a constant process of change are necessary for any company to stay on the cutting edge of competition and strategy. A lack of desire to change will ensure stagnation, institutionalize complacency, and create great vulnerability to more organizationally enabled competitors. In particular, businesses mired in the past will be unable to take advantage of new opportunities or to reduce net risk in the competition for strategic advantage and superior financial performance.

Prepared for the Unexpected

One very low profile but exceptionally insightful chief executive officer has long recognized these four organizational characteristics as key elements of global strategy. As chairman and CEO of a global network company, he has presided over a business that has established and defended a leadership position in a high-growth global business for over a decade.

The business had grown from a small team of entrepreneurial owners to a highly sophisticated network of operations to support an on-the-ground presence in over 200 countries. The massive supporting technology infrastructure rivals that of any complex global business and can track products and service levels in each part of a complicated international network from Saigon to Santiago or from New York to Tokyo.

The CEO often said that a great part of his strategy was to build the best organization possible and let them make as many decisions as possible within the parameters of group vision and strategies.

"In a high-growth complex international business within a dynamic industry, I can't foresee every issue that will arise, nor can I always be there when a crisis emerges. All we can do is build a highly capable organization, enabled by technology, and let them get on with it," explained the CEO. "To the extent possible, we manage what we can but recognize the need to be prepared for the unexpected as well."

Highly Effective Task Force Approach

Some years ago this philosophy was severely tested when a rival company unexpectedly bought out an operating partner in North America. The network organization sprang into action, quickly establishing a focused task force to recreate the missing link on a fully-owned basis. Within months, the business volumes were restored. The business again was in a leadership position, and was even stronger than before. Said the CEO:

"...that's the sort of challenge that cannot be predicted—the only preparation you can do is to strengthen the organization, get the best people in the right jobs, and support them to do what they need to do when the unexpected happens."

This example of a winning organizational approach created success out of crisis. The task force initiative paid handsome returns on past investments in creative organizational design and executive development. The close attention paid over the years to developing and preserving a culture of effective action in turbulence allowed this organization to reconstruct a leading and profitable business in a critical market in record time.

A Winning Approach to Network Leadership

In the future, enlightened leadership of this type will work well in responding to more complex challenges. In a network organization or interdependent set of alliances there are no longer any commanding roles, at least for long. Leadership requires, as it always has, mastery and success along five key dimensions. Yet in the more global and complex world of this new century, each element will need to be re-examined and adopted to fit a new set of challenges.

1. *Getting the Approach Right*: Involving the right people at the right time in the right way is a critical aspect of strategic effectiveness at all stages. This will span diagnosis, design and implementation, and include initiatives to ensure that capabilities for flexible future response are built in.

2. *Getting the Right Answer*: A large part of individual trust and collective effort will be driven by the single test of whether the path set out by leadership is correct and appropriate. A great deal of respect in a world increasingly driven by intellectual capital and individual "bandwidth" derives from an ability to process data, synthesize it, and draw the right conclusions and implications from it. Increasing individualism and declining loyalty will mean that every colleague is a critic and source of inefficiency unless convinced of the direction set out by the leadership.

3. *Setting Priorities—Focus on the Urgent and the Important*: In a complex world, it is easy to get caught up in long lists of initiatives and to start many interesting projects that cannot all be carried through to completion. One of the key attributes of an effective leader is to clear away the underbrush and focus the right balance of effort on the most pressing and the most important challenges. In business turnarounds, an experienced CEO states that no more than three key initiatives can usually be rolled out. Some organizations can only focus on one or two at a time. Concentration and consistent application of force is critical to strategic success in any system—commercial, military or societal. A capacity to focus and only push high-priority initiatives can turn into a major strength at a time of crisis or difficult implementation.

4. *Inspiring Individuals and Teams*: Connecting with the deeper elements of individual motivation—hopes, aspiration, fears, and desires—is the hardest capability to analyze, package, or teach. Often it is intuitive or natural. In some cases, the task itself is motivating or uplifting. But often it is the individual leader, willing or not, who embodies the initiative and can reach out to inspire individuals to new levels of performance.

5. *Getting it Done—the 80:100 Rule*: Simply put, many leaders— national, business or team—fail because they just don't execute. In one recent Fortune survey, 70 per cent of failed CEOs could be associated with a visible failure to execute and to deliver results from strategy. Results count. Even the best-designed and most eloquently articulated strategies are not valuable unless implemented. The 80:20 rule is a longstanding rule of Pareto efficiency. A new 80:100 rule is also becoming a basic truth of modern management: it is better to have a strategy that is 80 per cent right but fully implemented, than a strategy that is 100 per cent right but never implemented. The intellectual content of an 80 per cent strategy may not be as pretty as the 100 per cent and the execution could be rougher, but the results are infinitely more valuable.

Renaissance Requirements

Modern leaders need to master all aspects of leadership—combining the constituent elements in different patterns for each unique challenge, but also ensuring all bases are covered each time.

This comprehensive approach will require that leaders master more skills, add value in a wider range of situations and environments, and ensure that all of the complex elements of success are properly integrated.

In that more integrated role, the leader must operate more as a Renaissance man—mastering and integrating the disciplines of his time and providing guidance across all aspects of the challenge that complex systems generate.

Leadership is now often more about influencing then directing, inspiring more than commanding and integrating rather than building alone. The leadership contribution to each component and to the assembly of the whole must be relevant, understandable, linked to the overall purpose of the whole and, most importantly, implementable.

The Process of Next Generation Strategy

At a process level, Next Generation Strategy requires a different approach from traditional strategic planning. Next Generation Strategy is always bottom-up as well as top-down. Too often, past business strategy has been excessively one or the other. Top-down approaches have often failed because they do not incorporate sufficient input and learning from colleagues at the sharp end of the business. Bottom-up approaches often failed because they did not achieve the benefit of synergy, central direction, or the view of the whole of a business system. It is extremely difficult to muster a holistic strategy from the fragmented constituent elements of the mix.

In order to tap and to develop the full knowledge base of an organization, the strategy planning and execution process must also be broadly inclusive within an organization. A more comprehensive view will require a more comprehensive participation. The process will require more teamwork, and more time to brainstorm and test new models and approaches. A common failure in the past was to over-invest in the administrative details of strategic planning—compiling charts and completing templates—and then to under-invest in the understanding and use of the materials prepared. Often the last-minute rush to complete the required analytical charts and diagrams replaced a more thoughtful review of content, drawing of conclusions, and assessment of the broader set of strategic options the work implicitly suggested.

To be effective, the Next Generation Strategy process will require an earlier completion of basic linear models and their interpretation. The strategy process will require greater time spent in teams discussing the content of strategy and will leave more time for discussion of creative options and alternatives to redefine the business. Participation in the process will allow managers to reset and share ambitious but realistic goals.

Strategy is an abstract concept. Like all abstract concepts, it is difficult to define precisely. Each individual strategy will differ in concept, focus, and content, and will vary in structure and effect from situation to situation. Strategy is a process as much as a plan, and an art as much as a science. The logic and structure that generate the most effective strategies are often fuzzy in places—blending intuition, complex systemic insight and rational, fact-based analysis to yield a vision. This vision can define a forward path and a set of supporting actions and structures to achieve the overall objective of the organization or individual pursuing the strategy without overprescribing future action.

Good Process Makes Better Strategy

One of the fundamental principles underlying much of the Anglo-Saxon legal system was famously captured by a leading mind of American jurisprudence when he stated: "Good process makes good law." For many of the same reasons, it is reasonable to posit that good process makes better strategy. A sound strategic process will ensure that high quality information is available to inform and guide the development of strategy on a timely basis. It will also ensure that the pertinent strategic laws of gravity and fundamental principles of strategy are respected. In addition, good strategic process ensures that the consideration of goals, alternative action plans, and customer needs are debated in a wide and inclusive forum. Sound strategic process also ensures that the eventual output will benefit from thoughtful application of the full intellectual capital of an organization.

A proper strategic process and useful guidance will not only lead to the development of a better strategy, but will greatly improve the chances for implementation. If the value of a strategy is only seen in the results it generates, then good process and a constructive guide to content should inevitably lead to better results. A better approach can led to greater probability of achieving the super-ordinate goals of an organization and the personal objectives of individuals within the organization.

Gary Hamel, author of a number of leading books on strategy, is only partially correct when he says that we do not have a theory of strategy creation, and that we only know a good strategy when we see one. A good process and effective strategic construct will substantially illuminate the theory and practice of strategy creation. It will not guarantee that we will generate a good strategy, but will substantially improve the average content of the strategy process and increase the odds of a good strategy being generated and implemented. A random, unstructured, or highly constrained process is more likely to ensure the continuation of status quo than to lead to any breakthrough improvements in performance or value. An improved approach capturing the best of past learning about strategy and incorporating an approach to understand current and future risks, and opportunities can only improve the practice and discipline of strategy and improve its results.

Phasing and Staging

Strategies that are capable of implementation will not depart from a real understanding of the capability of a business to change, and at what pace that evolution can best be managed. A realistic implementation plan will be required which may even take years to implement fully, and will need to be phased and staged accordingly.

Comprehensive and Aligned

In addition to the top-down and bottom-up elements of the process, there will also need to be a final integrating phase of reality checking and alignment to ensure that the strategic program, once fully assembled, is realistic and that all elements are directed toward the same goal. Only after the entire program is checked and all elements fully aligned, can the program be communicated internally and implemented smoothly in the marketplace.

The output of Next Generation Strategy may exhibit some different characteristics from predecessor models. The two most notable differences may be seen in the resulting implementation plans. The implementation plans of Next Generation Strategy will be comprehensive in content, addressing and aligning all elements of the business system to ensure that the full set of objectives can be captured. All elements of the system, from channels of distribution to capital structure to compensation systems to communications, will need to be reviewed and aligned from a systems integration perspective. Contradictory or inefficient elements cannot be tolerated and will need to be ironed out in a final stage of alignment and direction confirmation from a top-down perspective. There will also be new measures of performance and reward that will need to be crafted to ensure that staff motivation and incentives are fully aligned with the vision and strategic goals of an organization.

A More Demanding Process

As the content of Next Generation Strategy is both more demanding and more complex than past models of strategy, the process to design and implement it is also more demanding and complex. There are more steps in the process. There are more people and perspectives that need to be taken into account. The design process must slide smoothly into implementation. An effective process to ensure management buy in and leading to detailed implementation will take longer and absorb more resource upfront, but the pay back will be higher and faster in following years. To ensure that the development of a new strategy has benefited from the full capability of an organization and the individuals within it, a few useful rules may set out the principles of approach, which can lead to the highest quality strategic process.

1. *Ensure an Effective Process*:   A new approach to the process of strategy will require longer lead times and the involvement of multiple groups to provide input and co-ordination with other business activities—marketing plans, year-end reviews, budgeting processes, rights issues, and other events that would benefit from fuller integration with the strategic process.

Rules of meeting discipline need to be respected. Many review and strategy development meetings will be less structured, more critical, and bolder in thought than past discussions. Ironically, this broader range of thought and greater depth of content requires basic meeting disciplines to be sharper. High quality materials and presentations need to be developed in advance and summarized clearly. Objectives for each meeting need to be set out and agreed at the outset. Attendance and distribution lists for minutes need to be defined thoughtfully. A summary of agreed points, points in contention, potential breakthrough ideas, prioritization of efforts, potential value, and agreed next steps need to be documented and circulated. Summary perspectives as well as agreed points need to be minuted and circulated, as do action steps. Promising thoughts need to be evaluated, distilled, captured, and circulated.

Perhaps the most important of traditional meeting disciplines to heed is listening carefully and ensuring a broad level of active participation within each meeting. The chairman's obligation is to ensure that all relevant views are heard and debate on perspectives held. Meetings dominated by a few individuals or characterized by incessant interruptions are unlikely to capture the full potential of the group's capabilities.

One of the frustrations faced by managers in complex modern organizations is an excess of data and a paucity of useful information. Distillation, simplification, interpretation, harmonization (the use of similar templates to enhance the comparability of information) and upfront summary of conclusions are essential characteristics of a process that creates deeper understanding and more effective strategic decision-making.

It is axiomatic that frequent, small corrections are far preferable to keep a missile on track than a massive effort to recapture a missile that has gone way off course. The energy required is less. The likelihood of reaching the target is greater. The risk of unforeseen catastrophe is lower due to a less intrusive set of corrections and interventions. The same is true for large transformation projects or strategic planning exercises. A constant flow of feedback—formal and informal—and quick response can keep the process on track. An effective and efficient process leading to superior strategy and implementation is the objective. Frequent corrections on content and process will improve the odds of achieving the overall goals of the exercise.

The principal architectural elements of Next Generation Strategy provide a checklist to ensure that strategic reflection has covered the full set of issues. The 7Cs, 9Ss, 8 strategic laws of gravity, and other models can provide different prompts and queries to stimulate discussion and ensure all relevant items are surfaced and integrated into the process.

The flow and evolution of multiple intersecting systems is extremely challenging to perceive and exploit. Yet to be successful in generating breakthrough strategies, a systemic view is essential. Capturing a systemic view does not mean discarding other basic viewpoints. Rather, it means adding a new and higher-level perspective. Systems and their intersection are revealed in dynamic patterns of behavior. Extrapolation from these patterns to a higher level of understanding and action will be necessary.

Dynamic systems behavior can be captured at many levels. Just as wave and particle physics can describe, from two different perspectives, the same phenomenon, systemic (holistic) and particular (atomistic) views can be equally valid and complementary.

One of the dangers in pursuing a new and more inclusive process of change is that over-enthusiasm will lead to too many people in too many meetings with too little effective output. A process that is carefully managed will avoid this risk and police the line between the interesting and the useful.

2. *Ensure an Inclusive Process—Break Down the Hierarchy*: A more inclusive participation in the development of strategy serves four objectives. First, the content of strategy is improved by increasing the amount of thought and perspective that goes into the process. In particular, the younger employees in an organization may be able to contribute fresh and unexpected views on key risks and opportunities. Second, the chance of effective implementation improves greatly. An organization's sense of ownership of a strategy will be greatly strengthened if broader sets of colleagues are involved in its generation. Third, the process provides valuable learning opportunities to the participants—adding practical tools and techniques while stepping up the level of overall integration within an organization. An inclusive process allows organizations to realize internal synergies between divisions, departments, and business opportunities that might have gone unnoticed. Finally, a broader process will increase the engagement of individuals within the overall enterprise. The challenge of engaging individuals within a collective effort is one of the most complex tasks a senior manager faces today. Improvements in this engagement will improve the entire morale of an organization: leading to higher individual satisfaction, better retention of key staff and customers, and a whole-hearted dedication to the vision and initiatives of a new business strategy from all relevant parties.

No individual or single level in the hierarchy has an exclusivity on the generation of good ideas. It was a secretary at 3M who contributed to the creation of PostIt, a highly successful and creative non-linear development in office supplies. At Asda, a grocery chain in the UK recently purchased by WalMart, the word "employee" has been discarded in favor of the term "colleague." At Asda, no one has an office with walls. The more collegial atmosphere created has opened new channels within the organization for new concepts in product, service, promotion, and supplier arrangements. Effective access to knowledge, intuition, and insight at all levels maximizes the use of intellectual capital in the organization.

The product of Next Generation Strategy is not an enormous tome that sets out in minute detail the activities and responsibilities of each individual for the next set of years. Business environments are too volatile, the future too uncertain, and individuals too independent (or at least the best ones are) to benefit from excessive direction and control. The final content of the strategic document should be architectural rather than exhaustive. It should describe the vision, principles, plan, goals, and outline action plans for departmental action. The plumbing, engineering, and detailed individual plans may need to be developed and implemented at a different level, in a fully co-ordinated manner but with an appropriate degree of autonomy and freedom.

Many strategic planning processes are set to work on an efficient rather than effective basis. Timetables are brisk. Review sessions are short. Feedback is focused. The process is repetitive, mechanical, and uninspiring. The linear and non-linear characters of Next Generation Strategy will require further discussion from fresh perspectives and more challenge on the underlying vision than past processes. More questions need to be asked, contrary positions played out, and new ideas explored.

As most strategies in the business world have been operating at a level of satisfactory underperformance, external examples of real excellence need to be tabled and examined. New growth and transformation models need to be described, applied, and challenged. A constant challenge from external perspectives and from a platform of full potential is required. Effectiveness as well as efficiency will need to be the dual objectives of the process.

3. *Set Longer-Term Objectives for the Individuals and the Group*: A deeper understanding of the systemic nature of business enterprises and the challenges they face will require objectives to be set for a longer time frame as well as for immediate action. Multi-year perspectives may be required on major initiatives, individual and group development plans, and organizational evolution. Perspectives are required on both the hard and soft areas for measurement and investment. Longer-term objectives could include revenue and profit targets, new product initiatives, departmental satisfaction scores, new systems implementation, team skills development, hiring targets, and individual skills development. Each area would have a specific target for one-year, three-year, and long-term (5–10 years) accomplishment. Consolidation and review of these objectives (which should also be linked to compensation) is one of the most important opportunities for senior managers to engage, direct, and motivate their colleagues.

Personal objectives will need to be carefully aligned with group objectives and a realistic development plan for each individual set to ensure execution. This set of phased objectives should be short, less than 10 per person, and each item measurable and actionable. They should be shared with colleagues and confirmed with a boss and relevant senior mangers. A clear hierarchy of objectives should be crafted so that each longer-term objective is fully supported by the next level to ensure full alignment of effort.

4. *Test the Logic and the Process*:   Good strategy can be characterized as an inexorable flow of logic from insight to action—a seamless web of facts, principles, decisions, and actions that will allow an organization to achieve its superordinate goals and generate extraordinary returns to stakeholders. All of the components of the strategic logic should be tested, cross-examined and challenged. Are the facts correct? Is the interpretation proposed correct? Does it give the full picture? Is the strategy truly MECE—mutually exclusive and comprehensively exhaustive?

An applicable example of best practice in process from the manufacturing world requires that strategists do not wait until the process is finished to assess the quality of the effort. At each stage of the process—in particular at mid-term reviews or other critical junctures—team members should step back and ask whether the process is correct, which areas need improvement and how the next phase could be improved. Good leaders and animators should solicit concerns from each member of the team and assess progress and performance objectively. One useful tactic is to end each major meeting with two questions which all participants are required to answer in one sentence per question: How are we doing? How could we have done better? The short answers to these questions take little time and may add great value to the process.

5. *Document the Strategy But Do Not Overprescribe*:   Strategies need to be documented for four reasons. First, the interactive process of writing down the strategy is one that inspires thought, insight, and focus. Conflicts and gaps are exposed. The true quality of thought—linear and non-linear—is captured. Second, a written document is essential for communication. Communication of selected elements of the strategy throughout the organization will be essential to create a sense of purpose and accomplishment. Third, future generations of strategy will need a reference point to understand the past and to assess success and failure of key initiatives. Finally, a cogent, crisp and concise summary of the strategy will provide the foundation for aligning group and individual objectives. The quality of organizational alignment will depend in great measure upon the clarity and communication of the vision and supporting strategy.

6. *Search for Non-Linearity and Creative Breakthroughs*:   At each element of the three-phase model, armed with a fuller understanding of risk, opportunity, and the patterns of complex systems behavior, it is essential to search for non-linear opportunities to generate breakthrough insights and actions. Dell focused on channel evolution and created a highly successful direct sales model. British Airways focused on customers and unbundled all elements of their value chain which were not essential for superior customer service. The Quantum Fund seeks out arbitrage opportunities for investment to profit from anticipated financial discontinuities. Stealth technology has driven a whole generation of military purchasing in aircraft, ships, and ground vehicles. Particularly as differing systems intersect, it is essential to look for opportunities to create or exploit discontinuity.

Leave room for intuition and creativity. Because of the nature and limitations of systems of human thought, our analysis and understanding of complex systems are often at their best at an intuitive level. The speed and capability of our thought can often surprise ourselves as we intuitively arrive at an understanding of systemic patterns not yielded by direct data-driven analysis. Intuition, schooled by an understanding of the basic strategic laws of gravity and informed by the full set of usable information, can often skip ahead of linear analysis, yielding insights on threats and opportunities of discontinuity, which a more linear approach would never uncover.

One broad implication for most organizations today is a need for fewer, but better people to perform the same tasks at lower cost and at a higher level of quality and service than in the past. Technology is only one enabler to underpin this positive evolution. Higher quality and better-trained people are also necessary. An upgrade of organizational capability will be expensive, but the results could very well justify the expense many times over.

One way to increase the creative output of a high quality organization is to break down internal barriers in the Next Generation

Strategy process. A combined team of finance, marketing, and line management looking at competitors may be far more effective than a purely marketing-led view of the opposition. Creative teaming may also break down external walls as well as internal. Involving suppliers and customers may elicit win-win opportunities and new sources of competitive advantage. One of the limitation of linear models is that they do not take into account the systemic trend of shared economics—Shintaro Hori's dynamic syndication principles—which is redefining the boundaries of processes, strategies, and competition.

There can be no sacred cow in the process of reformulating strategy. Every risk and opportunity will need to be pursued if full potential is to be realized. Rebirth and renewal will require destruction of past models as well as building of the new. Shiva, the 10-armed Hindu god of creation, has a tool in each hand: five tools of destruction and five for building, representing the two necessary halves of the creative process.

7. *Search for Win-Win Answers*:   Many breakthrough strategies are driven by new win-win approaches. New supplier relations, integrated logistics, alliances, and new business models bringing manufacturer and customer closer together have all created new paradigms and higher levels of reward for their creators. It is important to ensure sufficient time is allocated for fresh thought on entirely new win-win models, not just attempted optimization of the old antagonisms.

A Dual Challenge

By its nature, the Next Generation Strategy process is more inclusive and less hierarchical than preceding approaches. The output of the process is more visionary and may be less detailed in some areas. The content is more complex, and the design and implementation more challenging. The result is a new type of dual challenge. On the one hand, the leadership of an organization will need to lead from the front; setting out a vision, ensuring all elements of the business system are aligned, and that implementation is proceeding at a brisk pace. On the other, Next Generation Strategy requires senior management to lead from behind; supporting, enabling, and structuring without unduly influencing the free flow of ideas and initiatives. The correct balance of leading from the front and supporting from the back will vary, but leaders will need to reflect carefully on their own role and style throughout the process.

The Spirit of Shintaro

It is serendipitous that the insightful Mr Hori of Japan was named Shintaro by his grandfather, a former CEO of Asahi Chemical, a leading chemical and textile conglomerate. For Shintaro is an abstract noun in Japan as well as a proper name. Its full definition captures much (and then some) of the spirit of Next Generation Strategy: "a new vision; a fresh perspective that elevates an habitual experience; the process by which man conjures up the sublime in art, music, and cuisine; the creation of a loftier conceptual framework; what separates man from beast, what distinguishes the exalted from the mundane; a stimulation of the imagination that heightens the senses; a break in the conventional mold, leading to discoveries of countless joys; the essential way man is capable of contemplating the divine; the way man created the humanities; the state of mind leading to inspiration and poetry; a positive end result that stems from a search for new frontiers and horizons."

Getting Results—An Integrated Model of Solutions

The approach to the solution of complex issues—business, economic, social, environmental and even biological—will require our best application of creative thought. It will also require the deployment of our best models of strategy, the most appropriate structural approach to strategic design and implementation, and the exercise of effective leadership at the highest level. A strategy for solutions to the most critical challenges of our time will require a full application of the whole of Next Generation Strategy and all of its constituent parts—embracing a restatement of the basic vision, systemic response, net risk reduction, opportunity capture, and capability deployment.

Although turbulence, volatility, and systemic understanding do not throw out old models and principles wholesale, they do require a new and more comprehensive approach to problem solving. An integrated model of solutions is required which is based on a systemic understanding of the new paradigm and which achieves new goals through the development and execution of a fully integrated strategy. One-off responses rarely work well to respond to systemic challenges and volatile environments. The nature of systemic solutions is comprehensive, sustained, and aligned. At any particular level, tactical initiatives will need to be identified and implemented which can drive a strategy and vision to realization in the marketplace. A set of investments, initiatives, behavioral changes, and allocation decisions will translate the ideas, generated by strategy, into effective and different actions in the market.

Any effective strategy will need to be designed and implemented at three interrelated levels for effective changes to be made. At a systemic level, an overreaching vision will be required. At an intermediate level, an integrated approach to reduce the net risk assessment and improve the net opportunity calculus will be necessary. At a particular level, the tactics and implementation imperatives will need to be spelt out in fine detail and followed through to the generation of results in the real world. Throughout the process the organizational and human element will need to be addressed to lead the implementation of the solution.

That strategy will need to engage the problem at all levels on a fully co-ordinated and aligned basis in order to identify and implement effective solutions. That response will need to embrace a systemic component, which puts in place the most appropriate systemic response to the systemic nature of the problem. To analyze the true nature of the challenge and to identify the appropriate response will require a visionary, top-down view of the problem and an ability to see the patterns that characterize the discrete elements in an identifiable paradigm of behavior. An integrating vision of the solution will be required which provides direction to the strategy and allows individual corrective actions to be aligned with an overall direction and systemic objective.

Vision

The more complex and turbulent a problem, the more important the need for a clear and simple vision. This vision will need to be clearly articulated and promulgated to set a comprehensive new point of arrival—a new vision of the enterprise. Not only will the articulation of a vision contribute to the alignment of the resources of an organization, it will allow unanticipated questions to be answered consistent with the intended direction of change. One of the characteristics of a dynamic global system is that thousands of unanticipated risks and opportunities will arise in remote locations at unexpected times for which there is no rulebook or operating procedure. With a clearly stated vision, many of these risks and opportunities will be managed in a manner consistent with the overall redirection of the enterprise. The more complex the system, the more valuable a simple vision becomes to both direct and motivate groups and individuals. In a scientific language, a motivating vision will increase the energy available to drive change—each individual contribution will increase and the overall value and energy of the effort will increase as well.

Imperatives for Systemic Change

Most of the general principles of systemic management and imperatives for change, will be relevant across many apparently unrelated systems. At the same time, the dominant characteristic of any one system will create an imperative to emphasize a particular type of response. Although the prescription of a single response to complex challenges is likely to be inappropriate, focus must be brought to each corrective effort to counter the salient characteristics of a particular system and the risks it carries.

All of the rules of systemic change will need to be respected. Successful efforts for change will need to align resources, bring to bear sufficient resources on a sustained basis to make change, and provide insightful initiatives which focus on the most responsive or vulnerable elements of the system. Effective systematic change may require the exploitation of weak links or the shoring up of the weakest point to achieve a desired outcome.

Risk and Opportunity Management

At the intermediate level, the constituent elements of risk and opportunity will need to be addressed on both isolated and integrated bases. On a prioritized basis, each element will require a conscious strategy to manage. The scale of potential harm and likelihood of occurrence should be reduced. The capability to respond and likelihood of timely deployment of the response capability will need to be increased. As a corollary, opportunities for positive value addition should be captured, the ability to capture those opportunities will need to be developed and the likelihood of that capability being deployed increased.

Although relative net risk assessment can be an imprecise measure, its intellectual content is still extremely valuable. The real value in the relative assessment, however, lies not in the academic value of comparative analysis. Instead, the true value is in the impact that analysis could have on real investment decisions (and certainly marginal investment decisions) in risk management—reducing the potential scale of harm, reducing the likelihood of occurrence, increasing the capability to respond, and increasing the likelihood of timely response. The level and allocation of global resource to the different categories—once the systemic net risk and opportunities assessment is clear—is, at its core, a true reflection of our values and informed action on implementing priorities and objectives.

Positive and Negative Measures

In every volatile situation, there will be rapidly changing sets of risk and opportunity. In each unique combination of systemic behavior, of risk and opportunity, there will be a need for evolving negative and positive elements of a solution. Risky or undesirable behaviors will need to be suppressed. Actions or assets not consistent with the chosen vision will need to be realigned or removed. Contrary behavior will need to be effectively sanctioned. At the same time, positive responses will need to be captured to allocate and align resources and actions. Opportunities should not be missed to advance positively toward the vision, implementing the integrated strategy on the way.

Negative initiatives will consist of limiting proscriptive actions focused on suppressing the scale and probability of risk. Negative initiatives can also ensure that positive efforts are not limited by conflicting behaviors. Negative initiatives may have a powerful short-term effect, but also need to be balanced by more positive long-term initiatives and investments.

Positive initiatives may be focused on developing an opportunity or enhancing response capability. They may also be directed at a favorable adjustment of the probabilities of eventuation and response in the risk set. Positive efforts will also be focused on identifying the opportunity set, improving the odds of eventuation or capture, and enhancing the capabilities of the organization to realize the benefits presented by the opportunity. The major positive tools will be investment, reward, co-operation, alignment, consolidation and funding of effort, organizational development and prioritization. It should be also noted that positive engagement usually has a far greater impact in the long-term, although the deployment of positive tactics may be difficult in the immediate turbulence.

In all cases, positive and negative actions must be aligned with an overall vision and tied to a specific strategy.

Principles of Systemic Change and Management

Each system carries with it unique content. It is also characterized by a unique process of development and populated by a unique cast of characters. There is no pre-set format for systemic development or evolution that can be applied to each aspect of such a disparate set of phenomena, personalities, interrelationships, and complex behavior. There is, however, a common set of principles that can be identified, extracted, and understood. Any strategy that aspires to realize a new vision in a systemic context must draw from these principles of systemic behavior. No change is possible without an understanding of the particular nature of the system that is the object of change. At the same time, no change is possible without a full understanding of the general patterns and principles that will drive an effective and efficient set of strategies and tactics.

Newton's Laws

In all dynamic systems the rules of science and nature will prevail. Newton's Laws of Momentum will underpin all derivative observations. A summary of these basic principles describes those which guide efforts to change systemic behavior.

First Law (also known as the law of inertia): A body in a state of rest or of uniform (linear) motion continues to remain so, unless subjected to an external (impressed) force.

Second Law (also know as the law of momentum): Rate of change of momentum is directly proportional to, and in the direction of, the external applied force.

Third Law (also known as the law of action and reaction): Every action has an equal and opposite reaction.

In the observation of complex dynamic systems, these laws, as the laws of thermodynamics, will create a platform for understanding and action. But beyond the Newtorian basics, each of the ten observed phenomena of complex global dynamic system generates its own management imperatives and guidelines for effective response.

There are proven principles of systemic management and redirection based on the laws of behavior of force, momentum, and energy. These six principles provide a foundation for proactive change, for systems control, and for strategic management. Their application is inextricably intertwined with an effective model of solutions.

1. *Inertia and Intervention*:   Large, dynamic global systems have enormous momentum in a set direction. Change in the system's behavior, therefore, takes equally enormous, or even greater, amounts of energy and resource—time, money, manpower, thought, and action. Technically, the amount of force required to drive effective redirection or to alter the velocity of a moving system must equal or exceed the initial or accummulated force operating to drive the system along its current trajectory. The laws of momentum and thermodynamics apply to all types of dynamic systems—from "hard" systems of matter, moving physical objects and machinery with moving parts to "soft" systems of human and organizational behavior. It is only the nature and direction of the corrective or constraining force being applied which will vary.

Optimization without external intervention is a random (unlikely) event. In the absence of external intervention, systems will grow, evolve, decline, and even die out according to their own logic and natural development. Most will follow the path of least resistance toward established goals or a pre-set end point. An optimal state, as defined from an external perspective, can only come about as a purely fortuitous event unless system managers and operators implement effective change programs. Those change programs will require significant amounts of effort and redirected energy to bring about the desired changes.

2. *Alignment of Effort*:   Given the momentum described above, forces for change will need to be fully aligned to make the full potential impact. Fragmentation of effort or contrary forces in the corrective effort may very well result in insufficient force to bring about desired change. For many of the reasons highlighted by systemic management concepts a Harvard study showed that most efforts of large-scale business transformation fail. One major reason for that failure is a lack of full alignment of the forces for change (individual objectives, supporting resources, compensation, training, development, personnel quality, IT, etc) which dramatically affects the desired outcome. The full set of systems and subsystems of a business enterprise will need to be arrayed and fully aligned against the large and complex task of changing a large and complex system.

3. *Vision and Direction*:   Systemic thinkers and influencers need to determine a clear vision and think forward through multiple sequenced stages. Only long-term navigation will allow participants to benefit fully from systemic understanding and action to change the behavior of a complex system. Due to the complexity, pace of change and seamless nature of systems, thinking and acting based on a fragmented short-term perspective will not create significant change nor, in all likelihood, lead to a desired outcome. Abrupt, short-term redirection of a complex system can be both expensive, in terms of effort, and more turbulent and discontinuous than effective in redirecting an enterprise toward a longer-term goal. It may even be important for some systemic thinkers, for example CEOs of businesses in consolidating industries, to think all the way through to the "end game" of their industries. These end games or ultimate states may be decades away in the future, but action may be required today to emerge as a winner in a more stable and more consolidated industry system in the future.

4. *Understanding Feedback and Self-Regulation*: Every system contains within it a sophisticated set of feedback mechanisms which informs its evolution. The nature and functioning of the monitoring and response functions within a complex system contribute significantly to its development. It is a rule of systems behavior that "information is power" and that "what gets measured, gets done" on an unconscious or conscious basis. In order to drive significant and lasting change in any system, the measures and monitors will need to be set to manage those elements of the system's behavior which are intended to be changed. If an intelligent building control system is meant to monitor and manage temperature and light exposure, a set of sensors and actuators, monitored and managed by a central processing unit, will need to measure and respond to input in degrees and lumens. The responsive mechanism of a system only operates on measures which it tracks and can respond to. Understanding these feedback systems is extremely important to comprehend and to redirect the evolution of a complex system.

5. *Systemic Tools, Skills, and Capabilities*: If we are dealing with a different and more complex universe of systemic behaviors, it is not surprising that the tools and process to bring about change are also different and more complex. Strategy is more complex to diagnose and design. Implementation is more difficult to plan and execute. Individuals will need to develop a different way of seeing risks and opportunities, and will need to improve on capabilities and skill sets. Not all individuals, organizations or leaders will be able to make the leap required to master this new world. Those that do will benefit enormously from the opportunities a new perspective will create. Those that do not will fail to master critical challenges and despite hard work and good intentions may be truly consigned to a consistent and lasting level of satisfactory underperformance.

6. *Segmentation of Systems*:   Systems are of three fundamental types: those we cannot influence but can only seek to understand and predict; those which are under our immediate and individual control; and those intermediate, reflexive systems which can only be influenced by collective and concerted action. The pattern elements described above constitute a flow of events and phenomena that cannot, in some cases, be predicted, reversed, or stopped. As systems engineers and managers, or as visionary leaders of enterprises and nations, we can only realistically aspire to create change in systems that we can truly influence. Setting priorities based on real opportunity for change is a critical task in a comprehensive model of solutions.

An Architecture of Solutions

Each strategic solution will need to combine all of the elements of Next Generation Strategy on an integrated basis. The components of a comprehensive architecture of solutions from that expanded model of strategy will include:

1. A clear and compelling new vision of change;

2. A set of initiatives to reduce risk and capture opportunity on a prioritized basis. Necessary constituent elements are:

    a. A set of negative, or proscriptive, interventions which removes problems and stops or limits specific behaviors.
    b. A set of positive interventions that captures opportunities and enhances fundamental attitudes, beliefs, and capabilities.
    c. A systemic response that addresses the specific content of an issue and constantly respects the general principles and imperatives of systemic change and management.

3. A specific implementation plan to ensure potential for improvement is achieved. That plan must be driven by:

a. A set of effective institutions, dedicated task forces, funding sources, and organizational capabilities to ensure effective implementation and adaptation of solutions as necessary. Representation of all critical constituencies will be essential.

b. A program to build understanding and capabilities to address future issues and events which are not forecast, or are not yet forecastable.

c. A set of specific measures to assess success or failure and guide corrective management.

4. Leadership.

The elaboration of an effective architecture of solutions will include these four elements and ensure that a complex challenge is met with a comprehensive and best practice model of solutions.

4
Old Problems, New Paradigms

As we look beyond business and into the social context in which we work and live, it becomes apparent that many of the greatest threats to our well being arise from non-commercial areas. Our economic and personal welfare is at serious risk from sources that lie outside the borders of our business enterprises and industrial sectors. As businessmen and women, and simply as individuals, we can no longer ignore these escalating threats and the potential harm they represent. Providing better solutions to societal as well as business challenges would improve our collective performance and add immeasurably to the quality of our common future.

Application Beyond Business

As old problems assume new global dimensions, the archetypal pattern of systems, risks, and opportunities that surface countless times in the transnational business world can be seen in the non-business world as well. In many cases, the lack of firewalls in non-commercial areas is driven by the development of swift and effective global distribution systems which have emerged from the last few decades of economic prosperity and development of a global economic system.

The same underlying patterns and lessons learned in the global business world are seen in many of the significant challenges to our civilization. Businesses are rapidly globalizing as a result of improved logistics, the ease of executive air travel, access to global media, the development of electronic systems for the movement of capital, data and information, and a growing class of individuals willing and able to work in different environments outside their home markets.

Many of the major challenges faced by modern multinational companies are related to the opportunities and complexities of this new global model of business. Success in the modern world of international businesses is driven by an ability to understand, and master, these complex global challenges.

The same model of evolution of distribution and delivery systems across borders generates many of the new challenges in non-businesses areas. The drug trade is one of the most obvious, where criminals are using the full range of these new delivery systems to dispatch their illegal products to global markets. The spread of AIDS and other diseases is directly related to the greater mobility of individuals and the emergence of a global lifestyle. The environment is a third of many other areas where traditional national borders are not respected. Solutions to all of these problems will require a fully informed and new transnational strategic effort.

A Need for New Approaches

The Asian economic crisis and its resultant contagion, spilling over into East Europe and Latin America, demonstrated clearly the need to be receptive to new ideas, to discard old models, and to be aggressive about addressing the true sources of the problems. The human cost of the crisis was enormous as were the financial and political costs of the economic collapse. As the problems that emerged were new, solutions also had to be considered afresh and action taken swiftly.

The IMF, in the first instance, unwisely attempted to apply old solutions—raising interest rates, closing "bad banks," and imposing fiscal austerity. The result was the collapse of currency and capital markets, loss of confidence, social collapse, and an inattention to the full costs of the crisis. As a result, there was a consequent loss of faith in the IMF in particular and the West in general. Traditional national responses also failed. The World Bank was forced to sit on the sidelines. The US intervened too late in the process and has yet to provide a strong leadership in response to the crisis.

A new and more comprehensive model of solutions will need to respond to the full impact of the recent crisis and also prepare in advance for the next set of turbulent economic events. This model may be essential to non-economic areas as well.

No More Firewalls: Crisis Lessons from a Global Economy

Perhaps the most visible example of complex global systemic problems and the need for a new approach to solutions is this recent crisis of the economies in Asia, Russia, and Latin America. With currencies, banking systems, corporations, and governments toppling or being shaken, the crisis, which began with the collapse of the Thai baht on July 2, 1997, has proven to be a global economic warning shot that traveled with unprecedented speed and deep impact.

The Asian Crisis

The real problems in Asia which triggered the crisis existed long before the collapse of the Thai baht. Japan had already been in a long, slow decline since its own bubble economy burst in 1989. Fundamental problems in the Japanese financial system had been left unaddressed for over a decade. In South Korea, Malaysia, Thailand, Indonesia, and other countries, massive US-dollar-debt were built up in the private sector—unhedged, unmonitored, and under-analyzed. Asset bubbles in property and shares were growing in Hong Kong, the Asean countries, and even in some Chinese coastal regions. Licenses and businesses proliferated. Currencies strayed far from purchasing power parity values. Confidence in emerging markets was waning and concerned portfolio investors already fleeing the formerly vaunted Asian capital markets.

The detonation of this dangerous cocktail resulted in the collapse of many currencies and banking systems, a prompt bursting of asset bubbles, and a significant decapitalization of Asia. Currency speculators, capital flight from ethnic Chinese and other concerned parties in Asia's racially sensitive countries, departing "hot money," and an ensuing lack of confidence put enormous pressure on vulnerable currencies and over-leveraged economies. Like dominoes, a string of national economies cracked under the pressure one after another. Thailand fell first, followed by South Korea, the Asean countries, and eventually, Hong Kong. Russia tumbled next, with parts of Latin America following not far behind.

Many of the causes of the crisis are well known: companies with too much short-term debt; a mismatch between local currency assets and offshore unhedged, dollar-denominated borrowings; poor financial system regulations; growing current account deficits and failure to heed IMF early warnings of impending disaster; a large gap between market currency exchange rates and purchasing power parity values; and large unproductive investments in property and shares. A system of crony capitalism and outright corruption operated in many of these countries, further contributing to the inefficient distribution of scarce capital resources.

In addition, this simmering cocktail was further fueled for over a decade by an apparently inexhaustible supply of capital, an expectation of unending growth, and high domestic savings rates. International and local banks were eager to participate in the seemingly unlimited growth potential of Asian consumer markets, and a group of companies were allowed to operate with limited disclosure of the true state of their affairs. All of these factors contributed to the eventual crisis. The fallout from this collapse spilled over into Hong Kong, Singapore, China, and other countries in the region. The collapse further depressed the existing capital market problems in Japan. The short-term impact saw spiraling food prices in local currency prices, increasing unemployment, deep recession, social unrest, and political turbulence.

Lack of Effective Strategic Response

As the Asian crisis deepened and its consequences reached into Eastern Europe and Latin America, national governments and industry regulators faced a list of potential solutions, which lengthened by the day. These recommendations ranged from capital controls to market intervention to *laissez-faire* policies, and from objectives to raise or to lower interest rates. No consistency emerged, neither did any single effective approach to the crisis.

In the absence of clear international leadership, radical ad hoc tactics were adopted by embattled national leaders. *Laissez-faire* Hong Kong intervened in its capital markets. Free-trade Malaysia erected capital controls. Export driven China launched a $1.2 trillion domestic infrastructure program to provide employment to staff shed by inefficient state-owned enterprises, to underpin its 8 per cent growth target, and to keep the reform program afloat. South Korea, Thailand, and Indonesia agreed to pursue the IMF approach of high interest rates, reduced government spending, and continued adherence to free market principles, despite rapidly rising social tensions and unemployment, thereby threatening further progress. Adaptations to the original program and restored subsidies for basic foodstuff were quickly the order of the day again. Resentment rose against the West in general and the IMF in particular.

Clearly, the problems brought on by the economic crisis over-whelmed the existing approaches to economic, national and international management. There was no unified or consolidated approach taken by nations, which were united only by their common fragmentation. The best practice model was ignored and, in fact, no central vision, strategy or leadership emerged. The strategic and management approach produced a set of differentiated winners and losers at a national level—but at an overall level there were only losers. Intranational agencies had, at best, a unified record. International co-operative organizations showed their weaknesses. The liberal democratic capital model was bruised. Confidence in global leadership was reduced. The risks of reoccurrence are still higher than necessary. This risk is particularly worrying in the light of the full scale of the damage created by the recent round of regional and global economic crises.

The Scale of the Damage

In Asia, leading economists like Ken Courtis of Deutsche Bank estimate that there is in excess of $1.5 trillion of accumulated bad debts in Asia as at the middle of 1999, with non-performing loan levels continuing to climb. Half of this was in Japan. Equity capital markets in the region lost nearly $2 trillion in value from July 1997 to the fall of 1998. Trading volumes and initial public offerings (IPOs) plunged to record lows and remained low for two years. A further $3 trillion of lost GDP and expected GDP growth ensured that many businesses would operate in a negative environment of excess capacity, slack demand, rising unemployment, and low returns for years to come.

Traditional sources of new capital for recovery—domestic and international markets for debt and equity—quickly slammed their doors on emerging markets in general and Asia in particular. Credit lines were withdrawn, senior credit committees became extremely risk averse, and local bankers focused on collection for the first time in a decade. The price of scarce money rose as new risk calculations tripled premiums. Even sovereign borrowers were stung by ratings which dropped proposed issues to a level just one notch above junk bonds. From Thailand to Japan, leading domestic banks were driven to bankruptcy or were on the verge of insolvency as financial systems failed. At its nadir, the equity market capitalization—the value of all quoted shares in a country—fell from $128 billion in Indonesia in July 1997 to $12 billion by August 1998. Malaysia's market capitalization fell from $292 billion to $56 billion, South Korea's from $156 billion to $46 billion, and even Singapore's robust market fell from $174 billion to $66 billion. As a result, IPOs—primary equities issues to raise new capital—ground to a complete halt. The Japanese banking stock index fell from a 1989 high of 2,750 to below 750. Although some capital markets had recovered by the middle of 1999, many business, and investors, will never recover.

Banking Sector Failures

Many Asian banks are now illiquid or extremely conservative in lending practices. Non-performing loan portfolios in formerly blue-chip financial institutions in Indonesia and Thailand surged from a low of 10 per cent to a high of over 70 per cent. China raised $32 billion to restore the capital base of state banks struggling under 40–50 per cent bad debt ratios, or even worse. Indonesia's stated need for $60–80 billion for its banking sector was always unlikely to be met by either private or public funds in the short term. New credits written were often aimed at blue-chip multinational corporation (MNC) clients, with cash-strapped local firms left out in the cold. Many large international banks, particularly from Germany, the Netherlands, France, and Switzerland, had an Asian loan portfolio exposure equal to total group shareholder funds. A few expanded through acquisition (e.g. ABN Amro, BNP, and GE Capital) and increased exposure on the consumer side (e.g. Citibank and American Express). But most corporate lending banks and senior loan committees became far less expansive from a loan perspective. As one international bank CEO said recently, "these days my pockets are still deep, but my arms are a lot shorter."

Involuntary Renationalization

Contrary to desires and policies, the crisis forced great chunks of faltering economies back into the hands of governments. By taking over the banking system, most Asian governments will de facto take over the industrial assets used as collateral in non-performing loan portfolios. In South Korea, Thailand, and Indonesia, central banks, finance ministers, newly created asset management companies, and restructuring agencies have become the unwilling proprietors of vast piles of underperforming assets.

These assets proved more difficult to offload than initially expected. Failed auctions of the Kia Car Company in South Korea—originally saddled with $9 billion of debt—and of Indonesia's Semen Gresik reflected buyers' reluctance to meet initial seller expectations and domestic concerns over the social and business impact of the proposed sales. A depressed market for assets (from a vendor's perspective) or an excessively expensive and risky market (from a buyer's perspective) further limited the number of privatization transactions. Indonesia was forced to revise its target sales of stakes in state-owned companies from 12 to 10 and rolled back expectations of receipts from $1.5 billion to $1 billion. Even at this reduced target, investors were reluctant to put money into state coffers for existing shares, preferring the acquisition of new share issues to ensure that their capital remains within the undercapitalized companies in which they were investing. Little resulted from most of these Indonesian initiatives in the period of the crisis.

The net impact of this forced renationalization, expensive restructuring programs, funding of operating losses, thin privatization markets, and preference for new share issues provided little funding for empty government coffers. In addition, a need for clear business and industrial strategy and a requirement for governments to act as effective owners of many businesses in the short and medium term placed a severe strain on highly limited management and transaction resources in both public and private sectors.

The Human Cost of the Crisis

The related social costs of the economic catastrophe were equally overwhelming. Over 100 million Asians fell back dramatically in the economic status of their lives, many slipping back into a life of poverty they thought they had left behind forever. Over 10 million, perhaps as many as 20 million, jobs were lost. Millions of children were forced out of educational systems. Crime, suicide, depression, family disintegration, ethnic violence, and malnutrition rose steadily.

In some Asian countries, schooling is only provided for those who can afford to pay their children's education. Development experts speak of the risk of a "Lost Generation" of children to illiteracy and malnutrition as 20 million Indonesians slipped below the poverty line again, and school fees became an unaffordable luxury.

As a result of the economic and social problems, political tensions also rose. Relations between Singapore and Malaysia fell to an all-time low. Race riots aimed at the ethnic Chinese became a common occurrence in Indonesia. Japan lost stature by the day as it failed to resolve issues underlying the 1989 collapse of its capital markets and dithered over fiscal stimulus and demand packages. Confidence, for obvious reasons, fell across the entire region.

James Wolfensohn, president of the World Bank, summed up the tragedy when he was quoted in the *Financial Times*: "Countries that until recently believed they were turning the tide in the fight against poverty are witnessing its re-emergence along with hunger and the human suffering that it brings."

Unemployment

More than 10 million jobs were estimated to have been lost in South East Asia alone. For each percentage point of lost growth in China, an estimated three million potential jobs are lost. As high growth is required to absorb the millions of redundant State Owned Enterprise (SOE) workers, a slowing of growth would imperil the pace and sustainability of reforms. In South Korea, labor militancy marked an escalating level of unemployment initially forecast to rise from 700,000 to nearly 2 million. For the first time in recent history, the unemployment rate in Japan was higher than that of the US. A prescient article in the *Harvard Business Review* in 1993 warned of an excessive white-collar staffing level exceeding one million workers in Japan. Even with the unique Japanese approach to unemployment—transferring unwanted executives into affiliated companies, providing non-jobs for the "walking dead," and restructuring foreign subsidiaries by removing non-Japanese employees first—the ranks of the unemployed in Japan swelled to historic highs, placing heavy pressure on the unemployed, their families, and a system unaccustomed to reabsorbing newly unemployed older executives in particular.

It is worth remembering that the unemployment rate in the financial services sector in the US during a similar period of restructuring and bank failures exceeded the average national unemployment rate during the Great Depression. Major economic dislocations inevitably have a significant impact on employment, and the failure of many emerging countries to provide a social safety net amplified the total costs of this particular crisis.

A failure to act swiftly and effectively not only prolonged and deepened the crisis, but also increased the risk of a global economic meltdown and further destabilized an already volatile geopolitical situation. The failure to act effectively by global institutions trusted with the development and implementation of a recovery plan has reduced faith in current world leadership and further widened the gulf between the East and West for decades to come.

The Limited Capability of the IMF to Respond

As the frontline organization leading the region to recovery, the IMF has attracted much criticism of its role in the crisis. In particular, the early application of traditional models of crisis management proved costly and ineffective.

From a deeper perspective, another problem with the IMF's approach was not that it was, as claimed by some countries, excessively intrusive, rather that it was inevitably too limited. It was directly active in too few countries, was funded with too little capital, and was not able to take a direct approach to the largest economic problem facing the region—vast quantities of corporate debt and a shortage of equity capital in the private sector. Further, the opportunity was lost to co-ordinate the initiatives of various governments and international institutions to address the full set of issues on an effective basis across all of Asia.

The hard truth of the matter is that the IMF response to the crisis could only ever have been inadequate. There are five primary reasons for this.

First, the IMF, by the nature of its charter, was not able to provide the type of capital needed in Asia. The heart of the problem was excessive private sector debt and dramatic erosion of the private sector equity capital base in Asia. The IMF is charged with ensuring the stability of the international monetary system, not the recapitalization of troubled private sector enterprises. Traditionally, the IMF acts as a lender of last resort to bridge short-term crises in current account imbalances, and does not provide effective advice or long-term funds for structural reform and recovery. Longer-term programs are not the strength of the IMF. Nor for that matter, the feeding of a hungry population. This territory more appropriately belongs to the World Bank and the International Finance Corporation (IFC).

Second, IMF programs were only in place in Thailand, South Korea, and Indonesia. The Philippines was an old patient undergoing rehabilitation since the Marcos era. Crisis fallout in Malaysia, Japan, China, Hong Kong, Singapore, and other countries was left unattended.

Third, IMF funding was inadequate in the face of the capital vacuum created by the crisis. The total IMF package, to be disbursed over a number of years, amounted to a total of $100 billion spread over the three countries. Aid to Indonesia's 200 million beleaguered citizens trickled in in $1-billion increments, not nearly enough to restore health to an economy where the stock market declined 80 per cent and where the banking system had collapsed under bad loan rates that exceeded 70 per cent in some state banks. To put it into perspective, Indonesia needed to feed a population of 200 million, to recapitalize its insolvent banking sector, to support tens of millions of newly unemployed workers, to restructure and privatize a vast network of inefficient state enterprises, and to rebuild a collapsed distribution system which was previously dominated by ethnic Chinese. A $1-billion tranche of IMF capital provides $5 per person to apply against all of these tasks, far short of requirements to make progress against the daunting list of shortfalls in the country.

Fourth, the political and social costs of the IMF program were extremely high and the risk of major civil unrest was barely averted in South Korea, Thailand, and Indonesia. The IMF package of high interest rates, closure of entire sectors of financial services industry, price deregulation, and fiscal austerity is seen by some to have contributed as much to the problem as to the solution.

Lastly, was the resulting loss of confidence in the IMF. At a time when co-ordination and collective effort was at a premium, the IMF became a pariah in Malaysia and other crisis-damaged countries. The IMF solutions, when compared to the true sources and scale of the problem, have proved to be of mixed value and leadership opportunities were lost across the region.

Overall Capability to Respond

Throughout the deepest phases of the crisis in 1997 and 1998, response to the crisis was, at best, of a patchwork nature. In areas where co-operation would have been most beneficial—trade finance, currency support, interest rate policy, financial sector initiatives, multi-party debt restructuring, food programs, and regulatory reform—there was little co-ordination of effort. Only following the collapse in Russia, with its sensitive issues of geopolitical and military balance, and the threat of the collapse of the yen have the US and the G7 countries been seen to place a priority on the overall emerging markets situation. The risk of global meltdown and political instability finally drove the US and major free-market allies to understand and to act to contain the depth and potential impact of the continuing economic crisis of the emerging markets.

Risk and Opportunity for New Vision and Effective Solutions

Based on a full and accurate understanding of the problems set out above, a fully co-ordinated program for recovery was required which could have addressed all aspects of the emerging markets' crisis-related issues—social, economic, and political.

A comprehensive and effective solution to the full set of problems created by the crises in the emerging markets required a bold and innovative approach, involving billions of dollars of relief aid and private sector capital.

That bold and innovative approach would have required a high degree of institutional co-ordination, a far greater scale of engagement by the West, a more inclusive approach in the regions, and more effective leadership. Given the clear failure of the IMF to provide results along these dimensions, new leadership could take over the frontline responsibility in the next crisis to develop and implement a different and more meaningful architecture for recovery.

This crisis created a unique opportunity to cement relations between the developed markets of the world and the crisis-hit countries of the developing world. Unfortunately, that opportunity has now been lost and an element of mistrust has joined a sense of mutual participation in the global economy.

Failure to move now to prepare for the next catastrophe will prolong and deepen any ensuing crisis, increase the fragmentation of the regions, increase dormant geopolitical risk, and widen the gulf between Southern, Eastern and Western Worlds for decades to come.

Prior to July 1997, the world as a whole appeared to be moving peacefully toward a shared model of democratic market capitalism. There was little large-scale conflict on a global basis. The emerging markets crises unexpectedly upset this progressive trend dramatically. World leaders need, once again, to come together rapidly and effectively to stop a similar crisis from destabilizing the current global order and thus, creating a deeper and more lasting crisis around the world in the future.

In business terms, the crisis in the emerging markets in general and Asia in particular created a challenge familiar to many experienced executives—a set of troubled enterprises well positioned for a turnaround strategy. Asia's political leaders have struggled with the usual set of issues common to many turnarounds: economies burdened with too much debt; soft demand; excess capacity; fragmented industries; increasing global competition; lack of profits and cash flow; slowing investment;

unwilling (and unpaid) lenders; disappointed capital markets; and low levels of consumer confidence.

Unfortunately in the emerging market crisis, all of the critical elements of an effective turnaround strategy were missing. There was no agreement on the real problems, no common vision of the turnaround, no specific strategic plan, no single team responsible for the effort, no measures of success, and no strong leadership. Formerly accepted principles of free-market capitalism were discarded and ad hoc state intervention broadly sanctioned. This lack of a common vision and approach to a turnaround strategy created a strategic vacuum into which national leaders in emerging markets were driven to adopt one-off solutions tailored to serve short-term economic and political interests.

Creativity and Capital Controls

Creative solutions are often needed to respond to new types of crises. Despite dire warnings to the contrary, Malaysia's irascible prime minister, Dr Mahathir Mohamed, flew against the grain of traditional economic orthodoxy when he cut interest rates and erected capital barriers to protect the Malaysian economy from a capital-flight driven collapse.

Although now faced with a complex and delicate task of re-entering a free-trade economy, the controversial measures implemented by Dr Mahathir have proven surprisingly effective. Despite heavy criticism at the time of implementation, capital controls will no doubt be considered as a valid weapon against economic collapse in the future.

IMF-inspired interest rate hikes and forced closure of critical financial institutions were avoided in Malaysia. A creative alternative was implemented. A comparison to Indonesia, even Thailand in the early days, may well prove in the long run that the more drastic protective measure of capital controls may have been the best thing for Malaysia during the embattled years of the late 1990s.

Gaps in the Structure

The approach taken reflected gaps in the global architecture and shortfalls in the approach to crisis management. The crisis team was fragmented and the process of decision-making not fully representative. The cast of institutional characters included the G7, G24, IMF, World Bank, Asian Development Bank (ADB), EXIM Bank, International Finance Corporation (IFC), Asia Pacific Economic Cooperation (Apec), Asem, ICGI, and the individual development agencies of developed and developing countries. The private sector, made up of local and international banks and businesses, had no seat at the table, despite being at the heart of the problem and also critical to any real long-term solution. A consolidation of institutions and the creation of a private sector advisory council could have been valuable steps in the development of an effective crisis response.

There is, surprisingly, no credible body representing the interests of the business sector at a global level. There is a long list of business (and mixed business/government) organizations which includes international chambers of commerce, the Conference Board, the Club of Rome, the Trilateral Commission, the Council on Foreign Relations, but there is no global organization of any strength that is capable of representing private sector business interests in a crisis situation. One may well be needed before the next global crisis hits.

On hindsight, institutional consolidation could better have taken place in the recent crisis under the direction of the World Bank than the IMF. The World Bank is the lead institution in social programs and private sector restructuring under the International Bank for Reconstruction and Development (IBRD) and the IFC. Ultimately, a new Asian institution similar to the European Bank for Reconstruction and Development (EBRD) would have been ideal as it would be capable of providing private sector equity and debt funds, along with restructuring advice. This "ABRD" (an Asian version of the EBRD) could be developed as a separate trust under the World Bank (as recommended by ASEM2) or as a new multilateral development bank, as alluded to by the former US Treasury Secretary Robert Rubin in his press conference following the last round of G7 meetings.

A Private Sector Advisory Council for Asia, similar to that recently established in Hong Kong by Chief Executive Tung Chee Hwa, is also required at the most senior level. This council could represent the diverse interests of international and local businesses in Asia and ensure that the views of this critical constituency are fully represented in any discussion of solutions to this crisis or its inevitable successors.

It is clear that the IMF could not lead the path to recovery for the future, and Western powers will need to look for a more effective future leader for similar regional crises. A full recovery program would require a full and co-ordinated effort by the IMF, World Bank, IFC, G7, ADB, UN, the US Federal Reserve Board, and other institutions. Although the participants at the recent London session of ASEM2 generated a shortlist of sound economic principles to underpin a regional recovery, the proposed action list fell far short of real needs, underscoring the point that overall leadership out of crisis must come from more purposeful action, logically led by the US and the larger group of G7 countries. As the American intervention to limit the deterioration of the yen showed, swift and clear tactical moves, backed by capital and political resolve, can be successful in responding on a timely basis to short-term economic threats.

While the US may need to lead the design of an unexpected crisis recovery process, a new institution, free from excessive US influence, could be set up to implement recovery programs over the longer term.

It is possible to set up the suggested ABRD as a dedicated and well-capitalized institution, funded by the G7 and Asian governments alike. The 61 national governments which provided the Ecu 5 billion for Eastern Europe's recovery institution could also be logical core contributors to this dedicated Asian recovery institution. A virtual ABRD, set up as a dedicated task force along the lines of those operating within a state-of-the-art network organization, would have been ideal—it would have been less bureaucratic and less Japanese in flavor than the ADB, and it would have been tailored to meet the needs of the recent crisis. A task force model, involving public- and private-sector initiatives, would have suited well to implement and co-ordinate a comprehensive recovery program for Asia. The EBRD staffing approach of mixing nationals of the target countries and Western experts would also be attractive, as would the policy instituted under Jacques de la Rosiere of placing the bulk of the EBRD's staff into stricken countries.

This approach would have a number of attractive characteristics and would be unburdened by any negative history in the region. Like the EBRD, such an Asian institution could provide independent advice on restructuring, invest fresh equity capital (without the ability to take majority control of an investee company), lend and underwrite debt capital, and provide professional strategic advice for crisis-hit private and public sector companies. In addition, the commercial approach of the EBRD, which has generated profits over the past five years even with a Ecu 150 million write-off in the first half of 1998, would limit the political backlash in donor countries.

Given the importance of the situation and failures in Asia, it is clear that the US, as leader of the G7 countries, should step in swiftly to prepare a program that reduces risks and captures opportunities in the future. A World Bank-IFC-EBRD team could be appointed to jump-start the full set of necessary programs on a timely and effective basis. These existing institutions are already staffed by an international set of professionals familiar with Asia, experts in critical industrial sectors, and senior managers who are highly capable in the areas of privatization, restructuring, and management of capital funds.

Perhaps the greatest advantage of an ABRD is that it would be more acceptable to Asian leaders than the IBRD, IFC, or IMF, which are all seen, to some extent, as Washington's pawns in the international markets.

The establishment of such an institution would allow for the consolidation of activities by all the other institutions active in Asia, including advisory lending and relief agencies. If the US were to lead the establishment of the ABRD, it would then need only four key contacts for the successful implementation of recovery initiatives: the ABRD for all institutions and aid programs; the G7 as the lead for donor nations; Apec for recipient countries; and a Private Sector Council made up of representatives of banks and private sector companies from Asia and the international community. At the moment, ideas and entities are poorly co-ordinated across Asia. This inevitably leads to fragmentation of effort, and even to contradictory initiatives being undertaken.

Missing Measurements

As currency and economic volatility subsides and a number of key indicators show positive signs once again, it is surprising that such an intellectual vacuum still surrounds the issue of recovery.

The term "recovery" is used equally to mean an end of decline, a restoration of positive growth, a restoration of GDP to the 1996 (or 1995 or 1997) level, or a return to past high rates of growth. A more precise and common set of terms that identifies with precision the four stages of recovery is needed. There are, indeed, four separate stages of recovery for any individual country or industry sector. The first is an end to volatility and decline. The second is a restoration of positive growth. The third stage represents a subsequent recovery to former levels of GDP. The fourth and final stage would constitute a restoration of sustainably high growth rates (but lower than past debt-fueled growth rates). This clarity of vocabulary, coupled with an accurate measure of progress against each stage, would provide a more solid platform for informed discussion of the drifting issue of recovery.

The lack of adequate measures and understanding of critical

interrelationships contributed to the depth and duration of the recent economic crisis. Two years after the crisis began, a similar lack of information and understanding existed in relation to recovery. Given the risks of both unfounded optimism and excessive pessimism, it will be essential in the future to establish an accurate and usable guide to true recovery.

Overly rosy forecasts can diminish reform efforts in the areas of bankruptcy legislation and industrial policy. Much needed corporate restructuring could be put off indefinitely, with current proprietors hoping for salvation from a returning high tide in the economy at large. Barriers to the attraction of needed foreign capital could be resurrected. Dashed hopes left over from yet another false dawn could further damage consumer confidence and delay growth in demand.

On the other hand, overly pessimistic forecasts can deter the return of international lenders and investors to capital-starved markets. In the absence of a reliable construct to chart the true pace of recovery, once-burned providers of capital may well err on the side of conservatism, particularly at the decisive level of senior credit or investment committees.

No Recovery Index

It would be useful to have a simple summary of complex data showing where an economy or industrial sector is truly in the recovery phase.

One of the many insights that emerges from a cursory view of the economic predictors of the current crisis and recovery in Asia is that the factors that should have sounded alarm bells of an impending economic crisis are different from those that will trigger the all-clear siren.

The full set of economic factors and the interconnections which triggered the crisis are still being understood. Some are obvious—overly leveraged companies, currencies with wide deviations between purchasing power parity values and trading values, unhedged offshore short-term dollar-denominated borrowings matched against local currency cash flows and asset values, excessive unproductive investments in property and share speculation, excess industrial capacity in many sectors, and inefficient national systems for the distribution of capital which were driven more by cronyism or contacts rather than by rational market mechanisms. A number of these factors together with others combined to create a catastrophic phenomenon (to use the mathematical term)—collapsing demand, capital market values, currencies, personal aspirations, and threatening social stability in many countries.

While these more complex factors were moving collectively to create the combustible mixture that exploded in July 1997, the basics of economic performance were apparently healthy. GDP growth and confidence were high. Unemployment, bankruptcies, and non-performing loan rates were low. Billions of dollars of foreign direct investment were rolling in. Economics 101 certainly would not have predicted an impending crisis. A more thoughtful set of risk measures could have contributed to more effective preventive action, but no such comprehensive system was in place.

The current imprecise approach to the definition, measurement, and understanding of economic recovery may lead to a repetition of past mistakes. Isolated measurements are taken and broadcast, but without the benefit of a comprehensive monitoring and reporting system. A thorough and integrated set of measures of the economy—in crisis or in recovery—will be necessary to determine the true state of health of the economy. This data will also be required to aid important decisions and actions related to the recovery.

An accurate and comprehensive indicator for the economy would have significantly diminished the chance of an unnecessary delay in the recovery in Asia and other crisis-hit emerging markets.

An Architecture of Recovery

Based upon a full and accurate understanding of the problems set out earlier, a fully co-ordinated program for recovery was required which would have addressed all aspects of the emerging markets' crisis-related issues—economic, social, and political.

The key elements of the program that an effective task force could have designed and implemented are as follows:

1. *Social Relief Program*:   Immediate relief aid was required to provide food, educational funding, and health care on an urgent basis in the worst affected areas. In Indonesia, the most critical case, average income dropped from $1,000 to $200. Prices of basic foodstuff rose. National distribution systems collapsed as ethnic Chinese fled violence, rape, and arson. A thoughtful program to make food available and restore sustainable distribution systems was required.

In the longer term, a more positive environment will be required to attract back hesitant investors. Rice and other grains, palm oil, fishery, fruit and vegetables, and other foods will require long-term programs to ensure self-sustaining capability. These programs will need to be coupled with the resurrection of a functioning distribution system.

International, regional, and national relief agencies will need to be co-ordinated and balanced solutions will need to be implemented on a prioritized basis to achieve these objectives.

2. *Economic Recovery Program*: The fundamental economic needs in the Asian crisis were clear: more private sector and bank sector equity capital, more trade finance to unlock trade flows, the identification of investment opportunities with strong commercial potential, and the implementation of clear and effective business strategies for businesses with a real chance to survive and prosper. These strategic plans required businesses to consolidate, restructure their debt, focus their business portfolios, "rightsize," realign their organization around key customer segments, and build on profitable product lines to generate as much cash as possible from healthy operations. These needs may well be replicated in the next crisis.

The IMF response package had only an indirect impact on the critical needs of operating companies in the region. In particular, Asian corporations with healthy operations but high debt levels and no deep-pocketed parents, needed direct infusion of equity and fresh credit lines to keep afloat for the duration of the crisis. The key elements of a viable approach to fill needs like these in future crises could work out as follows:

a) Establish an initial fund of $50 billion
Contributions to a newly created Asian Recovery Fund could come from a broad number of sources, including the G7 countries, Asian governments, (especially Hong Kong, Singapore, Brunei, and Japan), the ADB, World Bank, IFC, IMF, and other sources of capital. In the recent Asian crsis, this fund would have provided an opportunity for Japan in particular to step up to the challenge of assisting other Asian countries escape the full impact of the crisis.

Parallel co-investment funds could also be put in place by national governments through institutions—like Petronas, the Employees' Provident Fund (EPF), Pensyen Nasional Bhd (PNB), and Khazanah Nasional in Malaysia and similar organizations in other countries— across the region. Co-investment funds, when properly focused by the regional fund, could reduce the local political costs of participation in the regional fund and accelerate the restoration of confidence in the country.

b) *Target direct investments to eligible opportunities*
A triage approach could soon segment investment opportunities into three categories: companies that do not need special assistance (e.g. oil and gas projects with Malaysia's highly profitable Petronas); companies that would not survive under any reasonable set of assumptions, and those that would survive and prosper with an injection of capital. New funds could be targeted at the latter category for the highest impact. In particular, businesses which are profitable at an operating level but are unable to service debt would be a prime segment for investment in the form of new equity, preferred shares, convertible bonds, or other hybrid instruments.

c) *Implement required preconditions*
Before deploying funds into specific businesses, target companies would need to comply with a strict set of preconditions: adoption of international accounting standards, improved corporate governance, debt restructuring, full operating transparency, elimination of artificial intergroup trading, and other improvements in operating procedures. In some cases, large-scale management and board changes would be required. In all cases, a thorough review by external experts would be required to ensure that a clear and credible strategy is in place to which the funds could be effectively applied.

d) *Adopt creative capital approaches*
With a limited amount of capital available, creative approaches to get the highest impact from the capital deployed will need to be implemented. Convertible bonds, preferred shares, zero coupon finance, trade and working capital finance, super-voting shares, and other approaches could achieve multiple objectives. Government or fund guarantees could further stretch the impact of the capital deployed, just as Chinatrust's Jeffery Koo had recommended in the past.

e) *Creative securitization*
Following investment, logical collections of similar investment securities (grouped by industry sector, risk profile, type of security or country) could be packaged and sold in global capital markets. Government guarantees of principal amounts could provide a higher level of security and increase the attraction of the funds being distributed. Proceeds from

the securitization could then be recycled into further investments, thus increasing the impact of the initial fund commitments. Pricing could be set at attractive levels on initial offerings to stimulate demand.

f)   Develop local capital markets
In all of the initiatives involving capital markets, attention would need to be paid to the development of local markets to avoid the recurrence of capital structure imbalances, which contributed so much to the initial collapse of the region.

3.   *Adoption of Asem Principles*:   Economic recovery programs will need to be developed along sustainable lines embracing, to the extent possible, the four key principles enunciated at the Asia-Europe heads of state meeting (Asem2) in London.

The key principles agreed were the need for openness and transparency, a commitment on financial restructuring both domestically and internationally, the importance of keeping markets open in both Europe and Asia, and absolute rejection of protectionism.

However, the implementable content of the actual initiatives (listed below) agreed at the conference of heads of state were insufficient when compared to the full set of needs of the crisis:

- creation of an Asem Trust Fund at the World Bank to help finance the technical assistance of the restructuring of the financial sector and in addressing the social impact of the crisis
- dispatch of high-level European business missions with a view to enhancing investment projects in Asia and Europe
- reformation of the international monetary and financial systems, particularly the need to reduce vulnerability of domestic financial systems to speculation.

It is interesting to note that the Asem list of initiatives assumes a greater role for the World Bank and the creation of a discrete fund for Asia, similar to the above program outlined during the crisis as a creative alternative.

4.   *Political Support From Asian Countries*:   The IMF standard reform program, while directionally correct in some areas, has now generated extremely negative social, political, and economic responses.

These responses have had a significantly adverse impact on the IMF's ability to make effective change. Because a great number of emerging countries have proven extremely prickly to deal with or to be inert in the face of needed action, a new, more collaborative and inclusive approach is required to ensure a higher degree of activity and co-operation.

5. *Political Support From Western Countries*: Support from Western nations for future crises could be maximized through the creation of a new institution under the direction of the World Bank, coupled with the co-ordination of existing sources of capital, advice, and management capacity. Global and local efforts could be well co-ordinated in a transnational model of change. A clear and convincing program of communication would have needed to put in place an effective approach to generate public support for a recovery program—highlighting the risks and opportunity from an international perspective. Difficulties faced by the IMF in raising much needed replacement funds could have been further reduced by addressing a set of key issues in advance:

a)   Ensure that ill-gotten fortunes are repatriated and employed visibly to address national issues. American and European taxpayers are unlikely to fund bailouts of countries where former (or current) leaders and cronies sit on large fortunes and enjoy privileged lifestyles.

b)   Suppress corruption at every level. A World Bank estimate of 30 per cent leakage through corruption in some past Asian programs is clearly unacceptable. IMF announcements regarding similar levels of theft in Russia during 1999 will only exacerbate these concerns. Past miscreants need to be identified, prosecuted, and jailed. An active auditing procedure will be required to ensure compliance with international standards. Excessive administrative costs or outright corruption will significantly reduce the willingness of donor nations or institutions to participate in needed recovery programs.

c)   Evolve ownership of businesses to international standards, including real estate, financial services institutions, distribution, and resource businesses. Protectionist approaches only depress prices, reduce efficiency, and deter investment throughout the entire business system. Ultimately, customers pay for protectionism, and key sectors should be opened sooner rather than later.

6. *Timeliness of Response*: The *New Straits Times* of Malaysia reported in August 1999 that: "A master plan to chart the future direction of the capital markets, define its objectives, and address pertinent issues is now in the works and expected to be ready by the end of the year." Two and half years after the crisis was ignited the first study was slated to emerge on a critical element of crisis response. A faster and more timely set of answers might have avoided earlier costs and catastrophes.

7. *Value and Virtue of a Task Force Approach*: A dedicated team could have been set up quickly to respond to the Asian crisis—far more quickly than the creation of a new multilateral institution. All constituencies could have been represented—public and private, national and international; donor and recipient—without threatening any existing institution. A limited set of priority actions could have been taken in concert. Support could have come from the East and West alike. Creative solutions could have been better received, fine-tuned, and executed. Much of the societal, political, and economic costs could have been avoided.

Failure to move now to prepare for the next catastrophe will prolong and deepen any ensuing crisis, increase the fragmentation of the regions, increase dormant geopolitical risk, and may very well widen the gulf between the Southern, Eastern and Western Worlds for decades to come. Setting out in advance a best practice model of response and incorporating a task force approach, would be a wise investment to make now to avoid great costs in the future.

Asian Crisis Goes Global

The crisis of 1997 and 1998 was not confined to a subset of Asian's booming economies. A year after the collapse of the baht, Russia was forced to devalue the rouble and default on international debt obligations. A faltering economy and reversal of recent increase in confidence contributed to an increase in political instability in Russia and other parts of the former Soviet Union. Brazil and other South American countries were also forced to devalue their currencies despite billions of dollars in support programs. As the crisis progressed, capital markets and rating agencies lost faith in emerging markets across the board, as reflected in large-scale sell orders on stocks and currencies. Interest rate premiums on bonds rose to 10–15 per cent, thus increasing the cost of funds to prohibitive levels. One Malaysian offer was rated slightly above junk bond status, increasing the cost to such an irrational level that the government canceled the needed financial initiative.

Systemic Challenge

Although each complex system will contain most of the ten standard elements set out above, each will manifest some of these characteristics more than others. In the case of the economic crisis of the emerging markets, the salient characteristic was clearly globalization. The lack of firewalls, irrelevance of national borders, impotence of national central banks, and the pattern of contagion and collapse set out in stark detail the new global nature of economics. The capital markets are global, the most controversial participants—hedge funds and speculative investors—are also global. Policy makers, on the other hand, remain locked in outdated national models of control and intervention. In order to implement an effective strategy, a clear and simple global approach will be required in institutional alignment, program content, measurable deadlines, and in leadership. A clear and simple (or as simple as possible) structure to the solution to future crises is necessary to counterbalance the complex, global and dynamic nature of the problem.

The clear need in managing risk and limiting future damage is to build an effective response to the global, nature of the risk. The scale of potential economic damage is increasing with globalization and the probability of occurrence (or reoccurrence in this case) is already high.

Unfortunately, the capability to respond and probability of deployment of an effective response have not grown at an equal rate. The clear strategic imperative in these areas is to build the capability to respond and increase the probability of deployment at a global level ahead of the next catastrophe.

Proposed Architecture of Solutions

A checklist of implied actions, reflecting the structure of a fully integrated model of solutions could logically contain some of the following elements.

New Vision: A global economy and capital markets carefully monitored and managed to a lower level of risk and a higher quality of response to challenges and crises.

Specific Initiatives: • Develop more comprehensive pre-crisis alert models and a useful recovery index.
• Pre-establish principles for consolidation of crisis response.
• Establish a pre-crisis task force approach involving international and local institutions, and the private sector on an integrated basis.
• Pre-establish sovereign bond rating impact of various actions, events, and trends.
• Develop local capital markets.
• Estabish transparent risk assessment measures for banks and corporations.
• Adopt free floating exchange rates (without hard or soft pegs).
• Create an alliance of donor and recipient country heads to diagnose, design, and implement a solution to problems or crises.
• Develop an Emerging Markets Development Bank and Fund to provide economic, technical, and social/humanitarian assistance on a co-ordinated and fully funded basis.
• Set up a broad economic oversight group with private and public sector representation to spot problems in advance and prepare for risk eventuation.
• Establish a Private Sector Council, global and regional, to represent manufacturing and service companies on key task forces.

It's Not Just the Economy

Unfortunately, the pattern of realized risk that is undermanaged by existing strategies and institutions is not confined to the economy. Other problems reflect this same pattern of globalization with inadequate response—in the areas of crime, disease, terrorism, the environment, deculturalization, economic disparity, the underworld, and even the military. Old problems have assumed new dimensions, and so old remedies are no longer valid. Systems have evolved. New sets of risks and opportunities are presented. Priorities have changed. Yet our capabilities to reduce risk, capture opportunity, and master complex systemic challenge have not kept pace.

The net result is a world of increasing risk and lost opportunity. As these problematic systems grow, intersect, and evolve, risk is compounded. The rising level of risk has created an unnecessary systemic volatility, which could possibly explode into a future crisis or catastrophe of unprecedented proportions. The risk of an unexpected crisis emerging from volatile systemic interaction is not the only cost of the current paradigm—the current level of satisfactory underperformance in each area carries with it direct costs and systemic risks as well.

The application of a new state-of-the-art strategic model can highlight the content of new paradigms and indicate some of the content of an efficient solution. Much of the specific content in each area will differ. But an approach reflecting the common nature of the challenges can address and master many of the strategic challenges leading to a solution.

Gaps in the Global Architecture

It is clear from the summary of performance against the critical challenges set out earlier that there are many problems with the current global architecture—the structures, and the principles which define the manner in which we go about managing our world today and building a better world for tomorrow. In order to rise above the threatening state of satisfactory underperformance into which we have fallen, it is essential to reset strategy, to restructure the institutional approach, and to redefine operating practices in the area of transnational problem solving.

On the institutional side, it will be important to address three interrelated problems—ineffective international institutions; weakness in the model of intranational co-operation; and gaps in the foundations of the global architecture—missing pieces in the design for improved global management. On the need for redefined practices, a new approach to shared vision, strategic design, and effective implementation will need to be developed on an expedited basis. These changes will be necessary to reduce risk, to take advantage of the opportunities presented, and to begin to move toward realization of full potential in the critical areas of transnational challenge.

Asian Crises as Living Examples of Risk Unbound

It is interesting to contrast parallel Asian crises of the late 1990s to see a recurrence of the pattern of globalized crises and universal inability to respond. The common thread in the fabric of each crisis is the globalization, or potential globalization, of a local event which was never adequately managed. Each, in turn, reflects a different kind of gap in the global architecture. The economic crisis, the haze, the Nipah virus outbreak, and continued piracy in the South China Sea all made the headlines in 1999. The drug problems of the Golden Triangle continued unabated. The environmental disasters in China (flooding), Vietnam and the Philippines (also flooding), and Japan (nuclear disaster) also reached new heights of concern over the risks in the future. The conclusion which inevitably surfaces from a review of these crises and corresponding responses is that we, as an intelligent people, can certainly do better than we have in managing risk and solving the systemic problems we have created. To quote the inimitable Pogo, "we have met the enemy and he is us." The only source of potential solutions, of an improved capability of response, must also be us.

1.   Ineffective International Institutions

The IMF clearly failed to solve the Asian economic crisis. In a survey of regional executives at one CEO Forum, 26 out of the 34 respondents agreed or agreed strongly with the statement: "The IMF has been a failure in handling the crisis." The IMF, World Bank, ADB, and other global institutions failed to halt the domino effect of the emerging markets crises or to limit the depth of its impact on fragile economies. Interpol has done little to suppress the rising tide of lucrative global crime—drugs, money laundering, piracy, theft of intellectual property, pornography and pedophilia, corruption, and other classically global felonies. Nato dithered for years over the brutal crimes committed within the collapsed Yugoslavia—reducing the value of its subsequent intervention—and incurring enormous human cost through delay.

The ultimate mission of many of these institutions have been called into question by recent events. The World Bank is embroiled in internal turmoil over a new comprehensive framework approach to development. Nato is seeking to redefine its role in the wake of the collapse of the former Soviet Union. The UN, underfunded and far from efficient in some key agencies, is as UN Secretary General Kofi Annan has said, "asked to do too much with too little." Recent progress in reducing international tensions by respected and charismatic leaders of the UN and their envoys in tense military and political situations have offset traditionally slow progress made by the more bureaucratic components of the institution. Refugee programs and other crisis support programs have proved valuable, but the frontline role of such privately funded institutions as the Nobel Prize winning Medecins sans Frontieres, Action Aid, the Himalaya Cataract Project, and other focused initiatives show the range of opportunities for the UN to act to address basic problems where funding and operating capability can be brought together.

Recent resignations in the European Commission over ethics violations, scandals within the International Olympic Committee, divisive battles for the leadership of the World Trade Organization, conflict within the World Bank and between the World Bank and IMF, and other visible signs of disharmony have contributed to a lack of faith in international institutions as well as an erosion in their effectiveness.

A Decade of Japanese Decline

A second economic crisis in Asia unfolding further in 1997 and 1998 was the continuing decline of Japan. Although the Japanese economy dominates Asia, with a GDP 30 times larger than that of Thailand's and 10 times China's, the long-term move "sideways and downwards" sidelined Asia's largest economy at a time when leadership was needed. With a set of large companies in need of restructuring, an inefficient and decapitalized banking structure laboring under estimated non-performing loans approaching $1 trillion, inefficient distribution systems, and a currency dramatically out of line with its purchasing power parity, the Japanese economy was vulnerable to further collapse in the wake of the Asian Contagion. The decline of Japanese power and influence had been visible from the bursting of its bubble economy in 1989. The stagnation of the economy created a new risk of accelerated decline in the fragile foundations of the economy. A dramatic decline in the value of the yen relative to the US dollar could have triggered a real economic implosion. In 1998, the yen dropped steadily from 110 to the dollar in the spring to 140 by mid-July. Some forecasters even predicted achievement of purchasing power parity rates at a catastrophic ¥180 to the dollar. Domestic politicians and bureaucrats continued to dither and international institutions were forced to sit on the sidelines as the Japanese economy (and hence the world's) teetered on the edge of disaster.

The risk of a collapse of the global economic and monetary systems was barely averted by the last-minute intervention by the US Treasury Department and the US Federal Reserve Board. These two US institutions were acting in concert, essentially performing the functions of a global central bank. They were able to shore up the yen and pull the global capital system back from the brink with a few timely and effective initiatives. Bold intervention by the US Treasury Secretary and Chairman of the Federal Reserve Board pulled the yen, and Japan, back from a systemic economic and social meltdown. The ineffective Japanese policy machine had done little to lead a response to their decade of decline. No wonder then that the Japanese finance minister was referred to by White House staff behind closed doors as "The Minister for the Destruction of the World Economy."

In this case, the US was able to act in lieu of an effective international institution, and to stave off disaster. The US intervention was successful, but it highlighted the gap in the area of international monetary and economic leadership. Subsequent calls by the head of the Bundesbank, and even billionaire George Soros, for the creation of an interventionist global central bank only serve to underscore the current lack of an effective institutional presence in this area.

2.   Weakness in the Intranational Model of Co-operation

A network of highly co-ordinated resources operating in a common design—in individual markets and at a level of transnational cooperation—can be the most effective model in managing transnational challenges. Yet the current set of intranational models—G7, G24, Asem, Apec, Asean, Organization of African Unity (OAU), the Andean Pact, and others—has shown little capability to deal with crisis or significant challenge facing member countries or entire regions.

Many of these associations serve a useful purpose, or have served a purpose in the past, but their proliferation, ineffectiveness, and time demands may actually serve to inhibit, rather than enhance, the objectives they put forward. A newly elected president in Latin America expressed frustration when he noted that nearly half of his first three months in office were wasted on international meetings with little benefit or results.

There are two interrelated factors underlying this weakness. The first is an inherent inability of bureaucratic institutions to respond effectively and swiftly to multiple masters. The second is the tendency of collective political bodies to cater to the most reluctant member, thereby ensuring that the institution only achieves the lowest common denominator.

If intranational co-operative bodies are to work well, they need to have a clear vision, a meaningful agenda, clear measures of performance, an alignment of resources to attack prioritized issues on a focused basis, and a need to engage in substantive challenges as well as to provide a set of forums for communication, discussion, and review. An intranational forum can provide some of the elements of a bridge over the fault lines of civilization. But it can also run the risk of taking up valuable space within the global institutional framework—absorbing scarce resources and providing little in the way of substantive measurable progress.

Asean and the Haze

The Asean response to the haze issue reflects the problems of intranational models of co-operation, and the risk of slow or lack of effective response to literally burning regional issues.

Following a number of years of suffering from episodic cross-border clouds of pollution from land clearance fires primarily located in Indonesia, Asean members promulgated a zero-burning policy, put in place a satellite surveillance unit, and created an approach to muster a four-nation firefighting force in the case of "hot spots" being detected.

Unfortunately, the response mechanism in any co-operative model is confined to voluntary implementation at member-state level. As Rodolfo Severino, the new Asean secretary general, observed: "This means that not all measures are in place or implementation plans carried out." He stated in a speech in 1999 that he hoped to have haze-reducing improvements in place before the next El Nino occurrence, predicted to be in September 2000, three years after drought conditions contributed to the worst ever state of regional air pollution.

There are, Severino noted, tough trade-offs to be made between land conversion and haze, and powerful lobbying interests to contend with at the local level. In the absence of authority over sovereign nation states, and in respect of the Asean principle of non-interference in fellow member states' affairs, Asean's response was limited to establishment of a monitoring and surveillance unit, to training of officials, and to providing an open forum among ministers to "encourage" change, in line with the agreed zero-burning policy.

A forum to discuss the comparative data and progress on agreed policies can support a more active and informed approach to transnational problem solving. But it frequently falls apart under the pressures of a crisis or in the face of recalcitrance of individual members. Co-operative models carry with them a significant risk of achievement of only of a lowest-common-denominator target. The approach may even institutionalize satisfactory underperformance, and achieve a response level as characterized by an organization that is slow and bureaucratic rather than fast and flexible, is internally rather than externally focused, and if not satisfied with the status quo, at least too comfortable with slow evolutionary progress in the face of needed swift and deep change.

The Asean response to the economic crisis also reflected these core problems, coupled with a high degree of fragmentation, lack of common policy or vision, and missing implementation capabilities. Two years after the crisis began, Asean had managed to put in place an economic surveillance unit in the Asean Secretariat, to accelerate the implementation of the Asean Free Trade Area (AFTA) trade barrier reduction by one year, with substantial prior progress to be made in tariff reductions by the original six signatories to the Asean treaty two years in advance of the AFTA's new 2002 target, a harmonization of definitions and standardization of customs on the free trade of goods, and a reduction of barriers to investment by Asean companies in other member states.

In addition, Asean ministers added a list of regular discussion items to their agenda including action taken to stimulate demand, reporting transparency and corporate governance, feeding the poor, and the mobilization of additional resources to strengthen the economy. Again, these were steps in the right direction, but were they sufficient to respond to a recurrence of the current crisis and to the needs of millions of Asean residents plunged back into poverty? Do they provide sufficient assistance to support or assist in, for example, the recapitalizing of Indonesia's banking system with a stated need of $82 billion? One of the risks of adopting a weak model of co-operation and voluntary directional alignment for each issue is that it stands in the way of more powerful, more flexible, and more effective approaches to the solution of problems which are either time sensitive or far deeper than those envisaged at the time of the formation of the intranational or regional model of co-operation.

3.   Missing Pieces

In some areas, there is no institution or co-operative organization to address critical problems or represent constituencies which are necessary to the design and implementation of needed solutions. For example, there is no global central bank to regulate a global economy, there is no environmental authority to limit and manage damaging behaviors and there is no entity to represent the collective interest of the private sector—banks and businesses—at a global level. These missing pieces create gaps in all phases of strategic development—diagnostic, design, and implementation—thereby considerably reducing the value of overall effort. The public statements made by the Japanese finance ministry prior to a recent G7 economic summit, which called for co-operation between public and private financial institutions to avert currency crises in the future, reflect the value of harnessing the power of the private sector in the pursuit of public goals.

4. Limitations on Deployment

As the six-month delay in calling in global experts to help respond to the Nipah virus outbreak in Malaysia demonstates, even effective institutions like WHO or CDC can be neutered by ineffective deployment procedures. The same is true of Nato in Kosovo. Effective capability, ineffectively deployed, does not result in a satisfactory outcome.

5. Limits to the Extent of American Intervention

In many areas, the operative influence for constructive response is the projection of US power and policy through initiatives that take place well outside the national borders of the US. Internationally placed agents of the US, such as the Drug Enforcement Agency (DEA), Bureau of Alcohol, Tobacco and Firearms, and the Federal Bureau of Intelligence (FBI) can fill some of the gaps left behind by Interpol and other international crime-reducing institutions. The Federal Reserve Board and Department of Treasury, acting in concert, stepped in to support an ailing yen at a critical moment of risk to the global financial system. US military forces have long provided a stiffening element to Nato as well as its leadership in the face of Soviet or other European aggression and expansionist tendencies.

The failure of the European Union to develop a meaningful response to Kosovo and in other areas of conflict has pushed the American resolve to the fore time after time in global military affairs, often with the sole support of the United Kingdom. This Anglo-US alliance also provided much of the strength for Operation Desert Storm, which effectively drove Saddam Hussein out of Kuwait. Although technically a UN resolution implemented by a coalition of Middle Eastern and global powers, the true strength behind the alliance was an English-speaking force led by US political capabilities and weapons technologies.

Although effective in a number of cases from Mexico to Japan in the economic sphere and from Kuwait to Kosovo in the military, the model of US projection of force on an extraterritorial basis, to compensate for the lack of international institutions or the lack of international will and co-ordination, has inherent limitations. Unilateral action by the US may not always be a welcome intervention by recipient nations. The Malaysian example during the economic crisis and the Nipah viral attack are examples of unlikely sources of requests for US assistance.

There also remain many traces of America's isolationist past. The result is often confusing to foreigners and Americans alike. Thomas Friedman captured this conflict in America's role as a global power with a self-defined role as leader of the world and as a non-internationalist anti-colonial power when he wrote: "Surely one of the oddest features of international affairs today is the fact that half the world thinks America wants to dominate everything and half the US Congress doesn't even own a passport."

Why Apply Next Generation Strategy?

As old problems assume new dimensions and responsive institutions fail to keep pace, both the scale of net risk and complexity of required solutions rise. Each global challenge, although unique in many ways, also exhibits a set of common characteristics which makes apparently dissimilar systems responsive to a common approach. As these challenges become more global, more complex, and more threatening, a fresh and comprehensive view is required to offset broadly accepted levels of satisfactory underperformance.

The approach and content of the Next Generation Strategy model necessitate a reconsideration of the basic elements of global strategy. The vision of the collective enterprise and the rules of engagement need to be reviewed and rewritten. A clear statement of the elements of the net risk assessment can help to clarify investment priorities and areas of opportunity for greatest benefit. The salient systemic characteristics will spell out the approach required for positive high level change. The tools and rules for the management and influence of complex dynamic systems can improve efficiency and effectiveness of the efforts invested in change programs. A review of structures and capabilities will identify specific gaps in the global architecture and operating weaknesses in global capability which can be addressed.

Highly effective and forward looking task forces can address crises in the short term. A better strategy will also define more clearly organizational, structural, and institutional needs in the future. Responding to these gaps and weaknesses will strengthen the potential for future improvements in operating performance, as well as in improving the quality of strategic diagnosis, design, and implementation today.

Finally, and most importantly, the application of the Next Generation Strategy model in each area would improve results dramatically. A statement of a more aspirational vision, a set of investment priorities to reduce risk and capture opportunities, a strengthened platform of structure and capability to deal with future challenges, a best practice approach to complex systems management, and effective leadership of a new approach can all, if properly executed, significantly contribute to the reduction of risk in this volatile era.

Through the application of the state-of-the-art model of global strategy, we are more likely to realize the full potential for improvement inherent in today's systems of risk and volatility.

Caveat and Content

Each of the following sections provides a brief overview, from one perspective, of extremely complex and multi-faceted social phenomena. The purpose of each section is not to develop a comprehensive analysis, nor to describe every facet of each area selected for exploration. The objective here is to establish some of the simple and common elements which can lead to a different and improved approach to the management of the risks they represent.

Within each area can be found a few of the elements which a fully fleshed out Next Generation Strategy would examine and analyze in greater detail: the costs of current underperformance, the net risk assessment, and an outline of indicated solutions.

In the compact edition of the integrated model of solutions appended to each area, the content can be linked back to the description and the diagnosis which precede it. A full set of diagnostics, strategic designs, and implementation plans would fill many volumes. A fully elaborated statement of a response—relevant task forces, institutions, skills, capabilities, and precise resources—would extend the content in each area even further.

For purpose of debate, each sector will set out an alternative and more aspirational vision of collective performance. Examples of the initiatives required to achieve the vision will be posited. Salient systemic characteristics are highlighted. Opportunities for improvement and better leadership will be cited.

In every area there is an opportunity to set out a new and more aspirational vision for collective pursuit, and new opportunities for more effective leadership at each level of strategic engagement.

The approach to each area also highlights in greater detail, a distinct element of the net risk assessment. The scale of potential harm is escalating dramatically in areas of crime, terrorism, and the environment. The probability of that harm occurring is escalating in the cyberworld and the environment. Our capability to respond is notably weak in areas of deculturalization and economic disparity. The probability of timely deployment is particularly low in the area of disease control.

In most cases there is a high cost to the current level of satisfactory underperformance. In all cases there are highly visible gaps in the global architecture which allow net risk to rise to unnecessarily high levels. In all cases a small number of high-impact initiatives, when well designed and implemented, would make a big difference.

Common Elements

Just as there are common threads in the analysis and characterization of the different challenges, there are common elements in the architecture of responses. The common elements of an effective architecture of solutions include:

- **Population control:** In the areas of disease, economic disparity, and the environment, a reduction in populations or even population growth would yield significant benefit and reduce the range and depth of critical challenges and risks.
- **Application of technology:** Whether the applied technology is statistical, as in the area of crime control, or process-specific, as in the area of environment, the use of modern technology can contribute to major improvements across the board.
- **Strategic alliance between different classes of states:** A unity of all affected states—rich and poor, large and small, donor and recipient—will allow better results to follow from improved

participation and engagement.

- **A dedicated set of ad hoc task forces to address urgent problems:** The UN and its related agencies, the World Bank, and other foundations of the current global architecture have contributed significantly in many areas. But they can also contribute both as individual institutions and as members of a set of new task forces, each with a pre-set termination date and precise set of deliverables. These specific task forces could work faster, more flexibly, with an external focus dissatisfied with the status quo, and capable of addressing both short- and long-term challenges on a co-ordinated basis.

- **Broader involvement in the solutions by those who constitute the "problem":** Creative combinations of large and small states, public and private interests, and other representative constituencies would ensure better performance in all areas of strategy.

- **A focus on the positive:** For all cases a thorough set of positive initiatives, as well as negative proscriptions, will contribute to the overall performance and management of risk in a given system.

- **Leadership and accountability:** In most areas of risk, there is no clear accountability and rarely does a leader emerge to claim the leadership role. A lack of ownership of the problem, a lack of leadership, and lack of results are major problems that need to be addressed in each area before meaningful change can be made to happen.

- **Agreement on the measures and definition of success:** Before progress can be made toward a goal, the goal needs to be identified and the measures of success need to be articulated. Progress against the objectives needs to be made. For most cases, a single scorecard—a "PSI" to measure and communicate progress—would be a valuable measure for participants in the effort and general population alike.

No Easy Answers

In each critical area, historic levels of satisfactory underperformance need to be reduced. To drive this change, better understanding, a renewed vision, new standards of performance, and a new set of strategies and structures are needed. In many areas, new leadership is also needed to improve performance, fill gaps, and drive toward a healthier future.

It is obvious that it would be inappropriate to only apply a single model—analytical or responsive—to challenges that have many fundamental differences as well as similarities. Yet a common flexible and thoughtful approach is needed to determine better strategy. This approach can, if properly applied, contribute to positive change.

Vision and idealism are important in a program to create new strategies, just as they are in improving existing solutions to challenging problems. However, we should be realistic about the nature of the challenge and the fact that there may well be no dramatic change overnight—setting out an effective process of change, not just immediate results, will define success in this area. In the medium and long term, overall measurable results will determine success. For now, all we may be able to do is to begin the journey with a clear direction, shared commitment, and firm resolution to carry through into the future.

Aspiration, Idealism, and Risk

There is, of course, a strong strain of idealism in this effort of applying global strategic models to societal challenge. The effort is admittedly imperfect in many ways. But without idealism and aspiration, we would make little progress toward a better vision of our future world.

There is significant risk in setting out a program of fundamental reassessment and redirection. Risk is always highest when new approaches are undertaken. But as TS Elliot stated: "Only those who risk going too far can possibly learn how far they can go."

Avoiding the painful conclusions and difficult realizations that effort surfaces would be unfortunate. Compartmentalizing our best models of global strategy and confining them purely to commercial application would remove a potentially valuable source of insight and creative solutions to difficult collective challenges. The analysis and recommendations set out in the following chapter are indicative of the sort of changes that could result from a better strategic program to analyze and recommend actions to improve on the current unsatisfactory state of affairs.

Crime

Crime and criminal behavior have been a part of our daily lives since the beginning of social order itself. From the beginning of recorded history, illegal behavior—whether violent or economic—has been a part of our collective behavior on an uninterrupted basis. Most crimes are of a petty nature, taking place at a local level and often the product of a personality type best described as "passive inadequate." Most violent crimes are also local in nature and will not be analyzed here.

The focus of this section is not about this bulk of criminal transgressions and disruptions to the social order from local sources. Of much greater concern is the accelerating risk of truly global patterns of crime and unchecked global criminal organizations.

Transnational Nature

Organized global activities in the criminal area make a long list, headed by illegal drugs, including heroin, cocaine, marijuana, ecstasy, amphetamines, LSD, and other narcotics. In addition to drugs and often related to it, are other elements of global criminal activities which operate on an equally systematic and organized basis—large-scale fraud, money laundering, piracy, software piracy, pedophilia, prostitution, cybercrime, corruption, and environmental crime. Other common global patterns of crime include the systematic criminal violation of the rights of women and minorities.

Using language similar to the transnational nature of the challenge and that used by other observers of complex systemic behavior, Paul Stares describes in his excellent book, *Global Habit: The Drug Problem in a Borderless World*:

"These [criminal] trends can be seen as a result of the interaction of local events in much larger global processes that are progressively bringing the world closer together or simultaneously diminishing the ability and, paradoxically in some cases, the willingness of states to exercise their sovereign prerogatives to control what comes across their territorial borders and what takes place within them. Revolutionary advances in communications, transportation, and information technology have made it possible for goods, services, people, information, and ideas to travel across international boundaries with unprecedented speed and efficiency...The drug trade, as a consequence, has increasingly become a transnational phenomenon, driven and fashioned in critical ways by transnational forces and transnational actors...And just as legitimate transnational entrepreneurs have been able to exploit the opportunities of globalizing free market economy, so have criminal ones, particularly drug trafficking organizations."

Costs of Satisfactory Underperformance

In the US alone, more than 1 per cent of its GDP is spent on maintaining law and order. With nearly one million private security guards employed, the unofficial policing system is even larger than that of the official police force.

Increasing insurance premiums is also a cost of crime, as are security systems in stores, closed-circuit video systems, and other expenses directly attributable to operating a business in a system of less than perfect social order. As early as 1980, the total cost of private security was estimated to exceed $20 billion, and this has risen rapidly ever since.

Federal, state, and local governments collectively spend over $30 billion to counter the drug trade. The annual social cost of illegal drug use is estimated to be $67 billion, "mostly from the consequences of drug-related crimes."

The full cost of the criminal drug trade spills over into the health care area as well. Over 500,000 hospital emergency visits per year have been attributed to drug abuse, not counting the full longer-term cost of other health problems such as AIDS, hepatitis, liver disease, malnutrition, domestic violence, and child abuse. The link between drugs and crime are irrefutable. In a thorough study completed in June 1991 involving 712,000 prison inmates, 62 per cent of the respondents admitted to regular drug use at some stage of their lives. Half of the respondents admitted to drug use in the 30 days prior to committing the offence which had resulted in their incarceration. Nearly one-third claimed to be under the influence of drugs when they committed their offences—17 per cent were in the pursuit of funds to pay for drugs when they committed their offences.

In 1994, as documented by a separate study, 66 per cent of 20,000 adult males tested positive for at least one drug at the time they were arrested. Across the US, drug-related charges have resulted in the arrest of over one million people per year. The consequent costs of incarceration, health care, impact on the family, and social order are enormous.

The cost of the drug problem is compounded as drugs, directly or indirectly, are linked to money laundering, corruption, violent crime, disintegration of the family, corruption of the judiciary and police force, loss of wages, and skyrocketing prison and health care costs. The full cost of the drug problem will not be limited to any one year or even to one generation. Another study estimates that every year, 375,000 Americans are born with a drug addiction, primarily to cocaine and heroin.

During the 1990s, 100,000 drug-related deaths were reported in the US. It is estimated that 20,000 Americans die every year as a result of illicit drugs. This can be compared to total American deaths of 50,000 during the entire Vietnam War. In 1993, a year when comprehensive data was available and well analyzed, Americans spent nearly $50 billion on illegal drugs, of which nearly $30 billion was spent on cocaine, $9 billion on marijuana, $7 billion on heroin, and $2 billion on other illegal drugs. As a result, the Organization for Economic Co-operation and Development (OECD) estimates that up to $100 billion is laundered through the global financial services world annually. A large piece of this comes from the proceeds of drug-related transactions. The drug business, at a retail level, is one of the largest and most profitable commercial sectors in the world.

Colombian Quagmire

Colombia now produces 80 per cent of the world's cocaine and is the source of 70 per cent of the heroin distributed in the US. Despite annual spending of nearly $300 million by the US to reduce the production of these two major opiates, land devoted to coca and poppy production has recently risen by 25 per cent.

With insurgent guerrilla groups guarding the fields which fund their war against the Colombian state, old solutions have proven ineffective in reducing a major threat to the US and other consuming markets.

A frustrated DEA, edging toward a "Narco-Nam" engagement of troops and direct military aid, continues to search for a more effective response to the transnational threat of drugs which has gone on so long unchecked by traditional approaches.

Corruption and Bribery

The Straits Times of Singapore reported that the worldwide figure for corruption and bribery now tops $222 billion per year. Of this, $80 billion changes hands in the developing markets. The problems of corruption and bribery are nothing new, and go back through the ages. Recently, Dutch archaeologists unearthed a list that identified corrupt government officials at a Syrian site dating back 3,500 years.

In recent times, there has been a significant amount of analysis and concern focused on the issue of corruption and its role in particular in limiting the development of emerging countries. A World Bank study estimated that 30 per cent of global aid to one country had been lost through corrupt payments to government officials and cronies. Corruption is not purely the province of developing countries. In southern Italy for example, and in other developed nations, corruption has played a major role in economic inefficiency: repelling legitimate investment and creating a massive governmental debt with little productive development to justify the liability.

Although not unique, the cost of corruption in developing markets is particularly acute. Indonesia's $77 million scandal in 1999 involving inappropriate payments to collect government guaranteed debts at Bank Bali imperiled the country's banking sector restructuring program in the wake of the devastating economic crisis of 1997. Vietnam, desperate for every dollar of foreign and domestic capital investment to restore its stalled economy, recently convicted 77 defendants of a corruption scandal with an estimated value of $280 million. In these small markets, large sums of this magnitude can stimulate or slow down the growth of an entire national economy.

Recent reports from the State Statistical Bureau in China reported that over $100 billion, nearly 20 per cent of all bank deposits, was public money transferred to private accounts. One foreign investor in China discovered early in the process of acquisition that a systematic program of theft in great part underpinned the economy of the village abutting his major production unit. When the new owner locked down the plant, villagers deprived of historic sources of income rioted at the factory gates. The response of the authorities, which eventually pacified the rioters, was that the plant was no longer government owned and so theft was no longer acceptable. In an economy as fragile as China's, where political reform can only continue in a robust economic climate, siphoning off this degree of wealth and liquidity is a major risk factor in the continued stability of the region. The full cost of bribery and corruption goes well beyond the moral and social costs of the act itself. The OECD concluded that: "Recent international financial instability, which hit the Asia Pacific region particularly hard, demonstrates that corruption has a devastating effect on investment and growth."

The withholding of IMF funds and other funding to Indonesia as a result of the Bank Bali scandal is but one direct cost of corruption. There are other costs as well. The OECD also noted that: "Behind many natural or man-made disasters, there is often a tragic tale of safety violations ignored, as corrupt officials are paid by corrupt businessmen to look the other way." Whether it is hidden bottles and cans weakening the foundations of buildings in Taipei or illegal logging and deforestation in Cambodia, the secondary cost of corruption can also be counted in lost lives and environmental disasters.

Money Laundering

Money laundering, according to the US Treasury Secretary Lawrence Summers, is "the fuel that allows criminals to operate." The *Los Angeles Times* reported in October 1999 that money laundering in the US had grown to as much as $1 trillion per year. One recent summary in the *Financial Times* estimated that $350 billion is laundered through the City of London on an annual basis. The risks of apprehension are minimal. Of this $350 billion, amounting to $3.5 trillion in illicit money passing through the city every decade, only $90 million has been discovered by police.

One of the many challenges of the transnational crime of money laundering is that it now takes place in a cyberworld which ignores national boundaries and flows through anonymous accounts in a complex web of corporate and banking entities around the world. The sheer volume and velocity of money flowing through the global system allows money laundering to grow at an ever accelerating rate and creates a significant barrier for investigating authorities.

The manipulator of illicit schemes can move money virtually on a daily basis, and on a minute-by-minute basis. Documenting each transfer can take investigating authorities months. A string of transactions can be completed in days which will take years to unravel. This ability to execute laundering transactions through a net of anonymous and short-lived shelf companies that hold accounts in offshore banks protected by banking secrecy laws can only continue to make money laundering one of the more attractive global crimes of the new millennium.

Some estimates of deposits in the private banking sector quotes the level of illegally obtained funds as high as 20 per cent of total assets under management. These funds reside in accounts in Switzerland, the Cayman Islands, the Netherlands, Antilles, Jersey, and other traditional offshore tax havens. According to *The Economist*, corrupt African officials recently had $20 billion in secret deposits in Swiss banks alone. The cost of bribes from German companies to win international contracts was estimated at $3 billion in the same study. The international arms trade is a business traditionally characterized by "commissions," local agent involvement, and back-door payments. The annual cost of corruption in procuring contracts through these channels was calculated recently at $2.5 billion—taxpayers' money skimmed off by buyers and sellers in the international arms trade.

Even in the US, huge sums of illegal funds wash through the banking systems on a daily basis. In one New York bank account alone, the Russian Mafia are alleged to have laundered $4.5 billion over a six-month period. This simple international program of money laundering linked together Russia, Italy, and other countries in a tangled web of fraud, extortion, and racketeering. Over a three-year period, the program is alleged to have laundered $7.5 billion through the Bank of New York alone.

The *Los Angeles Times* also notes that some experts believe that official efforts to reduce the flow of illegal money to the US are not pursued with full vigor by authorities due to the potential impact on the economy in general, and the real estate and stock market in particular. One trillion dollars a year allegedly buys a lot of ambivalence.

Cybercrime

The global web of 60,000 networks and its rising use as a commercial system provides fertile ground for amateur hackers and professional criminals attempting to exploit the vulnerabilities of this complex and rapidly evolving set of intersecting systems. There are already a minimum of 42,000 identified viruses. Three hundred new viruses are estimated to be invented every month. Some are harmless. Others can have catastrophic efforts on global software systems. But viruses are not the only source of criminal activity in the new cyberworld.

The military in the US already runs on a system embracing more than two million computers, 10,000 local networks, and 100 long-distance systems. Some illegal efforts to date have already been successful in accessing sensitive information, penetrating security systems and even hijacking one important defense communications satellite. Threats to destabilize Indonesia's fragile recovery by a group of hackers concerned over East Timor proved the reality of this threat in the middle of 1999.

Given the complexity of cybersystems, the improving ability to break codes, and the vulnerability of security arrangements, the potential is high for eventual penetration or misdirecting of these security systems. There are already over 1,000 estimated attacks per day on the security system of the US military computers, many from naive hackers rising to the challenge of military encryption systems. However, other more sophisticated threats are rising with time.

Authorities predict that new cybercriminals will range "from the dedicated sociopath working in isolation, to international criminal syndicates that access gigantic sums of cash, to undemocratic regimes sponsoring an offensive against specific targets."

The author of *World Boom Ahead* notes the risks of cyber-sabotage to future economic health and the ease of access to theoretically secure systems. A 1998 National Security Advisory exercise using software available on the Internet quickly gained access to the entire US power grid and Pacific military communications system. Dangerous amateurs tap into military computers, plant viruses, stop or diverge electronic funds flows, and commit other cybercrimes in the name of amusement and sheer technological challenge. Recent delinquent criminal activities, such as that of a Taiwanese student planting a new and dangerous virus in major computer systems around Asia, are only the beginning of a long history of harmful transgressions in the cyberworld.

Environmental Crime

Environmental crimes are often more easy to detect than money laundering, drug trafficking, and other criminal activities that are not openly exposed to surveillance. Deforestation, air pollution, water and soil pollution, illegal dumping of hazardous waste, and other activities are easily spotted through chemical testing and satellite-based observation.

In fact, many damaging environmental activities are not technically criminal at this point in time. Clearance burning of jungle land, rapid removal of the rainforest canopy, strip mining, overfishing or hunting, and other activities which are extremely damaging to the environment are not always against the law. In some cases, the pending arrival of environmental legislation merely accelerates damaging activities. Yet environmental crime has become a major contributor to deforesting activities in Asia and Latin America, as well as to worldwide air and water pollution and the extinction of endangered species.

Software Piracy

Outside the US, illegal sales of stolen software exceed $3 billion per year at retail level. Illegal software as a percentage of software use, according to the Business Software Alliance, was nearly 96 per cent in China, representing the equivalent of $1.5 billion per year in stolen software in 1997. Indonesia, with a rate of 93 per cent, reflects a value of $200 million lost through piracy. Japan, a generally law-abiding society, pirates $750 million per year in software or 32 per cent of the total software in use. Even in disciplined Singapore, pirated software is openly available in public areas for even the most casual of pedestrian shoppers.

Initially based on cheap copies of music cassettes and records, the illegal software duplication and distribution business now covers music, films, computer software, and other valuable intellectual properties. Thailand alone has a capacity to produce 60 million pirated CDs per year. Of these, 50 million are exported annually, representing an annual theft at retail price of over $500 million per year. The rise of the Internet will only increase the number of opportunities for software piracy.

It should be noted that software piracy is a complex business to police in many countries due to conflicting interests on the part of governing authorities and the widespread acceptance of bootleg software. Many developing countries, for example, will trade off the value to the country of developing broad-based computer skills through the use of software which many citizens would not be able to afford against the impact of software piracy on their own economies. Since most of the companies suffering loss are American or other Western companies, the impact on local companies is limited. The economic and social benefits of a more computer literate population are so valuable that governments are slow to track down and eradicate software pirates who are contributing to the average computer capability of the population.

Prostitution and Pedophilia

The globalization of prostitution and pedophilia is a relatively new phenomenon. Russia and the other emerging countries in Eastern Europe and Asia, notably Poland, Thailand, China, and Albania, have become the source market for female prostitutes in many of the developing markets around the world. One global estimate places the number of women and children forced into or voluntarily entering the sex industry at one million per year. Prostitution is often a traditional source of funds for criminal networks expanding into drugs and other illegal activities. Where it is not legalized, the sex industry is usually protected by a network of corrupt police, local officials, and tolerant judges.

A particularly repugnant aspect of the sex industry is child prostitution and pedophilia, which have been accelerated by the growth of the Internet and other global communications platforms. Information on sex tours and pictures related to the exploitation and abuse of children for sexual purposes is more readily available than ever on an international basis. A few internationally co-ordinated initiatives to arrest members from the pedophile rings have successfully resulted in arrests in the US,

United Kingdom, and continental Europe. However, the few initiatives that have been successful have been extremely expensive, mixed in conviction rates, and have generated little decrease in activity or increase in funding in many jurisdictions. Only recently did liberal Dutch officials join the international effort to suppress the generation and distribution of pedophilia around the world.

Adding to concerns, transnational and local sex industries are increasingly interconnected with other sources of risk behavior that exceed traditional concerns. In particular, the spread of AIDS, hepatitis, and herpes through the sex industry in developing countries such as India, Asia, and countries in sub-Saharan Africa has created problems on a critical scale. An increasingly mobile population traveling across borders in Africa and Asia has accelerated the spread of fatal diseases in countries of limited resources, simultaneously increasing both current costs and future risk.

Piracy

Modern piracy continues to this day, as characterized by increasing violence and the use of safe havens to protect the guilty. Every other day a piracy incident on the high seas is reported. The cost can be seen in an increasing toll of human lives, rising insurance costs, and the increasing wealth of modern criminals committing acts of theft and murder on the open seas. In 1998, 66 sailors were murdered by organized gangs in Asia, preying on victims in coastal and international waters.

The 1999 hijacking of the *Petron Ranger* off the coast of Peninsular Malaysia while in passage from Singapore to Ho Chi Minh City was yet another event in a long history of piracy in the South China Sea. The Japanese vessel *Tenyu*, sailing out of the Malacca Strait toward South Korea, was also hijacked with a cargo of 1,500 tons of aluminum ingots. Much later, the ship herself turned up under a different name in Zhan Jiagan, a port along the Yangtze River. The crew of the *Tenyu* have never been found.

Following the disappearance of the *Tenyu's* crew and the recovery of the vessel, the Hong Kong registered *Cheung Son* also became the victim of pirates in the Taiwan Strait. Unlike the crew of the *Tenyu*, a quarter of the *Chueng Son* crew eventually turned up, albeit in fishermen's nets off the coast of China.

Current treaties, for example the 1988 Rome Convention, which oblige nation states to prosecute piracy cases without exception, are routinely ignored and pose little threat to locally protected pirates. The highly publicized case of the hijacking of the *Petron Ranger* resulted in no initial prosecution at all. This breach of treaty generated condemnation of China by the International Maritime Bureau (IMB) for violating international conventions. According to a Lloyd's List report, the IMB even suggested that in organized privacy there was "a deep plot to cover up China's participation in criminal activities."

Although some arrests were later made by Chinese authorities in mid-1999—and the IMB has praised China's recent and more aggressive attitudes—the centuries old traditions of piracy are taking on a new international dimension as Indonesia and Chinese pirates continue to venture more deeply into international waters.

Captain Jayant Abhyankar, deputy director of the IMB, listed the obstacles to effective enforcement of laws against piracy. Addressing a Ship Management Conference, Capt Abhyankar cited the sheer size of the sea, impoverished governments, complex and multi-jurisdictional legal actions, problems in intergovernmental communications, and lack of co-operation of relevant authorities.

Crime Against Women

The US Department of Justice estimates that there are 3 million acts of violence per year against women in the US alone. Every 18 seconds a woman is physically battered in the US. According to Faludi's 1991 study, one in every four women has been sexually assaulted.

As women gain rights, education, and break out of age-old patterns, voices of protest are raised for the first time. New and more reliable data become available on this epidemic of violence against women. In a 1997 study of Japanese women conducted by the Metropolitan government in Tokyo, one-third of the more than 1,000 women surveyed stated that they have suffered some kind of abuse from husbands or boyfriends. The abuse described ranged from verbal attacks to violence and even rape. Although higher levels of education and economic status can lift women out of historic patterns of abuse, the current lack of literacy in developing nations—in Pakistan, only one-quarter of the female population is literate—will require fundamental educational standards to be raised as part of a program of change.

From India and Pakistan come regular stories of spousal abuse and even bride burning. In India, autopsies of wives burnt to death are a daily event which carries little risk of arrest and prosecution.

A recent study in South Africa showed that one woman out of five is abused by her partner. An epidemic of rape in that country has contributed to 1,500 new HIV infections per day and a reported level of 8 per cent of the total population being HIV-positive.

In the Middle East, the notion of family honor in a harsh, even medieval, context can lead to the murder of sisters and wives for slight transgressions in local behavioral standards. Even the appearance of the potential for immoral behavior can lead to death. Being left alone inadvertently with a man for a short period of time, has resulted in severe physical punishment and even death to protect a concept of lost honor and misbehavior. Human rights groups in Pakistan report that at least 286 women were killed in 1998 alone for reasons of family "honor"— with many more assumed to have gone unreported.

The systematic rape of Indonesian Chinese women, atrocities in Kosovo, documented abuses against women in East Timor, and the violence against women from tribal groups in Myanmar and other countries reflect a continuing failure to protect fully the rights of women in developing nations and the enormous cost in human suffering from a long history of abuse and unpunished criminal behavior.

Hate Crime

In 1997, more than 8,000 hate crimes were reported in the US. The new international component in the rise of hate crimes is generated by the global distribution of information via the Internet and the resulting creation of transnational "tribal" groups united by their common antipathies. This global set of hate-driven sub-cultures is a new dimension to the historic localized pattern of discrimination, violence, and other criminal activities targeted at religious, ethnic, or racial minorities. As nationally sanctioned programs of genocide by local or invading forces in the last sixty years of this century against citizens in China, Germany, Rwanda, the former Yugoslavia, and other parts of the world indicate, there is a real risk of racial, religious, and other group-specific targeting spilling over into mass murder on a national and transnational basis, if not checked at an early stage.

Salient Systemic Characteristics

There are in fact two separate segments of global crime: globally interconnected crime and crime of a repetitive pattern common to multiple nations. The salient systemic characteristics, constituents, and potential solutions to each vary. But both are united by their new transnational nature.

Globally interconnected crime would include drugs, money laundering, corruption, arms trading, pornography and pedophilia, piracy, software piracy, large-scale fraud, cybercrimes, and transnational environmental crimes. The common denominators here are the linking of products (for example, drugs, money laundering, and corruption) and the common presence of global criminal organizations (for example, the Sicilian Mafia, Jamaican yardies, Chinese and Vietnamese triads, Latin American narco-traffickers, Russian Mafia, Union Corse, Burmese and Thai warlords, and the Japanese Yakuza).

Crimes of a common pattern creating global cost and risk are the second category within which fit crimes against women, local hate crimes, and environmental crimes with no cross-border element.

We are seeing in both the organizational and product systems of global crime the full set of characteristic behaviors—convergence, blurring of boundaries between historically separate businesses, globalization, increasing complexity, and increasing acceleration along a number of critical dimensions. The response mechanisms, as in so many other areas, are limited primarily to national organizations incapable of meeting on an equal basis the global organization and product systems they face, and weak international organizations incapable of mustering sufficient force to counter the power of their global adversaries. Intranational co-operating organizations have equally failed to create any counter balance to the increasing power and wealth of these organized criminal syndicates.

Net Risk Assessment

Potential Scale of Harm: The scale of potential harm in the drug area alone is calculated in billions of dollars, and its impact on millions of lives. The scale of potential harm is increasing as new and instantly addictive drugs enter the market, and as the full impact hits all levels of economic and social welfare.

Even nations themselves are not immune to the consequences of systemic global crime. The existence of narcocracies like Colombia and Myanmar, the troubled and corrupt economies in Russia and Indonesia, and multiple risks to emerging countries like China attest to the potential scale of harm. China sits on a razor's edge of corruption on the one hand

and effective market participation on the other. The resolution of these tensions will have a major impact on the long-term health of the country.

Likelihood of Occurrence: The likelihood of continuing under-performance or realization of that harm occurring is high. Actual levels of crime reflect a certainty of continuation in all of the risk areas highlighted above, and the economic benefits to be reaped by escalating the harm potential—bigger and better weapons, more efficient and effective money laundering techniques, more addictive and expensive drugs— ensure that significant investments on behalf of global criminal organizations will continue to be made and that societal harm continued to be felt.

Capability to Respond: Our capability to respond has lagged well behind the escalating scale of risk and even the quantum of existing damage. The continuing flow of drugs, illegal financial transactions, pedophilia, arms trading, violence against women, and other global challenges to social order are proof that our response capability is severely lacking.

Probability of Capability being Effectively Deployed: The relevant responsible institutions are weak, ineffective, or even in some cases, corrupted. Even the more effective organizations have a handicap in the lack of ability to deploy responses on a timely and effective basis. Interpol, the UN, and other global agencies dedicated to the reduction of transnational crime have hardly made a dent in the continuing flood of criminal behavior. The extraterritorial projection of US capabilities through the DEA, BATF, FBI, and other organizations has had little impact on Khun Sa, Wu-Chi and the other warlords of the Golden Triangle.

The all-out attack on the Mafia at its Sicilian source by magistrates following the assassination of two prominent anti-Mafia officials has had an impact on the structure, but not yet a major diminishing impact on the global operations of organizations historically based out of Palermo.

Such institutions as Transparency International, a multinational group dedicated to the eradication of corrupt business practice in international markets, has had little impact to date on this age-old problem. The OECD as well continues to work toward obtaining full ratification of the code on corruption that has had little success or impact to date.

Recently however, local crime rates have been falling across the US. In the four-year period from 1993–1997, violent crimes in Harlem fell by 39 per cent and in the infamous South Bronx by 45 per cent. According to FBI statistics, crime in 1997 fell for all major cities. In large cities, violent crime fell by 5 per cent and property crime by 20 per cent. The rate of car theft is now lower in parts of the US than that in Britain or Scandinavia. The concern about crime has diminished in parallel. In 1990, 31 per cent of Americans saw crime as a major challenge. In 1997, this percentage dropped to 14 per cent.

There are many reasons attributed to this encouraging trend. One is the famous zero-tolerance policies pioneered in New York and the Metro systems in Washington, DC. The zero-tolerance policies, famously developed by William Bratton, New York Police Commissioner, and New York Mayor Rudolph Giuliani, have also been paralleled by effective reorganization of police departments, better equipment, and the deployment of more community policemen. Experts also point to an aging population which creates a smaller set of potential young criminals, and an increased use of incarceration, which has removed potential criminals from the streets.

Effective use of technology, notably in a statistical system as called COMSTAT, and an increase in the number of policemen on the streets have been associated with successful reduction in the crime rate. Increases in federal spending to support the new approach to crime control has also boosted budgets and increased the physical presence of policing resources. Other sources of reduced crime include an increase in the number of home alarm systems, increase in car alarms, increase in the use of private security guards, particularly in large buildings, and community engagement through neighborhood watch schemes.

The probability of effective deployment of the full response capability at a global level is unfortunately low due to cross-border confusion, red tape, evidentiary procedures that protect the guilty, court systems with unjustifiably long backlogs, limited policing budgets, and overlapping jurisdictions within nations and borders. There is no effective global institution or group of national institutions which has had a meaningful impact to date in the area. Even within a single nation state, intraagency co-operation is difficult. Scotland Yard and MI5, the FBI, DEA, BAFT, and state authorities, have all had public rows over territorial issues and conflicting claims to jurisdiction.

Not only is the intranational ability to respond limited but that limited capability may be encumbered by lack of co-operation, or even opposition from nation states which lie at the source of many global criminal initiatives. Response efforts are hampered by the support or tolerance—implicit and explicit, willing or unwilling—of some rogue states to the criminal enterprises resident within their borders. This list of troubled nations would include Myanmar, North Korea, Colombia, and a long list of small island countries susceptible to the attractions and threats of the drug trade and money laundering.

The resulting distraction, delays, and potential for unjust outcomes reduces the chance of even scarce responsive responses being deployed on an effective and timely basis. In addition, required funding relative to the accumulated wealth and power of target global criminals will make it difficult to match the force of the global criminal system on an economic basis.

Even Italy's prime minister is under investigation for alleged association with the Mafia during his period as national leader.

China, or its regions, have recently tolerated organized efforts at automobile thefts, sheltered pirates in violation of international law, and tolerated the theft of all categories of intellectual property, computer software, and music and cinema properties. China is also the source of a systematic abuse of the rights of women and female infants. Girl infanticide and sex selective abortions have become so widespread that there are now 35 million more men than women in China—a destabilizing ratio in any socio-cultural environment.

Lack of Measures and Understanding

The net risk assessment in this area is already extremely negative and getting worse.

In his book, *The Global Habit*, Paul Stares further notes with some despair that "....no in-depth forward-looking assessment has been carried out. In fact, despite worldwide rising concern, basic appreciation of the drug problems as a global phenomenon remains poorly developed." Noting that most studies have focused on local issues or only part of the problem, he demonstrates that the development of sanctions has been, in part, deprived of sound intellectual or data driven foundations. This lack of a sound diagnostic view of the problem may contribute to development of ineffective negative control sanctions rather than more productive "positive control" measures which could have a greater impact on a long standing and increasingly threatening drug problem.

It is not only a lack of analytical input which is of concern since: "The overwhelming approach to international drug control has clearly failed in its ultimate objectives, as the global market has continued to expand. Many of the negative control measures have also been perversely counterproductive."

Systemic Response

Perhaps the most important systemic characteristics of the criminal element of transnational behavior are consolidation and connectedness. The implied imperative and focus of effort then is first to develop a force equal to or greater than the consolidated systems whose behavior is to be influenced. This will require increased funding, an establishment of an effective international institution fully empowered to attack the consolidated system at its weakest points on a sustained basis. Failure to match the power and influence of these organizations on a global basis will allow them to grow and develop across the world. A second systemic response is to break the links that enable the system to grow through so many interrelated areas. The application of force to one aspect of the system on a concentrated basis may create a discontinuity in the whole which causes the system to lose momentum or even to collapse entirely. All levels of the system will need to be engaged, but a concentration of effort will have a far more powerful effect than a fragmented set of underfunded initiatives along national lines—one of the sources of the global underperformance in this area to date.

The need to consolidate and co-ordinate effort is clear, as is the imperative to enforce compliance with existing agreements as a first step toward improved results in the global fight against the costs, and risks of crime.

Proposed Architecture of Solutions for Crime

For each different area of transnational criminal activity, the exact set of required responses would vary in part. However, many of the elements of solutions would be shared. In the area of illegal drug use, for example, the set of proposed actions would serve as a model for others as well. The key elements of the architecture of solutions could contain the following:

New Vision: An international co-ordinated effort reducing additive drug consumption by 50 per cent over a 10-year period.

Specific Initiatives:
- Zero-tolerance policy to sales in user markets.
- Eradication of supply in drug-producing countries through negative and positive initiatives.
- Alternative "positive" treatment and therapy for habitual users to reduce demand.
- Alternative agricultural development policies in drug-producing areas to reduce supply.
- A concerted effort to break links to money laundering through intensive G7 effort at limiting bank secrecy and illegal transfers.
- Increased funding for the increased use of relevant technologies, e.g. COMSTAT.
- Abolish tax relief for bribes paid to corrupt officials—extending to a globally ratified version of the US Foreign Corrupt Practices Act, which curtails bribery and corruption.
- Establish a global drug agency—a drug Nato—with powers and prior approval to cross borders to eradicate supply and disrupt transit flows following international agreement.
- A series of rehabilitiation centers and support programs to help and treat users on a positive basis.
- Funding and development of local agencies to oversee alternative crop programs.
- A stronger alliance of national and local police forces to drive a consolidated and sustained effort at all levels of the transnational drug system—from basic production through distribution, including the elimination of visible and offensive street peddling.

Other areas of crime would have separate lists of positive and negative initiatives. But the balance of immediate actions and the development of future capabilities would need to be carried through in all cases.

Environment

The global environmental system is clearly one which is complex, global, and where destructive change is accelerating at an alarming rate. Air pollution, water pollution in rivers, lakes, and seas, acid rain, holes in the ozone layer, chemical and other hazardous waste leaks and spills, deforestation, species extinction, fish depopulation, and other destructive behaviors make a long and expanding catalog of current concern and future risk.

The expanding population of the planet, coupled with an increase in the consumption of resources per capita, have created a situation of unsustainable stress on the environment and brought on fundamental concern for future generations. Momentum is negative, with the extinction of plant and animal life taking place at an accelerating pace. The current wave of species extinctions, already identified by some as the Sixth Great Wave of Extinction in the history of the planet (and the only one which is man-made), is only one of many destructive trends which will disrupt the interconnected elements and overall balance of the planetary ecosystem.

The population explosion, together with an increasing demand for resources per capita, lies at the root of many problems, today and in the future. Since the 1950s, world population has doubled. Economic growth has increased fourfold over the same period, increasing the impact on consumption and environmental stress. As 60 per cent of non-European population in the world today is under 16 years of age, no significant change in expanding population trends is expected before the year 2050. Many experts forecast that by 2050, there will be 10 billion people on the face of the earth, nearly double the current population. This increased population, adding nearly 100 million people per year over the next 40 years, will create extreme stress on water, food, infrastructure, and social order systems.

Some analysts have determined that under past practice nations must achieve a per capita GDP of US$5,000 before becoming sensitive to environmental concerns and sufficiently motivated to make the trade-offs in favor of capital investment for increased pollution control against unfettered economic development and employment creation. Given current GDP levels which are well below this threshold for the vast majority of the world population of 6 billion, the potential scale of harm in this area is likely to continue to increase at an accelerating rate. A parallel observation that developing nations move away from a bicycle culture at $1,000 per capita per year to motorcycles at $2,000–3,000, and to automobiles at $3,000 and above, creates a disturbing extrapolation to a world of spiraling hydrocarbon consumption and greenhouse gas emission long before an environmental consciousness kicks in.

In particular, India and China, large countries on the verge of their own industrial revolutions, will contribute to deforestation, global warming, atmospheric, oceanic and local pollution, and other long-term environmental hazards. The rapid industrialization of the former Soviet Union, which was pursued with little regard for the environment at a time of Cold War priorities, yielded not only the Chernobyl nuclear plant but also refineries, chemical plants, manufacturing enterprises, and other Soviet scale investments which were built and run with little environmental concern.

Deforestation

Deforestation is a critical source of multiple types of ecological destruction since the removal of forest cover for logging or land clearance results in fertile top soil runoff, dust storms, polluted streams, flooding, salination of surface soil, and the reduction in the natural habitats of thousands of animal and plant species. It provides a common destructive core to a long list of environmentally damaging consequences.

As a percentage share of the original forest, the total remaining forest in Africa is one-third the size of its original ground cover. In Europe, the number is even lower than Africa, where only 1 per cent of the original forest remains in Europe. In Asia, the number is only 28 per cent. The world as a whole has lost nearly half of its original forests. Frontier forest as a share of the total remaining forest is only 40 per cent. The full cost of this centuries old trend is just beginning to be understood.

Paying the Price for the Past

The cost of illegal or excessive deforestation is paid through unnecessary floods, clogged waterways, parched soil, mud slides, property damage, and even in the deaths of flood or landslide victims who pay the ultimate price for underperformance in the area of environmental control.

In the Philippines, repeated flooding has been attributed to La Nina, a weather phenomenon which brings heavy rains. But the scale of the damage has been exacerbated by deforestation and a failure to heed the lessons learned in the areas of excessive logging and land clearance.

"The root cause of this problem is the denudation of our forests," said President Joseph Estrada, after surveying the damage created by a major period of flooding. "This is a sin of the past that we are paying for now."

It is not just Filipinos who are paying the price. In China, 4,000 people died in the widespread flooding of 1998. Premier Zhu Rongji conceded at that time that the environmental approach taken by China was "far from satisfactory."

Further dangers from past environmental damage can be seen in the rising bed of the Yangtze river, which has risen an average of one meter per decade over the past 40 years.

Asia's problems are far from over. Poor countries like Vietnam, Cambodia, and other Asean countries continue to clear land to raise cash quickly and to prepare land for valuable crops. Dak Lak province in Vietnam, for example, has seen its virgin forest cover cut back from 70 per cent to 15 per cent in less than 25 years. The immediate impact of top soil erosion, silting of rivers, and flooding are only the beginning signs of the damage done by such widespread and indiscriminate land clearance. At current rates of deforestation, some developing countries will shortly have no forest left at all.

Species Extinction

Species extinction is a growing concern as the number of species nearing threatened status or already in a threatened state is growing rapidly. The rate of vertebrates threatened is nearly one in three. Nearly 40 per cent of mammals are threatened or nearing threatened status. More than one-third of the fish, nearly one-third of amphibians, and 20 per cent of birds were designated as at risk in 1996. Many large animals that capture our imagination and affection face the greatest danger of extinction—the tiger, rhinoceros, panda, gorilla, eagle, and even the kiwi. Left unchecked, the current slaughter will soon leave these species residing only in 200s, photographs, and fading memories.

The problem is not new. As Paul Kennedy noted in his book *Preparing fot the Twenty-first Century*: "The author, Gabriel Garcia Marquez and other distinguished signatories sent an appeal to heads of states in Latin America nearly a decade ago, citing concern over the fact that by the year 2000, three-quarters of America's tropical forests may have been felled and 50 per cent of their species lost forever. What Mother Nature created in the course of millions of years will be destroyed by Man in little more than 40 years."

Air Pollution and Global Warming

According to the Environmental Protection Agency, 150 million Americans are breathing air considered unhealthy. Air pollution, acid rain, and global warming are linked problems. According to the carbon dioxide information analysis center at the Oak Ridge Laboratory, global carbon dioxide emissions from fossil fuels have risen virtually 500 per cent from the end of the World War II, with nearly 6 billion metric tons of carbon released into the atmosphere as a result of fossil fuel consumption.

Some of the worrying trends go back well over a century. Thousands of years ago, carbon dioxide levels were around 200 parts per million. By the early 19th century, carbon dioxide levels had risen approximately 40 per cent to 280 parts per million. This was the result of thousands of years of evolution and climatic change. It is interesting to note that the average temperature during the last Ice Age was only 9° Centigrade colder than today. Small changes in the environment can make a world of difference to its human inhabitants.

During the last century and from the beginning of the Industrial Revolution, carbon dioxide concentration in the atmosphere has risen a further 25 per cent. This increase has been accelerating over the past quarter-century. Current studies suggest that levels exceeding 500 parts per million, even up to 600, may be reached in the middle of the next century if corrective action is not taken. A disastrous impact of average global temperature on plant and animal life as a direct result of the flourishing of bacteria and disease, and other unexpected catastrophes can certainly be taken for granted should atmospheric carbon dioxide levels and global temperature continue to rise.

Global warming is already creating direct and unexpected non-linear consequences that extend into many environmental subsystems. In Alaska, for example, recent increases in temperature can be seen in reductions in the average ice thickness and increased spaces of open water, threatening traditional patterns of wild life behavior. Temperature increase has allowed unexpected forest diseases to destroy millions of trees as diseases flourish in the warmer climate.

Net Risk Assessment

These are only a very few examples of a very long list of proven environmental damage and risk of continuring harm to the environment.

From any perspective, the net risk assessment of performance in the environmental area is currently deeply negative and the overall risk of a global catastrophe racing toward a certainty.

Potential Scale of Harm: Holes in the ozone layer, an impending global shortage of fresh water, a loss of over half of original forests, and a continuing wave of irreversible species extinction are only a few of the examples of damage already inflicted on the environment. The scale of harm from a linear or a non-linear catastrophe has already reached a level of maximum concern.

Likelihood of Occurrence: As complex systems interact, as populations grow and as the demand for even higher levels of consumption continue, failure to reverse current trends will certainly result in mass catastrophes. It is purely a question of time. The global environment reflects all of the interconnected characteristics of complex global systems. Using language that describes some of the patterns and risks of the systemic character of the environment and the pure nature of chaos, Andrew Goudie concludes in the *Future of Climate* that "finally, it may well be that the atmosphere and the ocean possess a degree of internal instability which furnishes a built-in mechanism of change so that some small and random change to the operation of positive feedback and the passage of thresholds, might have extensive and long-term effects. Small changes might have big consequences."

Looking forward, clear analysis would indicate that there are two critical countries at the heart of the future of the environmental debate—the US and China. The US, which represents one-third of global consumption and production, is the major source of much residential, industrial, and vehicular pollution. The atmosphere, the water system, the land, and other major environmental areas are constantly at threat from the exhausts of the major engines of the world economy. At the other end of the spectrum, is China, the source of potentially the most pollution in the future and the source of much of the increase in pollution today. China, with its coal reserves approximating 15 per cent of estimated global reserves, uses this reserve to fund three-quarters of its energy needs. To date, China has had little success in discovering domestic sources of clean fuel or in building transport systems into China from more fertile areas of, for example, natural gas. With its low

GDP per capita and poor environmental regulations, China is well on its way to generating more pollution than developed countries have been able to remove from their own industrial base. At current trends, China will soon be not only the highest growth source of pollutants but will also be the largest in absolute terms as well.

In addition to the major environmental consequences of China's economic development, China is also the major villain in some of the most emotive areas of biodiversity risk. Resident and overseas Chinese are leading consumers of ivory from illegally slaughtered elephants in Africa, of internal and external organs, threatening species such as the tiger and bear, and other exotic animals whose skin, organs, and bones are allegedly useful in treating impotence, aging, and low energy through traditional medicines.

Costs of Satisfactory Underperformance
Paul Kennedy suggests in his book, *Preparing for the Twenty-First Century*, the need for reform and, even before that, for better understanding of the interconnection of the global changes now affecting our planet: "Just as we have to realize that the Earth is a closed system thermodynamically so also ought we to comprehend the linkages which our varied human actions—demographic, economic, social—have created. Because of the population explosion and humankind striving for high living standards, we may now be subjecting our ecosystems to more pressure than it can take; but as it shows increasing signs of stress, it in turn threatens us, rich and poor alike, with the consequences of having tampered too much with the Earth's thin film of matter."

Countries lagging behind the G7 are striving to achieve equal developed nation status and concomitant increases in living standards for their citizens. Should the developing countries of the world achieve this status, and assuming it is achieved through current policies of industrialization, investment, and unregulated emission, we would face an environmental catastrophe of unprecedented proportions. Should China, India, and other developing countries continue to burn crude coal as fuel for industrialization, operate factories with little regard to effluent content and dispose of industrial and residential waste in a haphazard manner, the world would inevitably become uninhabitable. Should the US and Europe continue a disproportionately high level of consumption and contribution to environmental damage, the same result will occur.

Capability to Respond: The proliferation of relevant governmental and intergovernmental institutions and their fragmentation characterize a system which, to date, has had unsatisfatory results at best. The poor state of the global environment and negative trends underscore the weakness of response capabilities in the international arena.

Some apparrently unrelated actions by governments, for example, providing subsidies to the fishing industry deepen the problem through the encouragement of over-fishing and contribution to irrationally high consumption, and depletion levels of marine stock.

Private foundations such as Earth Watch, the World Wildlife Fund, and other privately funded groups contribute to progress, but even successful efforts on small projects pale in comparison to the full scale of the risks and current damaging behaviors. Looking forward, this weakness in the response capability will be even more apparent as the core challenges and volatile mix will involve two of the largest and most complex nations on earth—China and the US—thereby increasing the scale and likelihood of a catastrophe eventuating.

On the other hand, when global interests are aligned behind the achievement of an aspirational goal, results can be achieved. Annual world production of chlorofluorocarbon (CFC) from the late-1980s to the mid-1990s dropped from 1,250,000 tons to less than 700,000 tons. Reversing a trend which began in the 1950s of accelerating growth in CFC production, global alignment behind a clear and ambitious goal allowed authorities and producers around the world to find substitute products, to change production processes, and to reduce measurably the risk to the ozone layer from CFC production.

With scientific evidence demonstrating irrefutable proof of a hole in the ozone layer over Antarctica, the threat to the world's environmental system was immediately identified as a clear and present danger to all countries. A specially modified U-2 spy plane, overflying the Antarctic, had confirmed the hole in the ozone layer beyond doubt. The 1987 Montreal Protocol was swiftly enacted, mandating that CFC production and consumption in the participating nations be reduced by half in a 10-year period. More than 100 nations were signatories to the Montreal Protocol and most began immediate actions to reduce the damage caused by CFCs in the upper atmosphere. With scientific data continuing to mount ominously on the depth and accelerating nature of the crisis, a second Montreal Protocol went into effect which moved the 50 per cent reduction goal forward to 1995 and added an 85 per cent target reduction by 1997. Aiming for total elimination of CFCs by the year 2000, the new protocol claimed nearly 100 signatories and also went into immediate effect. The risk of skin cancer in humans and damage to ultra-violet sensitive plant populations increased as information in the early 1990s reflected that the ozone layer, even immediately above the US, was thinning at a rate more rapid than formerly expected. Positive solutions were put in place including process management improvements, and internal yield-loss efforts by relevant manufacturers. Complementary negative initiatives of increasing prices and excise added to the effort's success.

Probability of Capability being Effectively Deployed: Ironically, in this area where there is a clear demonstration of the scale of harm, a high risk level of that harm eventuating and a proven ability to implement effective change, the probability of timely deployment is low. Although crises can pull together interested parties to respond to a flood, or to reduce an immediate threat, as in the CFC crisis, most longer term problems have evoked little or no effective response due to lack of interest or will.

Part of the problem is a gaping hole in the global architecture. There is no environmental police, environmental court, or few environmental sanctions in the courts of most jurisdictions. The politics of the environment are a study in complexity, conflict, and crisis. The sheer number of organizations concerned over the environment makes effective strategy design or implementation a difficult objective to achieve.

The United Nations Conference on the Environment and Development, the famous Rio Earth Summit of 1992, attracted 35,000 activists from nearly 9,000 organizations. Although the Earth Summit was a step forward in creating awareness of the environment and building a global level of concern, the large number of organizations with no effective leadership is, in the end, disheartening. Post-conference division is spreading more rapidly than coalescence.

Timeliness can also be an issue. The Convention on International Trade in Endangered Species of Wild Fauna and Flora (CITES) accords on the protection of endangered species were signed 13 years after the original proposals were tabled. Even as the accords were being put in place some local agencies and special groups were planning to ignore or bypass the accords.

Available Improvements

New measures in environmental accounting and new concepts such as intergenerational equity can clarify the debate and will help to inform the highly complex issues surrounding better management of the global environment. Potential responses to negative data are many and can fall both into the negative and positive boxes for action. Negative actions can include green taxes (for imports or domestic produce not complying with environmental standards), withdrawal of manufacturing licences from polluting enterprises, jail terms for violators, and other sanctions provided by the law and regulatory structures. Positive measures can include internal studies to optimize environmental and cost-efficiency of manufacturing processes, design to recycle, alternative material usage, rewards for increased recycling, and other measures consistent with improved utilization of the world's scarce resources.

In a famous essay entitled "Green and Competitive," Michael Porter outlined the possibilities for a more efficient model of overall business processes from design to procurement to manufacturing through to packaging and distribution which could yield significant insight into potential efficiencies in the process. Eradicating inefficiencies could result in both reduced costs and reduced pollution. Pollution is, by definition, a by-product from the burning, shaping, transporting, or transforming of goods in an inefficient way. In some industries with a high pollution sensitivity, successful investments have already been made in equipment and research to identify and realize potential environmental savings. One major multinational company identified more than 70 process changes that would create significant efficiencies in material processing and achieved dramatic reductions in dangerous effluents.

Positive and negative measures have proven to be effective in reducing vehicle emissions and CFCs in the atmosphere. Negative reinforcement mechanisms such as gasoline taxes, penalties, and fines for breaches of environmental legislation have been effective in a more limited set of cases. A broader application of that knowledge could lead to similar improvements elsewhere.

Deployment of response is not just an issue of effectiveness of global institutions. Much of the success or failure in the future will depend on the response of individual industrial enterprises. Bankrupt state enterprises in China will be far less likely to abide by policies than well-capitalized Western competitors. The effectiveness of deployment will depend upon global, national, and local actions to drive comprehensive change.

Despite the proven success of both positive and negative approaches, the overall status in the world's environmental systems is increasingly parlous. Many environmental criminals evade all but the slightest of penalties. Airborne pollution and fresh water problems increase by the day. There is still no clear global institution or leader to define and implement environmental rules. As could be predicted, the most reluctant participants in global protocols and treaties requiring decreases in environmental damage are the most advanced nations who produce the largest quantum of pollutants. The emerging nations perceive environmental regulations as an unacceptable hindrance to economic development or even perceive it to be an OECD plot to keep them from matching the living standards of the privileged world. The outcome of the global environmental challenges of the next century will be determined primarily by the policies adopted and implemented by the most advanced nations like the US and other G7 nations, and large developing nations like China and India. At both ends of the scale, much remains to be done.

Proposed Architecture of Solutions for the Environment

New Vision: An overall quantified goal of achieving a world where all major negative trends are reversed and a sustainable state of environmental stability is achieved in every area of the ecosystem: air, water, plant, and animal.

Specific Initiatives:
- Increased funding for population control programs.
- Formalization of CITES, the Rio and Kyoto Accords and assurance of implementation through sanctions.
- Rapid adoption of Californian standards for vehicles, for example, to accelerate deployment of effective response mechanism.
- Ban on clearance, cutting, and burning of original tropical rainforests (and enforcement of the ban).
- Increase in taxation on gasoline, coal, CFC, and other high impact pollutants.

- Imposition of green tax on emission intensive imports to reduce export of pollution.
- Development of an effective alternative to Chinese lignite burning by, for example, the building of a pipeline from Siberia or other resources of natural gas down to the mainland.
- Reforestation in the US, Europe, and in selected high potential emerging markets to offset tropical rainforest elimination.
- Scientific selection of species and implementation of replanting for maximum efficiency (certain species of bamboo appear to be a particularly useful source of improvement from a perspective of effective tropical environmental management).
- Prioritized reduction of harmful emission through improved engineering and control of vehicle engines, manufacturing plants, and rubbish recycling.
- Application of technology to relevant process and recycling efforts, e.g. provision of cost-effective cutting and clearing equipment to replace clearance burning techniques.
- Foreign aid linkage to adoption of low-cost environmental programs in emerging countries.
- Creation and funding of a single global agency with powers to bring civil and criminal action, and to implement global standards, measurements, and policies on environmental matters.
- Setting up of a simple set of measures, including the atmospheric PSI to measure and communicate progress (or lack thereof).
- Increased global monitoring and exposure of problems through the use of satellite and other new technologies.
- Regular forums at global and regional level to monitor progress against pre-set targets, track problems, and respond appropriately.

- Prior approval to global agency to impose obligations on national authorities to withdraw business licenses, issue injunctions, and levy significant fines—with a failure to enforce judgment by host state triggering host government's obligation to pay violators' fines.

Disease

From the beginning of recorded medical history, men, women, and children have suffered from waves of diseases and infections. Historically spread by armies and traders who travelled the world, disease is a risk which knows no national boundary or economic class distinction. Over the years, medical science has been engaged in a constant battle with a powerful foe. Matt Ridley stated that: "Medicine has underestimated not only the prevalence of infectious diseases but the resourcefulness of it as well. The enemy is not a static finite force, but an infinitely inventive complex of genetic combination engaged in a massive campaign of trial and error. That is what natural selection is."

Before AIDS and before the emergence of drug-resistant tuberculosis (TB) and more robust strains of influenza had caused alarm bells to ring again, the medical community seemed to have gained the upper hand over continuing waves of disease. The probability of old or new diseases spreading rapidly around the world also seemed to have been reduced. Our capabilities to treat new diseases and old had improved dramatically. The net risk assessment appeared to be improving steadily.

Recent History of Progress

Improved hygiene in crowded urban centers, better practices in hospitals and food processing centers, vaccinations and preventive medical care, urbanization and destruction of breeding grounds for traditional insect and animal carriers such as mosquitoes and rats, and a host of other improved practices and living conditions had dramatically reduced the risk of widespread distribution of infection. Our collective ability to respond to isolated crises had improved due to the adoption of effective practices developed by the CDC, WHO, and other national and international medical authorities. Better practices were deployed with great regularity across the world. These authorities to date have been more effective in the area of disease suppression than their sister organizations in other critical global challenges, who have less stellar records of success.

Smallpox and other diseases, which had threatened mass deaths in the past, seemed to have disappeared forever. While new and particularly virulent diseases appeared sporadically, most hemorrhagic viruses, for example, such as the Zairean Ebola virus and its related lethal cousins, seemed too lethal for their own good. Either because the vectors that carried them were particularly local in nature or because the diseases were so lethal that they soon extinguished their host, the highly lethal nature of these viruses seemed to contribute to reducing the possibility of spread. All major outbreaks have since been contained, although each catatrophic outburst of hemorrhagic fever captures the attention of the world and raises concern over the uncontrolled spread of the disease. The scale of actual damage to date from these past horrific maladies has been surprisingly limited. The potential scale of damage in the risk calculus appeared to be shrinking relative to past broad scale epidemics.

New and Old Diseases

As diseases evolve, continuous obsolescence and redefinition surface as a recurring pattern in the paradigm which may reverse recent successes in disease eradication or suppression. Drug resistance to TB and, worryingly, to AIDS is becoming a major problem in urban centers. While researchers are finding drugs which apparently limit the impact of AIDS, the virus is mutating in ways which make those drugs less effective. The sheer complexity of the AIDS virus and the mutations of other sources of disease raise fresh concerns by medical experts as to the eventual treatability of the disease.

The problems of resurgent old diseases is not academic or limited to any single disease. TB, which devastated central European cities for centuries, has been reborn as a major threat in the former Soviet Union. Particularly contagious in the cramped and unsanitary conditions of Russian prisons, this airborne disease spreads easily within confined areas. The diagnoses of many new and untreatable forms of TB are virtual death sentences for victims in harsh prison conditions. This death sentence may spread beyond the walls of Russian prisons, as each year 30,000 released prisoners carry a drug-resistant strain of TB into the population at large.

Arata Kochi, who is responsible for the Communicable Disease Prevention and Control program at the World Health Organization, is direct: "If it's not controlled [in Russia], it is going to spill over into Western Europe."

The validity of this concern is already evidenced in the case of a Ukrainian passenger en route to New York from Kiev via Paris. Dozens of passengers on his flight were infected with his strain of drug-resistant TB through inhalation of airborne germs in the few hours they shared together on the flight.

Other old diseases, if not completely eradicated, can reappear regularly over the years. In 1998 alone, three cases of bubonic plague were reported in the Arab Sea region. One 13-year-old boy died after being bitten by a flea which carried the contagious disease from infected rats.

AIDS

The current size of the reported AIDS population is only the tip of the iceberg. Although the problem has dropped out of world headlines in favor of sporadic reports offering hope through new drug and multi-drug treatments, the full tragedy of the AIDS plague has yet to be felt. As the number of full-blown AIDS patients in the US appears to be more in check, the number in the emerging markets of the world is exploding. Due to poor education, migration tendencies of single men, uncontrolled prostitution, poor medical care, limited advice, and resistance to the use of condoms, the AIDS problem in Africa and Asia is just beginning to emerge. The number of expected AIDS deaths in Asia and Africa is still rising with the number already in the millions. The unhelpful response by authorities in China and elsewhere raises concerns over a large-scale increase in the future infected population.

Ninety per cent of the existing 33 million HIV/AIDS cases are now in the developing markets of Asia, Africa, and Latin America. Almost all of the six million cases added in 1998 were in these impoverished markets. Eight per cent of South Africa's total population of 38 million are now reported to be infected with HIV/AIDS. AIDS is now the leading cause of death in Thailand where 300,000 deaths have been attributed to AIDS—both in adults and children.

Drug resistance, continued spread in emerging markets, lack of affordable or effective treatments will ensure that this unchecked epidemic is as much an issue of the next century as the past.

Hemorrhagic Fevers

The symptoms of viral hemorrhagic fever can be caused by four major tropical viruses—Ebola, Marburg, Lassa, and Dengue. All are potentially fatal infections which can spread rapidly from victims to new hosts. Ebola, perhaps the best known of these four viral families, killed over 80 per cent of its victims in an outbreak in 1995.

Like the bubonic plague, many hemorrhagic fevers are spread by rodents and insect carriers, through contact with rodent droppings, and infected blood or other body fluid products of victims infected with the disease. Particularly worrying is the possibility of these diseases spreading through aerosols, which float through the air in proximity to their victims. Traditionally spread from rural population sources, where poor sanitation and primitive living conditions bring individuals in direct contact with rodent excreta, outbreaks are then transmitted from one infected victim to another through blood, fluids, and aerosols.

Outbreaks of hemorrhagic fevers are characterized by high degrees of lethality, reaching a 90 per cent death rate in communities struck by one of the more dangerous strains of hemorrhagic fever. These virulent outbreaks are not restricted to a single geographical area or even continent. The African origins of the Zairean Ebola virus are well known. Lassa fever, the Ebola and Hanta viruses have their equivalents in related hemorrhagic fevers in other regions, such as the Bolivian and Argentine outbreaks. In Pakistan and Afghanistan, a limited outbreak was believed to be related to ticks transferring the virus from the local goat population.

In the past 20 years there have been at least eight short but deadly outbreaks in different parts of Africa. A number of common elements in the development of the hemorrhagic-fever phenomenon link bats, monkeys, and, ironically, modern medical treatment. The repetitive use of infected needles in poorly equipped hospitals accelerated the spread and lethality of Ebola. Well-intended mission hospitals, through the reuse of needles out of economic necessity, have spread the Ebola virus more effectively than mammals or insects. An estimated 75 per cent of Ebola virus victims in one Zaire outbreak are believed to have contracted the disease through reuse of infected needles. Of the 75 per cent who caught the disease this way, over 90 per cent died shortly thereafter.

Hemorrhagic fevers have also reached Europe in the form of the Marburg virus, which attacked staff handling monkeys in Germany. More recently a case of suspected Ebola was brought to Europe by a

German film maker who had apparently contracted the disease in the Ivory Coast in 1999.

The risks of one or more viruses breaking out of historically confined areas are high. Infections through bats and humans with a greater travel pattern than historic virus sources or carriers, and the global presence of similar viruses with no known transport link raise concern over the likelihood of a global epidemic of an untreatable hemorrhagic virus in the future.

Lifestyle Diseases, Lifestyle Cures

Like so many of the old problems assuming new dimensions, many of the risks and opportunities in the medical area are related to conscious decisions made individually and collectively. Heart disease, lung and other cancers, sexually transmitted diseases, traffic and industrial accidents, cancers, cirrhosis, AIDS, mental illness, and violence all take a high toll through the impact of human or social factors well outside the viral, bacterial, and amebic. Other lifestyle factors also reduce the length and quality of individual lives through the creation of toxic environments or adoption of harmful behaviors. According to a Reuters report, 66 million Americans carry at least one sexually transmitted disease. AIDS is now the fourth leading cause of death worldwide, causing 13 million deaths to date.

Mental health is a major concern. Recent growth in the older male suicide rate has contributed to a decline in life expectancy in 1998 in Japan. The average life expectancy of a male in parts of Russia is now less than 60 years. Alcohol abuse and depression are common contributors to short life expectancies.

As medical science slows in its rate of breakthrough discoveries in complex research-related treatments on disease, the next great stage of progressive action to improve health will need to include lifestyle cures—changes in individual and collective behavioral models which will have a positive effect on disease or injury eradication or diminution in effect. Clearly capable of being implemented, the likelihood of changes in lifestyle is purely driven by collective and individual will.

Costs of Satisfactory Underperformance

The arrival of drug-resistant TB, AIDS, and other diseases, spread through migration and travel, is of great concern. In 1996, three-and-a-half million people died from TB and three times this number is dying from AIDS. Spread to humans from goats in developing markets by ticks and other carriers, the re-emergence of TB and its arrival in wealthy countries through immigration and contact has raised many new and troubling questions. The treatment for a patient suffering from drug-resistant TB can take up to two years and cost $250,000 per year. In Pakistan, where TB has surfaced in numerous developing communities, the budget of $10 per year would do little to meet the treatment needs of the disease. The probability of deployment of effective responses, even where they exist, becomes increasingly remote where economic disadvantage is a fact of daily life. In many ways, HIV and new forms of TB continue to be problems of the underclass and thus less likely to attract the full attention of the global media or medical community. The recent economic crisis has further increased the human costs of disease in Asia. One Asian country has been forced to scale back expenditures for immunization by 26 per cent, for preventive programs against TB by 36 per cent, and similar programs against malaria by 27 per cent. According to recent Oxfam estimates the toll in unnecessary lost human lives as a result of these cutbacks is estimated to amount to 30,000.

Net Risk Assessment

Potential Scale of Harm: With the arrival of AIDS, we have seen again the very real possibility of unexpected "catastrophes" and new mass threats to our collective health. Increasingly promiscuous sexual practices, global travel, consumption of exported products, and movements of animals and insects across borders and even across continents will increase the risk of new threats being spread rapidly, just as cross-border travel and population movements throughout Africa, Asia, and Latin America have spread AIDS within a few short decades across these large continents.

Many medical experts write reassuringly of the rarity of epidemics or plagues which link easy contagion with high lethality. Although smallpox, measles, and influenza fall into this category of both widespread and deadly epidemics, none has maintained this deadly combination for an extended period of time. We are in many ways just beginning to understand the full systemic nature of bacteria- and virus-driven epidemics, and with each new discovery the range of potential risk increases. This model of new risk and accelerating distribution is one which increases significantly the likelihood of future risks being realized.

If nature's system of bacterial, viral, amebic, and other diseases is not enough of a risk to our human population, attempts to capture and "weaponize" anthrax, AIDS, and other biological agents only add to the risk. In addition to natural propagation of these deadly germs, new risks of accidents, misapplication, and release in a concentrated form for military or terrorist purposes further escalate the disease risk.

One high-level Soviet defector, Kanatjan Alibekov, announced recently that the former Soviet Union believed that two epidemics of hemorrhagic fever in a remote area of China near nuclear testing sites were in fact the result of accidents in a laboratory developing biological weapons. He asserted that even the *glasnost* government of Mikhail Gorbachev supervised a highly developed program of biological weaponry and delivery vehicles. Intercontinental ballistic missiles aimed at major urban centers, he claims, were armed with anthrax and other deadly biological weapons. In a highly sophisticated program of gene manipulation, anthrax, and other biological warfare elements were genetically altered to create even more powerful and dangerous weapons. At the top of the genetic agenda was improving the resistance of fatal germs to the most likely drug treatments. The risks of deliberate or accidental deployment of biological weapons could in fact create global epidemics where civilian response institutions would soon be overwhelmed by the magnitude of the diagnostic and treatment tasks.

Likelihood of Occurrence: It is impossible to eradicate the channels of distribution of disease in the modern world. Insects, contaminated water supplies, air currents bearing aerosols, global air travel and trade routes, and crowded cities will always provide effective distribution systems for viruses and bacteria. Sexual contact, hospital environments, direct contact with animal carcasses and live animals, and other behaviors mixing healthy and infected fluids will provide further channels for disease transmission.

These distribution systems, coupled with an ability of old diseases to constantly mutate and obsolete their past forms, create a risk of old and new diseases breaking out of their currently limited form. One example of mass death through mutation and evolution of a source of disease was the influenza epidemic of World War I. Apparently traveling from its source in Chinese wild ducks through domesticated ducks and pigs into humans, the H1N1 strain of influenza was particularly dangerous due to the evolution of its surface protein genes, which resulted in an ability to avoid historically developed defenses. Its more virulent nature allowed it to invade hosts in a new and effective manner. Not only did the H1N1 strain develop along particularly lethal lines, it caused a whole new set of populations to be at risk. Due to its mutations and transmission characteristics, healthy adults, notably young men serving in the armed forces during World War I, fell victim to this new plague in great numbers.

Capability to Respond: While the capability to respond has been improving for many decades, the intractability of the AIDS virus, and new strains of old diseases such as drug-resistant TB, have shown that our traditional remedies and approaches may be wearing thin. Drug resistance in particular may give a new life to old foes. And in the area of likelihood of deployment, the problem of haves and have-nots becomes a critical concern. Drug treatments or multi-drug treatments may become available for some of the more threatening of medical conditions but the costs of development and deployment can be overwhelming for poor countries. Even if a treatment for AIDS eventually emerges, capable of full suppression or eradication of the AIDS virus as it mutates and develops, the high cost of such a treatment could be prohibitive. Particularly in the emerging markets of Africa, Asia, and Latin America, the probability of deployment is severely curtailed by adverse economic conditions.

Probability of Capability being Effectively Deployed: A recent epidemic of Japanese porcine encephalitis in Malaysia in the spring of 1999 was another classic example of both risk realized and larger catastrophe avoided. Although more than 100 people died from the disease, which is transmitted from pigs to humans via mosquitoes, greater disasters were avoided. In addition to providing yet another example of mammal-borne viruses carried to humans through mosquitoes, the risk calculus in the disease area is proven to be susceptible to political elements which can delay or block the deployment of effective responses. In reflecting upon the four-element risk formula, the Malaysian example could provide worrying input into the analysis of the fourth element— the probability of effective deployment of response capability. In this case, the risk of a virus breaking out into the human population at the cost of many lives had already become a reality as the toll of victims rose in the pig farming areas, just outside the bustling capital city of Kuala Lumpur.

The capability of fighting epidemics of this type has been developed through the WHO and the Center for Disease Control and Prevention. However, the Malaysian response delayed access to that expertise for nearly half a year. During this critical six-month period, an erroneous diagnosis of simple Japanese encephalitis failed to discover a more complicated source of virus which had never been discovered before. In fact, the outbreak of the newly discovered Nipah virus was not offcially examined by global experts until the death toll reached nearly 100.

Although the disease was primarily confined to workers and residents living within 2 kilometers of the affected abattoirs—the effective traveling range of the mosquitoes—the outbreak under other circumstances could have spread far beyond the local communities it infected in the first instance. The small towns around Bukit Pelandok, where the disease was centered, was only 100 kilometers south of the capital. More worrying, the epicenter of the disease was only 15 kilometers from the new gleaming international airport which is a major hub for international travel to and from Europe and other major Asian destinations. It does not take much imagination to conceive of a similar outbreak in such close proximity to a major urban center and a major international distribution point spreading to a much larger population within the boundaries of one country and even to the rest of the world.

The overall chronology, as reported in the *Asian Wall Street Journal*, charts the course of the events and highlights the concern over delayed deployment.

September 29, 1998:	First case reported to Malaysian authorities.
January 1999:	Virus spreads to pig farms south of Kuala Lumpur; researcher posed suspicions about government diagnosis on the Internet.
March 3, 1999:	Malaysian government decides to vaccinate 2.4 million pigs against Japanese encephalitis; human death toll reaches at least 28.
March 7, 1999:	Malaysian scientist discovered virus that cannot be identified and traveled to the US to deliver samples to Center for Disease Control (CDC).
Mid-March, 1999:	CDC researchers ruled out Japanese encephalitis, concluding virus had never been seen before; death toll reaches 43.

March 19, 1999:	Death toll reaches 53; Malaysian government asks CDC for help.
March 20, 1999:	More than 2,000 soldiers and policemen start slaughtering pigs.
March 22, 1999:	CDC researchers depart for Malaysia.
Mid-April, 1999:	Death toll reaches 100.

While in some cases failure to deploy an adequate response may be due to economic limitations, politics can also enter into the likelihood of effective responses being deployed even where available. Lim Kit Siang, a prominent opposition politician in Malaysia, described the deaths as "unnecessary and avoidable" and "the result of criminal negligence and ministerial bungling."

The fact that a new and deadly virus could surface 15 kilometers from an international airport and the situation remain unattended by global best practice experts for nearly six months adds to the risk calculus and underscores the need for more thoughtful initiatives and procedures to manage risk in the area of global disease control.

Proposed Architecture of Solutions for Disease Control

| **New Vision:** | A reversal of growing trends of resurgent diseases in developed countries and a dramatic increase in the quality of health care in the emerging markets. |

Specific Initiatives:

- Establish pre-set trigger points where the CDC (or WHO) have the right to enter a country. Prior approval would reduce risk of contagion spreading.
- Create specific opportunities to reduce spread of disease captured at low cost by providing funds to vaccinate individuals, provide poor hospitals with sterile equipment, train and equip doctors to roll out proven technologies.
- Increase limitations on cross-border movement of untested livestock.
- Reduce the potential scale of harm by elimination of use and storage of toxic chemicals and biological weapons in G24 countries.

- Impose severe penalties on countries who propose or continue the development of biological or chemical warfare products.
- Increase funding to hospitals in emerging markets—public and private—to eradicate unsanitary procedures (e.g. reuse of needles).
- Promote acceptance of condoms as part of a global healthy lifestyle.
- Accelerate research and roll out program for less costly AIDS and TB treatments.
- Structure manufacturing and distribution accords with emerging countries to make expensive treatment affordable.
- Control and treatment of sex industry workers for AIDS.
- Regular health checks on workers in sectors involving high-risk contacts.
- Enhance capabilities of institutions and improve future response through consolidation of CDC, WHO, and other key public health services into a single responsive crisis task force with a new charter and rules of engagement.
- Establishment of a Global Health Council to set priorities and direct funding on eradication and suppression of diseases—new and old—in countries both rich and poor.

Terrorism

Sadly, the history of mass terrorism is just beginning to be written. With the easy availability of international distribution and delivery systems, the enthusiastic support of the international media community and access to weapons of mass destruction—chemical, biological, and nuclear—the potential scale and impact of a major terrorist incident is achieving new dimensions.

With reported access to weapons of mass destruction now an accepted fact in the intelligence community, the potential scale of damage done by any well-funded terrorist organizations is mounting at an alarming pace. The proliferation of terrorist groups, the ease with which a single horrific incident can propel a group into international prominence, and the apparently impenetrable structure of newly emerging terrorist groups increases dramatically the probability of new levels of damage actually occurring. Our ability to undermine, block, capture, or convict terrorist groups is diminishing as they fragment and move into a more unpredictable and isolated set of groups with intractable grievances. And given the complex national, religious, and political background of countries caught up in the terrorist phenomenon, effective deployment of even that limited capability is reduced.

Costs of Underperformance

To date, the perception of terrorist harm has been much larger than reality. In 1988, the year of the Lockerbie bombing, close to 300 individuals died as a result of terrorist violence. More than 90 per cent of these individuals were passengers aboard Pan Am Flight 103, which exploded over Lockerbie, Scotland, killing all on board. That same year, the chances of any citizen in the world dying in a terrorist sponsored act of violence were lower than the reported risk of being killed by a dog.

In 1985, over 6 million American citizens travelled across borders. Of these international travellers, 6,000 died while abroad as a result of natural causes, accidents, and violence. Of these 6,000 international travellers dying abroad, only 17 were victims of terrorist violence.

The Rand Institute, a highly secretive think-tank located in the US, completed a two-year review of the causes and impact of terrorism during a two-year period. From 1988-1989 the Rand Institute surveyed the actual impact of terrorism and its perceived risk. In 1988, there were 203 Americans killed in violent terrorist incidence. In 1989, the number had declined to 23. Most of the differences were explained by the large number of Americans who were killed in the Pan Am flight 103 bombing incident. Of the 259 passengers on board, a high proportion of the passengers from London to New York that day were, as always, American. The total American death toll from terrorist violence during the two years surveyed was 226. During that same time period, 92,669 Americans were killed in road accidents. Despite the minute risk of physical harm occurring through a terrorist incident and the relatively low cost of human lives, the impact of the widespread and emotional communication of the limited number of terrorist incidents struck at the heart of many Americans. In a survey during this same period nearly one-third of Americans said they would not travel abroad as a result of terrorist threat.

At one point during the 1980s, the American media had become so enthralled with terrorist violence that more time was devoted to terrorists, terrorism, and violent terrorist acts than to poverty, unemployment, and non-terrorist crime combined. With a few bombs taking a relatively small number of innocent lives, Islamic or other terrorist groups discovered an ability to dominate world headlines for weeks, change travel patterns and elevate the level of fear and concern of millions of citizens around the world. This reaction raised the status of a small group of criminals to a level of global influence.

Even from a small base, the numbers of incidents declined through the mid-1990s. According to the Rand-St Andrews Chronology, the number of international terrorist incidents had risen to nearly 500 in 1991. Following this peak in the year of the Gulf War in Kuwait, the number of international terrorist events fell to 343 in 1992, 360 in 1993 and 353 in 1994. By 1995, the decline continued with only 278 incidents reported. This decline in number was counterbalanced by an increase in the subsequent scale of terrorist incidents with the Oklahoma bombings, Ayum sect nerve gas attack, and attacks on American embassies in various parts of the world.

Net Risk Assessment

As we move forward into the next millennium, we will be facing, for the first time, real threats with an enormous potential scale of damage, high likelihood of occurrence, a significantly weakened capability to respond to the risk created and a low probability that even a reduced capability to respond will be effectively deployed.

Potential Scale of Harm: A summary statement from Bruce Hoffman's definitive book, *Inside Terrorism*, captures the changed nature of this risk element in the terrorist arena:"In spite of the non-proliferation treaty (NPT), technology continues to develop and the rudimentary nuclear weapon is now within easy reach of any group which has a few hundred million dollars to spend. The shortest way to access fissile products is through trafficking which is thus more of a temptation than ever..." So far the number of serious cases of trafficking identified is small and no foreign country has been caught flagrantly trying to buy. However, this trade is now falling into the hands of the organized Mafia. It has been estimated that, to date, about 30 kg of fissile material has been stolen—enough in theory to make at least two or three nuclear bombs.

A worried commentator continues this train of thought as he wrote: "For the first time in history, a fanatic movement can get hold of modern weapons, including the kind of chemical weapons of mass destruction used by the small group in the Tokyo subway. The inquisition did not have chemical or biological weapon; Hitler did not have the atom bomb. I can imagine no greater danger than the combination of old fanaticism and modern weapons." The stockpile of nuclear weapons in Russia, estimated to exceed 10,000 warheads, consists of a high percentage that are past their "due date." Theft is a significant risk. The difficulty in decommissioning these weapons—in part due to a complex integration of conventional and nuclear explosives—will extend the time as well as the scale of potential harm.

The role of religion in terrorism has, ironically, increased the scale and lethality of the terrorist threat considerably. Analysis of new statistics reflecting the full set of international terrorist actions during 1995 show that religious terrorists were only involved in one quarter of the terrorist incidents but were responsible for more than one half of the deaths. Of those incidents that resulted in eight or more persons being killed that year, 100 per cent were the result of acts of religious terrorism.

The intersection of global systems—distributive, capital markets, computer systems, and other critical components to the current world order—also creates a highly volatile mix that could be detonated by a focused and deliberate attack on an urban area, cyber-system, or defense capability. Both the access to weapons of mass destruction and the compounded impact of concurrent damage to multiple interacting systems magnify the potential scale of harm.

Likelihood of Occurrence: As we move into the new millennium, we are also moving forward into a new generation of risks from international terrorism. In the section of his book entitled *Terrorism Today and Tomorrow*, Bruce Hoffman summarizes: "...compelling new motives, notably those associated with religious terrorism, coupled with increased access to critical information and key components, notably involving WMD (weapons of mass destruction), leading to enhanced terrorist capabilities, could portend an even bloodier and more destructive era of violence ahead than any we have seen before."

The diaspora of impoverised Russian scientists, many of whom are highly skilled in nuclear weapons, security, and control technology can only add to the risk of weapons of mass destruction falling into the hands of well-funded, technologically enabled terrorist organizations.

Capability to Respond: With the advent of religious support, and state sponsorship or protection, international terrorism has changed the rules of the game. The ability to interdict well-protected terrorist groups acting from within the borders of sponsoring rogue states is far more limited than historic control capacities available in, for example, Northern Ireland or northern Spain. By its nature, terrorism is a movement of a few individuals creating violent acts for political ends. The supporting network of modern international terrorism now includes rogue states, well-funded Islamic individuals, religious sects, a compliant and willing international media community, and large vulnerable groups open to being terrorized. The core actors in the terrorist realm are a few highly secretive and highly trained individuals who are difficult to identify and even more difficult to stop if not carefully monitored.

As Hoffman says, "there are a series of interrelated objectives pursued by terrorist through acts of apparently random violence. Unlike ordinary crime, which is apparently organized but frequently random and disorganized, terrorism, which appears random is in fact a highly organized and complex system when operating in this international sphere." While there will always be Unabombers, and lone psychopaths operating in isolation, the bulk of terrorist activities, particularly the lethal activity of religious terrorism, is of an organized and systemic nature which creates a new type of vulnerability for those organizations. It is possible to deny terrorists the media value and global platform which is the objective of their activities. The rational nature of the terrorist threat can provide some avenues for change.

Given the systemic nature of terrorism, and the spiralling risk that intersecting systems now represent a new approach to intelligence gathering, suppression, and response is being developed. Only by building an effective systemic counteractive set of measures can the escalating threat of terrorism and resulting risk be reduced to a more manageable level.

A positive program to deny terrorists the benefits of a global platform would go a long way to limiting the value, and hence the likelihood, of terrorist actions. Other negative approaches of interdiction include penetration of national borders to attack resident terrorist centers, for example, the Osmana bin Ladin headquarters in Afghanistan or Pakistan. These attacks, usually US-led or Israeli-led, are a part of an effective program to "terrorize the terrorist" which has led to curtailment of terrorist operations in Libya and elsewhere.

However, as in the criminal world, the most effective approach is likely to be positive rather than negative, constructive rather than destructive and proactive rather than reactive. The full understanding of the systemic causes of terrorism and intelligent response to the concerns and attitudes which have created violent behavior can, in many cases, reduce the risk of terrorist violence to a considerable degree. Commercially inspired terrorist acts may fall outside this area of action but constructive engagement with the causes of terrorism may be just as valuable as a stern response to the act of terrorism, once perpetrated.

More information is needed, more funding required for intelligence gathering operations and a more thorough analysis of the causes of militant activities necessary. Although the fundamentalist beliefs driving religious terrorism are apparently uncompromising and inflexible, positive action will need to be as much a part of the risk management of terrorist systems as a negative response to counter terrorist acts once the risk is realized.

Ill-prepared for Biological Attack

Recent actions and initiatives may provide hopeful signs of an increased ability to respond to terrorist attack using biological weapons, although the starting point is distressingly low. Mr Peters of the CDC captured the increase in awareness of new forms of terrorism: "Bio-terrorism is like syphilis in the 1950s. Nobody wanted to talk about it but now, the genie is out of the bottle."

Doctors at a special Interscience Conference on Antimicrobial Agents and Chemotherapy were more scathing in their comments. "Our policy makers don't get it at all," said Dr Michael Osterholm, a specialist in infectious diseases who believes officials and politicians are out of touch with the reality of the new level of risks and potential harm. A lack of training of medical staff on acts of bio-terrorism was cited as a major area of concern at the conference. Dr John Bartlett, head of the specialist unit at Johns Hopkins, noted that no training was planned for response to bio-terrorist attack and only one institution was actively studying the potential of bio-terrorism. Key concerns now focus on risks from anthrax, bubonic plague, and tularemia, as well as a host of aerosols and nerve gases.

Probability of Capability being Effectively Deployed: The probability of effective action being taken by international organizations in this area is remote. In some cases, the organs of a core group of nation states which should be the chief instrument of limitation and interdiction are actually the sponsors of terrorist activities. The projection of US and Israeli force across borders has had a mixed record, and even raised concerns over the accuracy and legitimacy of such attacks. The fragmentation of the response and the complexity of the causes make a concerted and effective effort at a global scale an unlikely outcome.

Proposed Architecture of Solutions for Terrorism

New Vision: A model of control where weapons of mass destruction are not deployed and terrorism fades as a means to global publicity.

Specific Initiatives:
- Focus on reducing scale of potential harm through limiting acquisition and deployment of weapons of mass destruction, especially by the Russians.
- Reduce the likelihood of risk events occurring by removing value of publicity.
- Ban use of names of terrorist organizations and individuals on grounds of national security—depriving any terrorist movement of the publicity it seeks.
- Increase engagements between Islamic and Western nations to reduce causes of terrorism.
- Reduce causes of terrorism through proactive engagement in economic develop-ment of key source countries.
- Monitor cults with counterbalancing messaging where possible.
- Integrate global counter-terrorist operations into one single leading global task force to focus on reduction in primary risk areas.
- Increase intelligence, human and electronic, on key risk individuals and groups.
- Specially trained for medical staff for biological and chemical weapons treatment.

Deculturalization

The apparent assault on local value systems by a so-called Western, American, or universal set of values has and will continue to generate much *sturm und angst* as global distribution and delivery schemes carry primarily American, but certainly English language, images, words, messages, and values around the world.

Prime ministers and presidents from France to Canada to Africa to Asia are expressing concern over the overwhelming impact of Western values on fragile and long-established local cultures. The erosion of traditional values, habits, languages, and social order continues to generate resentment and concern on a global basis—driven by an accelerating fear of irreversible cultural colonization.

In Singapore, for example, Lee Kuan Yew extols the success of creating an alternative to the American model of individualism and lack of social order: "those who want a wholesome society safe for individual citizens to exercise their freedom, for young girls and old ladies to walk in the streets at night, where the young are not preyed upon by drug peddlers, will not follow the American model."

For many, the cost of exposure to an American cultural model exceeds the full set of benefits. Violence, individualism, materialism, and liberal sexual, community and political models may be unacceptable to many non-Anglo Saxon cultures. An unfettered ability to challenge a system which may rest on more fragile foundations than American institutions may be seen to create unacceptable political or security risk.

There are many sides to the culture wars. On the one hand are the advocates of "universal civilization," primarily from Western countries, who share a fundamental belief in individualism, market economies and liberal democracy. Associated with these fundamental tenets are notions of free trade, free speech, open markets, gender equality, and human rights protected by an independent judiciary system.

On the other side of the argument are those who believe that American cultural dominance poses a unique threat to a world better characterized by cultural diversity and retention of traditional values, standards, and behaviors.

Rising Cost of Satisfactory Underperformance

Opponents of alleged Western cultural hegemony point to statistics such as the 70 per cent of movie revenues in Greece that are derived from

American films. That percentage rises to 80 per cent in the Netherlands and 92 per cent in Britain. In the prominent Paris theatres, 7 out of 10, and sometimes even more, theatres will be showing American films at any one time. Although the US accounts for less than one-tenth of global production of feature films, this 10 per cent of volume represents 65 per cent of the value of the worldwide market. Numerous commentators reflect on the danger of American or Anglo-Saxon cultural imperialism and the onset of a culture of lowest common denominator through the blitz of US-sourced mass media.

There is a consistent set of concerns expressed by smaller, and less tolerant cultural environments. Major concerns include increased disruption to social order through violence, disrespect, crime and increased use of drugs in a social or habitual context; sexual promiscuity and decline in family structures; a change in the role of women; a rise in individualism at the expense of conformity and social alignment; and a decay in intellectual and educational standards, resulting in low levels of educational aspiration and achievement.

Resistance to Western norms and cultural contents can be seen in more personal commentary as well. Essayist Nury Vittachi, writing in the *Far Eastern Economic Review*, has also raised the issue of defining a role of heroes and characters in the eyes of Asian children. "Our comic books—which surely encapsulate some of our favorite dreams and fantasies—capture the reality of what we really think on a subject: Caucasians are superior, and we want to be like them. Every comic on the news-stand outside my office in Hong Kong depicts heroes of round eyes, straight European noses and fair hair. Not a single one of the 17 publications for sale features a hero or heroine with Chinese features. No character has straight black hair, narrow eyes or small, flat noses like the ones my children have."

Shimon Peres broadens and deepens the same debate when he declaimed: "a country is not just some land within borders, it must have a spiritual and moral identity. Just as we have concentrated so much on defending our borders, we must concentrate on defending our heritage."

A Sense of Identity at Risk

Proponents of a protectionist approach to cultural diversity believe that it is essential to protect, as Costa Gavras states, "what is essential about humanity." As the world develops, proponents of cultural protectionism and diversity return frequently to the value of culture in the context of an individual and national framework. As national borders become less meaningful for business, media, and the full array of distribution vehicles—hardware and software—the need to protect fragile cultures and historical memories comes to the surface time and time again. Often related to debates on local language versus English as an international mother tongue, or at least as a language of international transactions, the debate on culture and diversity contains within it many fundamental ideas of what we are, where we came from and how we will get to our future social destination with a sense of meaning and identity intact.

Japan's noted social commentater and economic guru, Kenichi Ohmae, talks about a new generation of Nintendo-kids creating a global culture through habits and exposure that links them to their generational counterparts around the world more than to past generations within their own cultures. "Children and teenagers are, at deep levels of sensibility and world view, becoming much more like their counterparts in other societies than they are like the older generation from their own culture. The essential continuity between generations, upon which every society necessarily depends for its integrity and survival, has begun to fray..."

An Inevitable Convergence of Cultures

Many adherents to either side of the inflamed debate will see the cultural world as a zero-sum game—where one side can win only at the expense of another—and see systemic evolution on a cultural front as something new and threatening. During the 1960s, when the cultural wars reached new heights of militancy, one Sioux Indian in the US struck a defiant tone when he stated "we are fighting for ideological survival. Our ideas will overcome your ideas. We are going to cut the country's whole value system to shreds."

Yet systemic analysis will show that neither opponents of universal culture or defendants of the status quo will win out. The cultures of the world will inevitably evolve and converge as a result of intersection, interaction, and learning. Ultimately the dynamic nature of cultural evolution will sweep both forward into a future where both global and local cultures forge new links, respond to each other and grow—together and separately.

Oscar Handlin has described the forging of an American character and culture as the result of a process of "brutal filtering" of immigrant cultures. Immigration, transplantation, and reconstruction in a New World tested and refined cultural values and norms from a number of well-established cultures around the world. Some of these cultures survived intact; others were changed beyond recognition in the process of adaptation to the new American reality. Just as cultures were forced through Handlin's "brutal filter" in America, cultures around the world will be forced through an equally brutal filter as globalization tests the value, sustainability, and relevance of an even larger number of cultures and their salient characteristics. Fukuyama's astute prediction is that cultures will emerge through the process of globalization in different forms. Some will emerge intact, others will evolve and adapt in order to survive, and others will not survive the pressures of the new global order and eventually disappear.

Risk and Opportunity

Rather than arriving at the end of history as Fukuyama so famously said, we may be instead beginning an era of broadened global cultural diversity, transnational experience, and a fundamentally healthy testing and change in basic value systems. With the retreat of Western colonialism, beginning in the 1920s and reaching a peak in the period following tWorld War II, and with the collapse of the Soviet Empire, the diversity of nations and cultures has increased and the imposition of foreign structures taken a significant step backward.

Individual, national, and tribal cultures have been able to emerge in geographies formerly dominated by colonial powers. Particularly in the Islamic world, a new wave of return to historic values has emerged, despite years of colonization, conflict, and development. National cultures in Eastern Europe, Malaysia, India, the southern Islamic republics in the Soviet Union, and in northern Africa have all experienced resurgence following decades, and even centuries, of foreign domination.

Potential Scale of Harm: The greatest harm could arise from an artifical suppression from one extreme or the other—resulting in a futile attempt to limit global cultural evolution or to unnecessarily submerge valuable and different local cultures in a flood of US experience.

Ultimately, there are two reasons to encourage and manage the rich diversity of culture that we can experience in our lives. The first is individual and selfish—the desire to live in a world of choice and different experience in order to enrich our own lives, to inform our fundamental choices, and to create a choice of where to live, how to live, what to learn, and what to teach our children. At a second and more collective level, cultural diversity must need to flourish in order to allow civilizations to evolve constructively, to merge where appropriate, and diverge where necessary. An enforced unity of cultural environment will only submerge alternatives which will fester, increase in pressure, and, unless the suppressed culture is extremely weak, explode in violence or revolution in the future.

In this complex set of systemic evolution, particularly in an area with such profound impact on our lives as culture and social values, it is of the utmost importance to allow full debate on an experienced basis, with participants in the debate fully exposed to the merits and problems of the alternatives they face. The calcification of a living culture and a desire to stop its evolution may only serve to discredit the culture it is meant to preserve. By insisting on a preservation of values and cultures as they exist at any one point in time, the full value and richness of a dynamic culture can be lost. Individuals may be forced into a black and white choice when cultural evolution creates many shades of gray, many opportunities for personal development, and many opportunities to integrate the values of yesterday and today into the cultures of tomorrow.

In the 1950s, Lester Pearson warned that humans were moving into "an age when different civilizations will have to learn to live side by side in peaceful interchange, learning from each other, studying each other's history and ideals and art and culture, mutually enriching each other's lives. The alternative, in this overcrowded little world, is misunderstanding, tension, clash, and catastrophe." Today's cultural conflict can in fact be seen as cultural skirmishes on a forefront of potentially great battles. If cultural dynamism and diversity is not allowed to flourish, then the "real clash" between civilization and barbarism will become more fully engaged. If diversity and dynamism are not allowed to lead to co-existence of civilizations, cultures, and value systems, then the supporting and subsidiary systems of religion, art, literature, philosophy, science, technology and morality are even more at risk.

Likelihood of Occurrence: Contrary to the views of many critics, there is nothing unique in the pattern of development of the Western or universal model of civilization as it has developed in Europe, the US and, to a more limited extent, in other nations of the world. As stated in *The Clash of Civilizations and the Remaking of World Order*, "the development of the West to-date has not deviated significantly from the evolutionary patterns common to civilizations throughout history..."

Although the West can be seen to be different in that it has had a more significant impact on other civilizations since around the 16th century, Western civilization is itself a result of a cultural consolidation and convergence over a millennium of mixing of Islamic, classical, semetic, Judaeo Christian and other cultures on an evolutionary basis. The allegedly monolithic western culture, itself drawn from diverse roots, is in a constant state of evolution and transformation according to the rules of global systemic behavior

Systemic trends of convergence, continuing obsolescence, globalization, and dynamism will continue to exert an influence on the cultural platforms of our lives. The likelihood of change or of divergence from the current model is a certainty. The likelihood of that change creating harm rather than benefit will come from extreme attempts to calcify or to submerge more fragile cultures in a simplistic application of a zero-sum model against an opportunity for win-win outcomes.

Capability to Respond: In the summer of 1998 Sheila Copps, Canadian Minister of Cultural Heritage, brought together representatives of 20 countries to address the issue of US cultural exports and the social impact of violence and aggressiveness in the US film and television industry in particular. The European Union, constantly involved in trade skirmishes of the US, has established a "cultural exception" in order to protect the unique cultural systems of Europe, and, not coincidentally, to protect their own film and television production businesses. Results, to date, have been at best, mixed. The Academie Francaise battles in vain against the popular use of "franglais." Cultural ministries attempt successfully to preserve the past, but have little effort on an apparently uncontrollable future. The true ability to respond arises more from the populations that embody the culture than from more formal institutional guardians.

Probability of Capability being Effectively Deployed: A balanced approach can only come about through a deeper understanding and tolerance of cultural dynamism and diversity by a people at large. Given historical antecedents, the likelihood of active cultural fusion and reasonable standards of cultural tolerance emerging is greater than most critics would allow. Even American recognition of its own multi-cultural roots can be built into the process of globalization of western civilization. Similarly, governing Islamic conservatives will eventually, by a natural process, be forced to take into account the inevitable modernization of the world and their own populations. By no means, in either case, does this mean a headlong rush into a single global culture of lowest common denominator. On the contrary, it can mean a healthy encouragement of diversity, an exploration of the different, an appreciation of varying races, religions, languages, and ethnic and racial traditions. In order to explore the full potential and meaning of our common humanity, a diversity of experience can be spread via the enabling technologies of modern distribution, delivery, and translation. It is now possible, more than ever, to explore the past in ways that will enrich the future. The modernization process can bring us not only forward into a new era of understanding and richness of a diverse, life but also backward into a more diverse, understandable and usable past to enrich our lives and inform the lives of future generations.

The Singapore Model

In addition to its well known business and economic prowess, the three million citizens of Singapore already live within an intriguing model of cultural diversity and coexistence. Made up of Chinese, Malay, Indian, and international cultures, modern Singapore comfortably embraces Christian, Muslim, Buddhist, Hindu, and Jewish communities. Each major religion shares national holidays—Vesak Day for Buddhists, Deepavali for Hindus, Hari Raya for Muslims, and Christmas for Christians. There are neighborhoods in Singapore which reflect a dominance of each of the primary cultures—Little India, Chinatown, and Geylang for Malays—which act as a hothouse to preserve the unique language, religious, family, and culinary traditions which make up Singapore's diverse cultural foundations.

At the same time, there is a conscious attempt to create an international platform across all ethnic groups—a state-of-the-art capability in technology, acceptable standards of English for all citizens, respect for the highest standards of law and order, and a world view which reflects the realities of global competition while retaining the unique cultural flavours of its constituent communities.

Representative of the multicultural nature of modern Singapore and its acceptance of a range of spiritual practices, the inter-religious organization reflects a national policy of religious tolerance, understanding, and multi-racialism. Bahais, Buddhists, Christians, Hindus, Muslims, Sikhs, Taoists, and Zoroastrians from the 50-year-old organization co-operate with the Presidential Council for Religious Harmony to reduce the risk of racial violence or cultural intolerance.

The successful inclusion of the diverse racial communities within the concept of Singapore's "one nation and one people" provides a fascinating model of both international cultural evolution and local preservation within the borders of one small island state.

Proposed Architecture of Solutions for Deculturalization

New Vision: A world of choice where local cultures are preserved, nurtured and protected alongside a modern global cultural option which expands naturally without offending against local standards.

Specific Initiatives:
- Promulgation of multi-cultural model which allows a range of choice in a naturally evolving framework.
- Ban on distribution of media product which offends against local standards of violence, language, and sexual behavior
- Development of local content—films, music, books, poetry, dance and drama—funded through cultural tax on US media imports.
- Production of high quality local language media productions by US, European, or local enterprises.
- Increase in level of cultural content in educational systems—teaching the value of local and foreign cultures.
- Increase in evels of cultural, youth, and artistic exchange programs.
- Link of Academie Francaise, cultural ministries with other relevant institutions in a network model styled Council on Global Cultural Integrity and Diversity.
- Adoption of general statement of principles of cultural preservation and evolution by the UN.

Economic Disparity

The world's three richest men now have more wealth between them than the combined GNP of the 43 poorest countries. But the stark fact of this enormous gap is not the only perspective of the gap between rich and poor. There is a gap between the developed markets and developing countries of the world. There is another gap within countries, between the rich and the poor. There is an increasing gap between the international super-wealthy and an emerging global underclass which creates an unsustainable and dangerous social dynamic as well as a morally challenging state of material differences between individuals. This gap is exacerbating social tensions at a time of increasing American affluence and decreasing hopes in emerging markets suffering from the after-effects of the market crises of 1997.

Increasing Differences

The problems of poverty in America and around the world are marked by an increasing concentration of wealth in the top end of the world's wealthiest population. In a world where 40,000 children die every day from starvation, malnutrition and disease, there were 538 billionaires in 1995 who between them possess as much wealth as half of the world's population. At the same time, there were over one billion humans living on less than $1 per day. Eventually, the debate on economic disparity, the difference between the haves and have-nots of the world, is a debate that goes beyond economics of income distribution and into interrelated areas of disease, crime, racial tension, violence, and other elements of social and moral order.

Although leading commentators have written eloquently on the risk of conflict in the "faultlines" between civilizations, and "faultlines" between conflicting religions, primarily Christian and Islamic, the "faultline" between the rich and the poor has already become a widening chasm which carries the same risk of social disruption, national or regional conflict, and spiralling risk of repeated patterns of civil violence should current trends not be addressed. The information revolution has allowed even the poorest of citizens of the world to see how "the other half" live. In the areas of famine, disease, and other problems endemic to an underprivileged underclass, the current state of relative global calm could provide a window of opportunity to adjust problems before they grow into unexpected catastrophes in the world of tomorrow.

Despite the economic boom of Asian tigers and other emerging market "miracles," the gap between wealthy industrialized nations and poorer developing countries actually increased in the period from 1960 to 1989. In 1960, the richest 20 per cent of the world's nations controlled 70 per cent of global gross domestic product. By 1989, despite decades of rapid growth in eastern Asia, and large investment flows to other parts of the emerging economies of the world, the percentage of world GDP controlled by the wealthiest 20 per cent of nations had increased to 82.7 per cent.

Looking forward, the increasing growth in the world's population is only forecast to exacerbate historic differences in wealth distribution. At current rates of population growth, within a century the population of the less wealthy developing regions could be up to five times the size of the developed regions. The potential impact on world economics, environment, politics, and social risk could well shift the net risk assessment significantly in the future. The rate of growth achieved between 1985 and 1990 was just under 100 million people per year. This is double the absolute rate of growth in the 1950 to 1955 baby boom period after World War II. Lower birth rates in the developed world, coupled with faster population growth in developing economies, will respectively slow the growth patterns of developed nations while accelerating those of developing countries.

Solutions to the problem of inequalities in wealth will extend into priorities in government spending, education, crime and disease control, and continue to extend to questions of the role and legitimacy of the modern state itself. Any attempt to resolve the issues of haves and have-nots will need to attack the causes well as the effects of income disparity. In the past, progress has been uneven. It has been said by some expert commentators that, in the period from the early 1960s to the first term of the Nixon Administration, America waged a war on poverty, and poverty won. While there is some truth to this cynically stated view, a deeper analysis of the situation and systemic approach to the problems can indicate a hope for a future strategy which has greater success in addressing the causes and effects of economic disparity.

Costs of Satisfactory Underperformance

A Fortune magazine article in the late 1980s defined underclass communities as "urban knots that threaten to become enclaves of permanent poverty and vice." This dark vision of the underclass is later described in broader terms as "a state of mind and a way of life. It is at least as much a cultural as an economic condition."

President Lyndon Johnson's eloquence at the commencement for Howard University on June 4, 1965 signalled the nature and challenge of the gap between haves and have-nots in America and outlined the costs of disparity that transcended the purely economic. When describing the spiralling problems of black America, President Johnson concluded "despite the court orders and the laws, despite the legislative victories and the speeches, for them the walls are rising and the gulf is widening..." the poverty of black Americans, increasingly urban, increasingly separated from white communities, "is not white poverty. Many of its causes and many of its cures are the same. But there are differences—deep, corrosive, obstinate differences—radiating painful roots into the community, the family, and the nature of the individual."

The issues of poverty and race in America are profoundly interrelated. In a powerful essay entitled, *The Black Family In America*, the costs of being born into the underclass for black children are clear and disturbing. The author, Marian Wright Edelman, points out that black children are "twice as likely to: die in the first year of life; be born prematurely; suffer low birth rate; have mothers who receive late or no prenatal care; see a parent die; live in substandard housing; be suspended from school or suffer corporal punishment; be unemployed as teenagers; have no parent employed; live in institutions.

Black children are three times as likely to: be poor; have their mothers die in childbirth; live with the parent who have separated; live in a female-headed family; be placed in a educable mentally-retarded class; be murdered between five and nine years of age; be in foster care; die of known child abuse.

Black children are four times as likely to: live with neither parent and be supervised by a child welfare agency; be murdered before one year of age or as a teenager; be incarcerated between 15 and 19 years of age. They are five times as likely to be dependent on welfare and twelve times as likely to live with their parents who never married.

On a national basis, Edelman, founder and president of the Children's Defense Fund, also pointed out "we invest in children because the cost to the public of sickness, ignorance, neglect, dependence, and unemployment over the long term exceed the cost of preventive investment in health, education, employed youth and stable families." The positive economics of investment to address many of the causes and symptoms of poverty and the underclass can be clearly set out through effective juxtaposition of costs of prevention and risk redirection against costs of risks once realized. Immunization costs $47. Institutionalization of a mentally-retarded child costs $25,000 per year. Comprehensive prenatal care costs $600, a neonatal intensive care unit costs $1,000 per day. Preventive check-ups cost $40 per year, avoidable disease treatment through hospitalization costs $600 per day. Family planning services to sexually active teenagers costs $68, prenatal care and delivery costs $3,000. A summer job can cost $1,000 per teenager. If institutionalized in a juvenile center, costs rise to $20,000 per year.

Higher Costs in Developing World

The costs of satisfactory underperformance are even greater in the lesser developed countries. According to The World Health Report in 1995, a baby girl in a least developed country, "will not share in the global, upward trend of increased life expectancy. She can expect to live until at most age 44 if she clears early hurdles: one in three chance of being malnourished and under weight all her life; a one in ten prospect of dying before the end of her first year; a one in five chance of death by the age of five. In some African countries this baby's chance of being vaccinated and protected from diseases like cholera and tuberculosis will be less than one in two. Her chances of schooling 'at least enough to read and write' are one in three. She will be chronically anaemic and over worked; puberty will only add to her problem."

The element of population growth will only accelerate the concerns over the gap between the haves and the have-nots in the next generation. Although forecasters vary widely in estimated world population by the year 2050, in all cases the population will be significantly larger, perhaps double, what it is today. Many forecasters, including the World Heath Organization and the United Nations Population Fund, estimate that the world population will virtually have doubled by the year 2050. This forecast assumes a continuation of our current rate of adding nearly one billion people to world population every decade. As this growth is increasingly in the poor areas of the world, we are increasing the population of disadvantaged and underprivileged citizens which, in all likelihood, will further reduce the quality of life in emerging markets. The shallow pool of wealth in emerging markets will be spread more thinly over an even broader base. Already, particularly in large urban centers in both the developing and underdeveloping world, the basic infrastructure is either creaking or breaking down entirely.

Salient Systemic Characteristics

In the late 1970s, American social scientists appeared to have discovered the threatening American underclass yet again. *Time* magazine in August 1977 described the American underclass in stark terms: "behind the ghetto's crumbling walls lives a large group of people who are more intractable, more socially alien and more hostile than almost anyone had imagine. They are the unreachables: the American Underclass...their bleak environment nurtures values that are often at odds with those of the majority—even the majority of the poor. Thus the underclass produces a highly disproportionate number of the nation's juvenile delinquents, school dropouts, drug addicts and welfare mothers, and much of the adult crime, family disruption, urban decay and demand for social expenditures." Continuing with the inflammatory tone, the *Time* magazine cover-story went on to describe a group of underprivileged in America who had become "an underclass unique among the world's poor people." Nothing could be further from the truth today.

With the rise in international travel, a parallel development of economies, and other reflections of a new global paradigm, the problems of the underclass are no longer restricted to America. As the insightful work of Dr Douglas Shenson and other human scientists has revealed, the related medical and social problems of the underclass in London, Paris, and New York (the South Bronx in particular) reflect a high degree of sharing. The problems of drug abuse, AIDS, malnutrition, and other problems of the underclass are now a shared global phenomenon. Dr Shenson's work demonstrates that the problems of a global underclass are pulling further and further away from the lives of their well-to-do compatriots, the high-end of the "haves" in the same cities with their common international purchasing patterns, brand affiliations, and lifestyles. Just as a global underclass is developing a consistent pattern of behavior and values, the global privileged classes commonly purchase Swiss Rolex watches, German-made BMWs, holiday through international airline travel, make reservations on global reservation systems, charge their expenses on American Express cards, and bank with new prestigious global powerhouses like Citigroup. Ultimately, the new global haves and have-nots are developing parallel value systems and cultures as well as economic behaviors.

The language used to describe a newly redefined urban underclass is remarkably similar to that of a quarter of a century earlier used by Michael Harrington in his seminal work, *The Other America*. Harrington's description of the poor in America, more publicly associated with Appalachia in the 1960s than in the inner cities of the 1970s, reflects the depth of the challenge and the lack of progress despite decades of investment. He concluded that "poverty in the US is a culture, an institution, a way of life...the family structure of the poor is different from that of the rest of the society...there is...a language of the poor, a psychology of the poor, a world view of the poor." These observations, valid in America at the time of writing, are now true at a visibly global level of application.

Net Risk Assessment

Potential Scale of Harm: Acceptance of the current state of difference between the haves and have-nots within a country or a single global community, is clearly untenable: untenable for practical economic reasons, untenable for reasons of preservation of social order and security, and also untenable for moral and spiritual reasons. As Harrington stated in the 1960s, attacking the newly discovered deep poverty in America, would, through the effort itself, make the US an improved nation "when we join, in solidarity, and not in noblesse oblige, with the poor, we will discover our own best selves... we will regain the vision of America."

Likelihood of Occurrence: The costs of not engaging in a solution would eventually be wrenching and extensive. The risk of divided societies being pulled apart is always present. Whether it is modern-day Rwanda or pre-revolutionary France, divided societies are more easily pulled apart through external influences or through unsustainable internal dynamics which create tensions that go beyond the purely economic. While periods of adversity can strengthen the bonds of a unified group, misaligned or chronically divided societies are more likely to crumble or explode into violence than pull together in moments of greatest pressure.

Capability to Respond: Michael Porter, the leading author on issues of business strategy and competitive advantage, has also highlighted the problems of poverty in America and the crisis of the inner city: "the economic distress of America's inner cities may be the most pressing issue facing the nation. The lack of businesses and jobs in disadvantaged urban areas fuels not only a crushing cycle of poverty but also crippling social problems, such as drug abuse and crime. And, as the inner cities continue to deteriorate, the debate on how to aid them grows increasingly divisive. The sad reality is that the efforts of the past few decades to revitalize the inner cities have failed. The establishment of a sustainable economic base—and with it employment opportunities, wealth creation, role models, and an improved local infrastructure—still eludes us despite the investment of substantial resources."

The systemic requirements of sustained and focused efforts are clear. In a concluding section, regarding the prevention of adolescent pregnancy and the solution for larger social issues, Mrs Edelman stated "certainly public attention is more ephemeral than it used to be, but strengthening the family and preventing teen pregnancies requires the same concerted efforts over the long term as the earlier struggle for social progress. A setback this month, this year means little. The struggle will take many years. Nothing less will make a real difference". She is joined by Michael Porter in her call for a new and more effective approach.

"The time has come to recognize that revitalising the inner city will require a radically different approach. While social programs will continue to play a critical role in meeting human needs and improving education, they must support—and not undermine—a coherent economic strategy.

We must stop trying to cure the inner city's problems by perpetually increasing social investment and hoping for economy activity to follow. Instead an economic model must begin with the premise that inner city businesses should be profitable and positioned to compete on a regional, national, and even international scale. Our policies and programs have fallen into the trap of redistributing wealth. The real need—and the real opportunity—is to create wealth."

In all cases, estimates of the appropriate response to the development of an underclass revolves around the need to create sustainable employment. If the cycle of poverty, family disintegration, crime, poor health, and despair from lack of opportunity is to be broken, effective and sustainable employment is the beginning of the end of an American underclass.

The solution to these gaps is not to address one aspect or another of the economic gap separating the haves and have-nots. A more systemic approach needs to be taken to bridge these gaps with a sustainable model which is properly designed, a vision which is fully shared, and an implementation program which allows lasting changes to be made. As a number of commentators have proven, fragmented efforts and efforts not fully sustained have yielded little results. As time goes on, the problems deepen and spread. What was once perceived as a uniquely American crisis is now a spreading global phenomenon reaching beyond the G7 or G24 nations into the entire population of the world.

Probability of Capability being Effectively Deployed: *The Undeserving Poor* by Michael Katz expands on Harrington's vision and summarizes the sad facts on likelihood of deployment of a capability to respond. An expert, but disheartened summary captures the essence of the challenges: "reconstructing the way we think about poverty is partly an intellectual challenge. As such, it draws on creative resources in which America is rich. Acting on those ideas is another matter. It requires material resources, which America also has, and political will which it lacks." The rules of systemic management will require a deep and sustained program of total engagement. The political will, so fundamental to the solution, has yet to be sufficient to implement effective change.

The need to address the problem on a global basis is increasingly evident. The gap between rich and poor nations is unsustainable, and the cost of raising living standards in the developing nation may carry with it unacceptable environmental and social costs around the world. The gap between the haves and have-nots in a single society is equally unsustainable and carries with it the risk of social disorder, increasing crime, and even the rise of an "anxious class" eternally caught between the apparently unending cycle of poverty of the underclass and increasingly entrenched and isolated global over-class capturing a disproportionate share of the benefits. The greatest risk is of a social short circuit which bridges the gap with violence and social disorder.

Proposed Architecture of Solutions to Economic Disparity

New Vision: A reduction in poverty and more equal access to opportunity on a global basis—eliminating hunger, the diseases of poverty, and the trap of long-term structural unemployment.

Specific Initiatives: • Population control policies.

- Increased education, access to global market for business opportunity and sustainable "framework for development" mooted by the President of the World Bank.
- Tax credits and other incentives for inner city employment creation.
- Workfare to replace culture of welfare dependency.
- Mandatory education of children to continue government economic support to parents.
- Consolidation of buying power into useful lobbying effort to attract businesses to low income areas
- Debt forgiveness by rich countries to free the power from the burden of interest payment and capital.
- Strengthened street security to allow businesses to operate safely and profitably.
- Revival of interest in VISTA, Peace Corps and international counterparts as examples of global service from the developed world.
- Cross-border forum for exchange of successful practices in poverty reduction.
- Full integration in major cities in US and in developing countries of government programs with key businesses to ensure highest value added.
- Alliance of wealthy and poor nations in programs of mutual growth.

Technology and the Cyberworld

It is difficult to understate the impact that technology already has on our lives and will have into the foreseeable future. Medical technology has impacted the ways we care for ourselves, cure our ills, raise our children, and even change our appearance. Recent advances in genetics promise a future where DNA manipulation will be able to alter our genetic code, eradicating disease, removing physical disability, and prolonging life well beyond any prior expectation.

Cloning is a reality in the animal world and threatens soon to become a common practice in the human arena as well. Biotechnology, so much the rage at the beginning of the 1990s in the stock market and in the news headlines, has changed the way we produce our vegetables and meat products, changed the nature of the grain we plant and consume, and promises lower risk food with longer shelf life and higher nutritional content. Advances made across all areas of human endeavours from aerospace engineering through robotics through stealth technologies have all changed the nature of the world around us in a way which can never be reversed.

Salient Systemic Characteristics

Technological advance on a linear and non-linear basis is nothing new. The stirrup once charged the nature of warfare. In the transportation area the steam engine and steam boats were introduced in the middle of the 18th century, shrinking distances and enabling commerce and travellers to explore new parts of the world for the first time. The development of the railroad system in the early 19th century quickly added another similar dimension to land travel. In 1886, the internal combustion engine contributed to the Industrial Revolution and allowed transportation technology to become more reliable, more individual and more affordable. During World War II, under the intense effort to develop technologies to be applied in the military arena, the practical jet engine emerged as the next leap of technological progress. The initial introduction of each of these new technologies created a discontinuity in the system of transportation and power generation. Between these watershed introductions of new technology, constant progress was made along a number of internal axes which enabled the new technology to work more effectively and more efficiently to achieve the fundamental goals of its practitioners.

One of the recent breakthrough technologies that will have a non-linear or discontinuous effect on our world is the emergence of the cyberworld—the emergence of standalone computing power and an interconnected network that enhances the opportunity, and the risk, provided by that computing capability. Either of these two factors, on its own, would be significant. Together they provide an access point to a whole new and unexplored cyberworld. This brave new world is characterized by vastly extended computer power; decreasing price and increasing simplification in the user interface resulting in mass adoption of portable and home PCs; the integration of intelligence and computer capability into networks of appliances and environmental controls connectivity of systems and enhanced applications through low-cost Internet connections; shifting consumer behavior; radical new organizational designs; online acquisitions and transactions; expansion of communication options with acceleration of digital data, voice, and image transfer; object-oriented programming for customized software and increasing computer literacy in the population at large. While these trends and similar sets of descriptors capture some of the drivers of today's and tomorrow's cyberworld, they also capture many of the costs and risks inherent in the rise of the cyberworld and the compounding of risks at the increasingly common intersection of complex systems.

New and Intersecting Risks

There are three categories of risk which have emerged as the cyberworld systems develop and intersect. The first set of risks are driven by the immediate consequences of the exclusionary nature of the Internet—"geek chic" as it has become known in the US. While the Internet will create many benefits for a few technologically literate users, it will have little impact on the poor and undereducated. An initial gender gap, where men dominated the use of the Internet, has declined with the arrival of a number of portals and sites targeted at woman. Yet many minorities in developed countries and residents of emerging economies may still find the Internet an unaffordable luxury. This will exacerbate the differences between the haves and the have nots, between the limited beneficiaries and the vast population excluded from the benefits of the Internet and the new global cyberworld.

A second set of risk evolves around the intersection of complex risk systems, the increasing probability of a catastrophic event, and the increase in scale of damage which can be created by that event. Not counterbalanced by a commensurate rise in our capability to respond or an increase in the likelihood of available response mechanisms being deployed, the net risk equation is increasingly moving in a negative direction.

One final set of risks is created by the sheer size, magnitude of impact, and unregulated growth of these large and complex cyber systems. As the natural development of systems proceeds, it will be increasingly difficult to police, manage, and respond to unexpected consequences as complex systems grow, merge, mutate, and absorb subsystems previously independent and more manageable. The year 2000 and the famous Y2K risk may be only the first unprecedented risk we face at the beginning phases of this emerging new world. As we enter the next millennium it is perhaps auspicious that the first second was a moment of unknown risk of potentially enormous consequences. Computer networks around the world were at risk which drove traffic control systems, intensive care unit medical systems, PC calendars and clocks, defense systems, business records and financial systems, and the whole gamut of computerized systems developed over the last few decades of the 20th century.

The apparently benign rise of the Internet and its impact on business also has a dark side which is infrequently discussed. It will, as we have seen above, increasingly separate the haves and the have-nots, creating yet another barrier for the lesser developed economies of the world to achieve parity with the developed nations. It will contribute to a concentration of wealth and its benefits to an educated elite inhabiting only the more developed nations of the world.

There is also loss of human contact in the development of remote transaction systems. There is an inevitable consequence of significant job losses once the efficiencies of an Internet business are realized. Although unemployment from large company downsizing has so far been absorbed in the US through the rise of small and medium companies, the full effect of the Internetization of businesses has yet to be determined. While the Internet does break down many borders between privileged people and farsighted businesses, it also depersonalizes interaction to a new degree.

Another cost is the loss of privacy. The development of offshore databases continues the unregulated development of electronic intrusion into the private lives of consumers and citizens.

Further, lack of regulation threatens to provide objectionable materials to unwilling adults or unsupervised minors, and a flow of primarily American information and debate to non-American citizens around the world.

Net Risk Assessment

Potential Scale of Harm: As we enter the new millennium, we are forced to the realization that this will be a period of new risk as well as new accomplishments, of new challenges as well as new opportunities in the cyberworld. The rise of the cyberworld will create a new set of risks to computer systems on a stand-alone basis and as a compounding of risk due to the intersection of complex systems such as the Internet and the capital markets. The potential for deliberate attacks only makes the potential scale of harm even larger at these vulnerable points of intersection.

"Our concern about organized cyber attack has escalated dramatically," affirmed Jeffrey Hunker, the National Security Council's director of information protection. "We know of a number of hostile foreign governments that are developing sophisticated and well organized offensive cyber attack capabilities and we have good reason to believe that terrorists may be developing similar capabilities."

A few recent headlines can serve to raise our level of concern significantly as new technologies create risk on their own and multiply that risk in their intersection with other systems. A report released by the Center for Strategic and International Studies (CSIS) warns that US defense capabilities and its economies are practically at the mercy of computer mercenaries, "cyber criminals" and "cyber terrorists". The CSIS estimated that 30 computer experts, strategically located around the world, could bring America to its knees at a cost of only $10 million. "Virtual corporations, cashless electronic transactions and economies without inventory...will make attack on data just as destructive as the attack on actual physical inventory...Bytes, not bullets, are the real ammo." The report listed only a few of a long number of potential disruptions as computer systems link up the fundamental structure of the economy, defense systems, and capital markets. The report cited the rising vulnerability of telephone lines to deliberate overloads, disruption to the operations of air traffic control, scrambling of software used by major financial institutions, life threatening alteration of formulae for medication at pharmaceutical plants, and intrusions into control systems in nuclear power plants.

Likelihood of Occurrence: With complicated instruments, and an electronic currency market trading one trillion dollars per day, there is a clear vulnerability of domestic capital markets to organized assaults and a constant risk of criminal intervention. It is extraordinary that these risks to date have not resulted in any profound catastrophes. Many experts believe it is only a matter of time before theft, blackmail, disruption, the insertion of a destructive virus, or other exploitation of cyber-vulnerability will create havoc in the increasingly vulnerable electronic capital systems expanding around the world today.

"The rise of computer systems and the Internet has thus created new risks in systems heretofore protected from only the crudest of criminal intervention, internal systems failure, and local mismanagement." With the rise of complex systems and accelerating number of complex systemic intersections, the risk of catastrophic events, deliberately or innocently caused, is increasing exponentially.

The story behind the sentencing of Kevin Mitnick to a 46-month prison sentence in 1999 highlights the level of vulnerability of modern computer systems. Arrested by the FBI in 1995, Mitnick was accused of penetrating sophisticated computer systems at Motorola, Sun Microsystems, Nokia, Fujitsu, and NEC. Even the systems of leading providers are not immune to sophisticated hackers.

Reports from the newspapers in UK of an unrelated "hijacking" by cyberexperts and redirection of a communication satellite deployed for defense purposes show the even more extreme risk inherent in the intersection of criminal systems with computer systems, communication systems, and defense systems.

In April 1999, the *New York Times* reported that the energy department had suspended all scientific works on the computer containing America's most sensitive weapon secrets at three nuclear weapons laboratories over fears that security lapses make these computers vulnerable to espionage.

The reports hastened to add that "the computers are connected together in networks that are not linked to the outside world..." However, one basic security flaw, according to officials, is that secret information about nuclear weapons can be copied from these sensitive computers onto a computer disk and then sent out as electronic mail among the thousand of emails that circulate every day through separate, unclassified computer systems!

An internal review by the Energy Department, which owns and oversees the computer and laboratories in which the work is pursued, determined that security measures at these three research sites were adequate at best. Two laboratories had received security ratings as "marginal" in performance while only the Sandia unit received a rating indicating a satisfactory level of security clearance.

Reviewing the risk situation, John Browne, Lab Director at Los Alamos, was quoted as saying that information security and complicated risk management structures could even get in the way of achieving the basic objective the labs are pursuing. "We have to look at threat to information security from a risk-benefit standpoint and put in place additional procedures that make sense...We can't raise the bar so high we can't get any work done. That affects national security too."

Even the security measures in the complex new cyberworld can, in turn, become risks themselves.

Capability to Respond: The new cyberworld is still in its infancy. Effective policing or responsive capabilities at a global level have yet to be born. Worryingly, one report on high-tech criminal behavior indicated that US law enforcement agencies are "5–10 years behind the transnational crime curve." The report went on to highlight the slow and bureaucratic nature of relevant institutions, citing a 49-month period to buy and install new computer systems versus a 9-month period in the private sector. An extensive proposed monitoring program, to be overseen by the FBI, calls for the creation of a Federal Intrusion Detection Network, or Fidnet, and specifies that the data it collects will be gathered in a centralized data center at the National Infrastructure Protection Center, an interagency task force housed at the FBI. The highly controversial US Administrations' plans to address the weakness in responsive capabaility has already met with resistance from civil rights groups.

In the extraordinary book, *Cybertrends*, by David Brown the completely new legal risks of the new systems are spelt out clearly in a section entitled Risk Unbound. The author cites Anne Brenscom, a lawyer who states that "the ease with which electronics impulses can be manipulated, modified and erased is hostile to the deliberate legal systems that arose in the era of tangible things."

In addition to clarifying the risks inherent in the intersection of dynamic and complex systems, *Cybertrends* points out the limitations of responsive mechanisms and regulatory schemes that exist today: "The emerging system is clearly more complex. But this stems primarily from the fact that high speed data communication tools have created a potentially boundary-less global space without the basic rules needed to ensure its stability. Countervailing regulatory powers are still fragmented along national lines." With such feeble enforcement mechanisms, the capability to respond, to date, has been extremely weak.

Probability of Capability being Effectively Deployed: Concerns over free speech, privacy, and limitations on free trade provide one set of limitations on effective deployment. Lack of an effective legal and enforcement infrastructure is another source of limitation. Lack of effective institutions, standards, and funding compound the problem. As the new cyberworld grows, crises and challenges will force a test and improvement in both capability and likelihood of deployment of that capability. Now, at the early dawn of a new and volatile era, the net risk assessment is only now becoming clear in its full and worrying form.

Proposed Architecture of Solutions for the Cyberworld

New Vision: A liberated Internet and cyberworld free of criminal threat, viruses, unlimited access to pornography, and with secure personal data files.

Specific Initiatives:
- Reduce the potential scale of harm through more effective modeling, control, and security at systemic intersections.
- Impose stiffer penalties for virus development or distribution.
- Resolve clearly personal data ownership and access, requiring prior specific approval of the individual with updates on content for confirmation.
- Increase access to racial minorities and to undeveloped countries through roll out of low-cost cyber-centers and greater investment in education.
- Establish "Net Police" with high-power processing and tracking capability with the power to warn, track, and arrest abuse of cyberworld systems.

China on My Mind

As each area of critical challenge unfolds, the swing role China will play in the pursuit of effective solutions emerges as a common element in virtually every area set out above. The economy, the environment, disease, crime, and other key challenges will be significantly affected by decisions made by China's rulers. This raises the importance of effective engagement between China and the West to a level of the utmost urgency and concern. To date, the history of that engagement has been mixed, at best. Current tensions in the relationship between the US and China reflect a lack of common foundations, the mutual suspicions of two differing civilizations with a patchy record of engagement, and inevitable turbulence at points of intersection of the two vastly different systems. The reactions in China to the US bombing of the Chinese embassy in Yugoslavia show how volatile and fragile the base of the current relationship is.

One recent editorial in the *New York Times* described the current state of relations as two parties "in a diplomatic fog attempting to negotiate a path toward a common goal with few common reference points and no understanding where the other party was." Occasionally bumping into each other, the leadership of China and the US often find themselves placed on a collision course by political or media forces on both sides of the Pacific. The media or contrary political forces can be seen to be operating to a very different agenda from the positive engagement favoured by Zhu Rongji and the Clinton Administration.

A Different Perspective

From a Chinese perspective, the US is often seen as bent upon "hegemonic domination of the world." This view is "proven" by the embassy bombing, support for Taiwan, protest at the treatment of Tibet, Nato bombing of Yugoslavia, broadening of alliances with countries bordering China, interest in oil and gas fields surrounding the Spratlys, hedge fund attacks on Asian shares, currencies and economies, and even the arrest of General Pinochet. These events are all seen as heavy handed attacks on national sovereignty in general and China's future integrity in particular.

Although unrelated and even innocuous for China when seen from a Western world view, these events take on a different meaning when seen from the perspective of a country that has been force fed opium by the English, brutally colonized by the Japanese, and cast into economic exile by the capitalist countries for nearly a half century.

Attempts to reconstruct a Russian-Chinese alliance and promulgation of the view that the US is attempting to control the world—and hence China—through a vast pincer movement involving alliances with Nato on the West and Japan on the East reflect a deep-rooted feeling of isolation and powerlessness.

US military exercises with armies in Tajikistan, Kazakhstan, and Kyrgyzstan and visits to the US by Mongolian officers have fanned the flames of concern. All of these countries share a border with China. The fear of being encircled or invaded led, in part, to China's attack on US forces in Korea in 1950. A better understanding of interest and resolve on both sides early on could avoid a large scale conflict at a later date.

Within China itself there are many complex factions. China's New Security Concept, a proposal of a more aggressive approach to foreign policy, is the brainchild of some of the more hardline factions within the military and government hierarchy and reflects but one of the contending forces that make leadership and reform in China one of the world's toughest balancing acts. In Jiang's own words captured in a *Time* magazine interview in October 1997: "In the past few years, the Chinese people have scored very exciting achievements. But there are brain-breaking questions and problems for us. It's hard for me to tell what's the biggest challenge."

The history, culture, and nature of the two systems—Chinese and Western—are so fundamentally different that the perspectives held by each often share little in common. The point of departure for China is a highly complex, centrally administered country of one billion citizens inhabiting diverse regions and enjoying vastly different levels of economic benefits and prospects. The entire system is struggling between conflicting tensions of an old, centrally controlled economic and political system and a new reformist drive toward modernization, economic liberality, and greater human rights. The imperatives for economic growth to underpin the reform movement are essential for an understanding of Chinese politics and economic policy. The system is characterized by a constant battle between advocates and forces of reform against conservative elements motivated by a desire to preserve the power and security of the old order.

Underlying these modern tensions is a four-thousand-year history of the Han civilization. Attitudes toward money, religion, fate, diet, medicine, family, language, central authority, the state, and even life and death are coloured by a rich and deep vein of history and collective experience stretching back over millennia. The concept of the Middle Kingdom, a vision of a China suspended between heaven and earth, is also an enduring part of the Chinese view for the future. Yet, also, memories of past losses and humiliations remain close to the surface. This complex mix of confidence and insecurity will require deeper understanding and more thoughtful engagement by the West to move forward together on a balanced path of peaceful progress. The complexities are not purely Chinese. The US government is forced to navigate in the treacherous space between a One China policy and a Taiwan Act which requires protection of Taiwan from mainland military adventures.

Kipling's famous phrase "The East is East, the West is West and n'er the twain shall meet" is a dangerous prescription when so much of the world's future lies in a successful joining of the twain in a mutual effort to build a sustainable new global balance.

Systemic Nature of Chinese Development

It is instructive to review the nature of China's current status from the full set of paradigm principles. For each principle there is a fit with important aspects of China's current point of departure. The increasing globalization of China's trade patterns, investment sources, and political influence is perhaps the most salient characteristic of the systemic development of the world's largest country. The inherent complexity of China is equally evident—its languages, political structures, religion, beliefs, collective memory, and fundamental world view.

The recent appearance of the Falungong spiritual movement as a major societal force caught many by surprise. The government's harsh words and relatively gentle initial treatment of the individuals involved in the mass demonstrations revealed a new layer of complexity within the society at large and even within the government itself. The country is carefully stepping out into a liberal free market global trading system but yet continues to suppress internal dissent and political opposition as of old.

The apparent contradictions are not, by Chinese standards, inconsistent. A unique blend of feelings of strength and powerlessness can only be understood on Chinese terms. The dynamic and accelerating pace of change is reflected in a century of dramatic swings in political, and economic structures from a feudal base one hundred years ago through agrarian communism and the tribulations of the Maoist era, to a modern reforming Communistic structure operating on the threshold of a new millennium.

Through waves of war, colonial oppression, rebellion, occupation, starvation, uprising and growth, the Chinese system has demonstrated a pattern of obsolescence and reinvention, constantly reinventing itself and recasting the structures of modern society on a foundation of millennia of old values and beliefs. Over time, the Chinese system is converging toward a more international set of economic principles, discarding inefficient doctrines of state intervention in the economy, and using the resulting growth to consolidate the country's disparate regions to the fullest extent possible.

Vaclav Suvil, a professor at the University of Manitoba, has summed up well the resulting systemic volatility in an essay entitled "China's

Unstable Past and Future", published in the *International Herald Tribune*. Noting abrupt and dramatic changes in policy, he identifies an underlying instability in many fundamental policies and draws the appropriate systemic conclusion: "…there is very little likelihood that the country's future will be a linear extension of the recent past, a matter of continuity, and stability. The lessons of the past tell us to anticipate more great reversals."

New business like China.com and a highly educated and technology literate population will accelerate this convergence through participation in the international culture of the cyberworld. The operative model has moved from the static to the dynamic and accelerating reforms are making up for lost time. Eventually new leadership will emerge in China, replacing the Old Guard of the 1949 Communist era. A more independent, worldlier, and more flexible approach is expected to emerge. Li Qiang, sociology professor at the People's University in Beijing, described the emerging new generation as better traveled, more tolerant of other cultures as a result, and most strikingly "they automatically accept reform; they know it must happen." The transition of leadership from Old Guard to New Generation is yet another complex element in understanding the changing face of China.

Internal and external turbulence also characterizes modern China—internal turbulence as a result of change, as new systems clash with old, and external turbulence as a historically self-contained Middle Kingdom steps out carefully into a global economy, a global communications net, and an increasingly global value system.

Ultimately, the Chinese system is essentially rational, seeking to find the most effective relation of means to its own shifting ends, but only pursuing those ends on a basis of a uniquely Chinese rationality. These means, ends, and the logical and historical structures linking them together cannot be fully comprehended from a western perspective—any more than a Chinese perspective can fully apprehend a Western system.

Complexity and Closure

In every system, the complexity of reaching an effective decision increases geometrically with the number of parties involved. In China, hardline, centrist, and reform factions all crowd the space for input on China-US relations. On the American side of the issue, the House, the Senate, the Administration, the media and the electorate all wade in on delicate issues of bilateral relations. Even when the leadership of the two nations approach agreement, the complexity of reaching closure conspires to keep the parties apart. During Premier Zhu Rongji's 1997 trip to the US, this problem of complexity arose as a major obstacle in the closing stages of obtaining a WTO clearance for China.

"In my view, the gap between the two sides is really already not very significant," a frustrated Zhu said at a joint White House press conference with Clinton. "If you want to hear some honest words, the problem does not lie with some big gap, but with the political atmosphere."

Of course, Zhu knew that before he arrived in the US, but could do little to redirect the forces aimed at stalling the approvals. Clinton also struggled awkwardly to temper the media's feeding frenzy. "We cannot allow a healthy argument to lead us toward a campaign-driven cold war with China," he warned shortly before Zhu's arrival. "No one could possibly gain from that except for the most rigid, backward-looking elements in China itself."

A Very Modern Model

As the Chinese economy steams ahead, building vast reserves of dollars and piling up an enormous trade debt with the developed world, Chinese military capabilities are rising at nearly the same pace. Only recently China successfully tested a new ground-to-ground missile, allegedly the Dong Feng-31 which is capable of delivering a single nuclear warhead 8,000 kilometers—or nearly the distance required to reach the mainland of the US. China already has nuclear and neutron bomb capability.

The combination of major trade and economic influence, coupled with a growing military capability, make China a force to be reckoned with on both fronts in the future.

To date, President Jiang Zemin and Premier Zhu Rongji have masterminded a highly charged and risky rush to the future—balancing reformist and hardline political factions, and responding to a nationalistic sentiment while steering China more firmly into the currents of a global economy. At times, the balancing act has wobbled dangerously, notably after the embassy bombing when the Foreign Ministry announced it would cease co-operation with the US "in the fields of proliferation prevention, arms control and international security." Highly vocal, and inaccurate, allegations of a deliberate attack on the Chinese embassy in *The People's Daily* and other mass publications highlight the need for better channels of communication and a platform of improved understanding and trust.

Rules of Engagement

The risk of not building bridges over the faultline between the world's largest and the world's most powerful countries is enormous. At a simple level, it is obvious that the world's largest and the world's most powerful countries should be engaged in broad and deep dialog on a full range of issues. The current three pillars underpinning the US approach will need to be extended and deepened by a full range of bridging initiatives: a One China policy; active dialogue; and peaceful resolution of issues.

The period following the 1949 Revolution, which cut many of the ties that could have bound the countries together, will need to be counterbalanced by far more action and a wider range of compensating initiatives consistent with a vision of a more fully engaged pair of nations in the future.

Now, with the legacy of that historic division leaving many gaps that should have been filled, a new opportunity is created to build bridges unencumbered by the past. It is possible to design a new policy of engagement that takes into account the systemic nature of the two countries and the full set of opportunities to build constructive bridges between the two cultural and economic foundations. The ties that bind the countries together are still too few and too weak, and both sides are too ready to sever even these flimsy points of contact.

Not Just the Economy

In the economy, China's emerging trade deficits, currency management, capital markets influence, market access, governance practices and protection of foreign investment are all issues which will require engagement for appropriate resolution on a mutually beneficial basis. An internal need for capital, job creation, technology, and open trade relations will bring China to the table on other issues as well.

In the area of crime, China will play a pivotal role in the global response to piracy, software piracy, corruption, drug trading, women's rights, and triad expansion.

In the environment, China's rising use of CFC, potentially catastrophic use of lignite, deforestation, and other environmentally unsound practices are of concern to Chinese citizens and neighbors alike. In the military sphere, Taiwan, the Spratlys, and other flashpoints will need to be carefully managed to avoid regional, or even global, military conflagration.

On the cultural front, China is one of the few civilizations to have a comprehensive set of cultural attributes which have survived the tests of time and the travails of transportation into new lands. The Chinese language, literature, medicine, philosophy, arts, architecture, cuisine, religion and belief system, family structures, performing arts, martial arts, clothing, and other pillars of the Chinese civilization have remained intact and influenced the West for centuries. The need to retain the essence of this civilization, while moving forward in inevitable social evolution, is one of the major cultural challenges of the coming centuries.

In the spiritual world, China's colonialist incursion into Tibet and systematic suppression of new religious sects is a major blemish on the world's religious and spiritual landscape. In a perverse way, the brutal suppression of Tibetan Buddhists in their Himalayan homeland has actually served to bring a powerful spiritual message into the major currents of global consciousness. Despite the benefit this spiritual diaspora has created outside of Tibet and China, the challenge to restore Tibet to its independent status is both a political and religious challenge.

Parallel Pathways

This list of challenges should not be taken to single out China for special criticism. The same criticisms and risk assessments would apply (and have throughout this book) to the major nations of the West. Even the colonization and suppression of Tibet has an American parallel in the expropriation of native American homelands, tribal genocide, and brutal suppression of ancient systems of belief. Rapid deforestation in China, which contributed to recent flooding which adversely affected 300 million people, has a historical precedent in America deforestation one hundred years ago—at a similar stage of industralization and development. Substantial engagement will require a deep and honest understanding of both pasts in order to move forward toward a sustainable common future.

This list of potential areas of constructive engagement can provide part of an agenda for progressive and comprehensive engagement by China and the West. A failure to build more points of contact between the two systems will inevitably place too much pressure on the few that are in existence today.

The momentum, power, and combined force of the Chinese and Western systems can follow one of two paths. One path leads to separation, conflict, and eventual catastrophic collision of the two. A new global duality between China and the US is already emerging which could lead down this path and replicate the costs and risks of past bipolar follies. A second path leads to constructive engagement which can provide counterbalance in advance to the strains and stresses of change and of the inevitable non-linear or catastrophic discontinuity in the future.

The list of risks and challenges provides, in fact, a significant opportunity to address major future risk, and to build effectively toward a better, and more united, world for tomorrow.

Bridges over the Faultlines of Civilization

China is not the only source of looming future risk. The highly popularized impending conflict between Christian and Islamic civilizations is only one of the many other "faultlines" in the current global topography. Just as the movement of tectonic plates and continental drift can create collisions, catastrophe and turbulence in the natural world, the evolution of the systems of the major religions, economic and political alliances, and cultural orders of civilization in the human sphere can create conflict, upheaval, and new sources of unmanaged risk in economic and societal systems. Many analysts and thinkers—most notably, Raymond Aron, Samuel Huntington, and Paul Kennedy—have documented these faultlines and predicted the impact of impending collisions. It is now incumbent upon us to find more effective strategies to manage these gaps and collisions—to build sustainable bridges over the faultlines and intelligent buffers between the colliding forces of civilization.

The religious source of civilizational conflict is only one of many areas of critical concern at the systemic intersections of the new world order. All need understanding and attention to reduce the inherent risk and capture available opportunities to build buffers and bridges toward a better future. Religious faultlines are joined by national conflict, economic differences, longstanding tribal divides, the conflict of dissimilar political systems, and the clash of cultural traditions which have evolved separately over hundreds, and even thousands, of years of separate development.

Although the Christian/Islamic divide has received the most attention as the archetypal collision of civilizations, the risks and opportunities for improved response afforded by a longer list of fundamental challenges and conflicts may be ever greater.

Without bridges and buffers, meeting points and intersections will inevitably be turbulent, catastrophic and conflictual. With a more generous and enlightened vision and a practical strategy aimed at building a more harmonious world for the next generation, we can reduce that conflict and turn risk into opportunity. Building bridges between religious civilizations in a search for win-win solutions is an important step in creating a world of diminished risk and enhanced opportunity at a collective level. It is also an important step to open new vistas for individuals seeking their own pathways through life. At that non-violent intersection of differing systems we have an opportunity to explore different combinations, to understand different religious and spiritual beliefs, to see our own lives differently, and to select from a more diverse set of ideas and practices.

The opportunities for dialogue, discussion, increased choice, and improved self-understanding are obvious. We are currently locking ourselves away from the richness that diversity can provide, and blindly following well-trodden pathways that can lead to increased risk and escalating conflict. Building bridges over the most visible faultlines of civilization is indeed possible. There is a resulting need for a thoughtful, balanced search for engagement of all parties to explore all positive opportunities and to reduce risks along a long list of faultlines and other sources of potential conflict.

Russia and the World Community

The constructive engagement of China with the world community has already been highlighted as a critical factor in the development of a safer world for the next generation. The same is true for Russia for many similar reasons: its role in the environment, military conflict, crime, economic development, religion, and a range of other challenges will push the global engagement with Russia's beleaguered people and their leadership to the forefront of the global agenda for Eastern and Western countries alike.

India and the World Community

The sub-continent comprising India, Pakistan, and Bangladesh is already populated by over one billion people and will play a key role in the same issues—military, religious, economic, criminal, and environmental—as China. As India's population surpasses China's, Asia's "elephant"—more lumbering but much larger than the Tiger economies—will play a larger role on the world stage in the future. In 1947, when India achieved independence, its population was 345 million. Having nearly tripled in size in only a half century, India is poised to replace China as the world's most populous nation by the middle of the next century. The economic role of India will also grow in importance as the world's largest democracy builds on an English-speaking and technologically adept population, a functional Ango-Saxon legal and administrative system, and a valuable network of Non-Resident Indians in Asia, Africa, Europe, and the USA. Just as the Overseas Chinese—the much vaunted Lords of the Pacific Rim—provide a base for growth and influence for China, the NRI population will build India's presence, and global influence, on an accelerated basis.

Other than regional military conflicts, notably with Pakistan over the national borders established in 1947, India has been relatively self-contained and has played less of a pivotal role in affairs outside of the confines of the subcontinent. Trade and investment flows have been more limited than with other Asian countries and the isolated nature of the economy has limited much of its impact on world economic or political affairs. However, as global systems evolve and national borders fall, India will inevitably step out onto the world stage as an increasingly important player in economic, environmental, technological, cultural, medical, and even military affairs.

North/South and East/West

The disheartening epigram from Rudyard Kipling of an unmet twain captures much of the nature of engagement, or lack thereof, between fully developed economies and the emerging markets of Asia, Africa, Latin America, the Caribbean, and other underdeveloped parts of the world. The human costs of economic disparity, disease, deculturalization, and other systemic challenges are sharply felt in the lesser developed markets of the South and the East. The need for support and development from one side and the creation of attractive markets of the future on the other side can create opportunities for mutual benefit if properly pursued with a long-term view in mind.

Rogue States and the World Community

The slaughter, rape, and genocide in Kosovo which captured so much of the world's (and Nato's) attention during 1999 is but one example of a rogue state transgressing global norms of acceptable behavior. North

Korea, Iraq, Libya, and Myanmar among others make up a group where the response of the international community to their transgressions will define to what extent national leaders will be held to a common world standard of behavior. Policies and practices in this area will set limits on sovereign state actions which operate to protect their citizens, their neighbors, and the global community as a whole.

Constructive engagement is the most successful and least expensive approach to bridge the gaps between states where behavior transgresses acceptable global norms. Military force, to use an old expression, is deployed both where it should be and where it can be effective. In the case of rogue states, it is possible that creative constructive engagement could be effective in many key areas to provide greater leverage and an ability to make greater change than that allowed by our current isolating approach.

Risk and Opportunity for Change

Each of these challenges and global faultlines reflect the common patterns of systemic evolution, risk, and opportunity highlighted above. The unique character of each turbulent intersection will lead to different approaches, different timeframes for the resolution of issues, and different content in dialog and resulting actions. Yet, effective response to the key systemic challenges set out above will build many bridges over these faultlines of civilization, will create buffers for the absorption of conflict and contention. A better approach can generate better strategic solutions to the major challenges of our time. Faultlines can fade and heal as we exploit opportunities to resolve differences on a more comprehensive and constructive basis.

In building these bridges, it is not always the correct way to play safe. Risk and occasional failure is necessary to test the limits on the possible. Experimentation and discovery are an integral part of a process which cannot be driven by a fear of failure. We learn through experience. We gain experience through actions. Acting is therefore the foundation of knowledge. We must be willing to accept risk in our actions to add to our present store of relevant knowledge.

In building bridges, and in testing alternatives to the current state of satisfactory underperformance, we shall not always succeed. But failing to take on greater risk in our endeavours is a guarantee of failure to achieve our full potential.

5 Next Generation Strategy for a World of Risk

Each of the preceding sections reflects a piece of the overall design of a better approach to global strategy and potential improvements to the global state of affairs. Improved results in the individual areas of the economy, crime, terrorism, disease, economic disparity, the environment, deculturalization, and the cyberworld can each make a contribution to the commonwealth of all nations.

Strategy, Structure, and Leadership in Tomorrow's World

The overall concept for a more effective global strategy in tomorrow's world advanced here is to adopt today the state-of-the-art model of transnational strategy developed in the business sphere and apply it to systemic global challenges beyond the purely commercial. In every application of Next Generation Strategy there is an explicit need to establish a new vision, to reset objectives, and to pursue the full potential inherent in even the most challenging issues and crises on a more creative and effective basis.

The full set of constituent elements of effective strategy has been elaborated in Chapter 3 and can be adopted to suit the particular needs of an enterprise or specific endeavor. In each area of societal challenge, new strategies can be designed and implemented to realize a more aspirational vision than the unsatisfactory standards of the status quo.

Full Strategic Approach Required

Each of the preceding examples was built along a single element of Next Generation Strategy—the net risk assessment. Much more is required to capture the full benefits of application of state-of-the-art strategy. The full program of Next Generation Strategy should be applied prior to the final promulgation of a new vision, the determination of a strategy, the elaboration and execution of a tactical implementation plan, and the establishment of an effective system for monitoring and response. A thorough diagnostic will need to be completed taking into account the full set of relevant internal and external systems. A consolidated view will need to integrate both into fully understood points of departure, points of arrival, and all of the steps inbetween. A vision is not, on its own, sufficient to drive change. The resource requirements of the strategy and the capabilities of the relevant organizations will need to be addressed as well to provide an integrated strategic design which will support the realization of a new and more aspirational vision.

Before significant initiatives are undertaken, it will be important as well to ensure that all aspects of the system are fully aligned and integrated to have the full force of available effort brought to bear.

As part of an integrated strategic process, an implementation plan will be elaborated and executed. Pre-set measures of performance will need to be promulgated and performance tracked against the targets. New, simple, and more creative measures will be needed. Results against performance targets will need to be assessed accurately and communicated on a timely basis to inform decisions on resources, course correction or even fundamental strategic redirection.

Successful strategies will incorporate the full set of systemic, structural, process, and organizational elements of strategy. The organization that creates and implements the most effective strategy will exhibit the characteristics of a winning organization—long term in outlook, fast and flexible, externally focused, and dissatisfied with the status quo.

Monday Morning at 8am

The value creation of any strategy begins with concrete action. At the end of every strategy project, one critical test of practical value needs to be met. One practical question needs to be answered: What will the organization do, or do differently, Monday morning at 8am?

Following the analysis and hypotheses set out in the preceding chapter, there is a clear set of actions which can be taken specific to each area of challenge. Another set of actions, at a more general level, will drive the process of initiation and oversight. The individual actions are spelt out in the relevant sections of Chapter 4. The highest priority actions that could be taken at a general level to create a forum for specific change would include the following:

1. *Leadership of the Effort*:   In order to ensure broad involvement, support to the leadership of a new global strategy should come from a core team of G24 heads of state, representatives of the private sector, and a highly selective set of international institutions. The US, supported by World Bank, the UN and European Union, could be a logical initiator, supported by a representative section of large and small countries. As for all complex leadership challenges, the individuals involved would need to demonstrate vision, courage, world-class communication skills, and effort.

2. *Determination of the Core Team*:   An operating sub-committee of the G24 could provide analytical and financial resources to fund the effort. The core team to lead and co-ordinate issue-specific's task forces would itself operate as a specially commissioned task force at an oversight level.

   For the purpose of debate, the core international institutions could be represented by the UN, World Bank, and IMF. High level representatives from the EU and Apec would also be welcome, as would the head of the World Economic Forum and Club of Rome as the private sector institutional representatives.

   The US should initiate the effort. A rotating head of state from among the G7 could chair the group, aided by two vice chairmen: one vice chairman would come from a newly created Private Sector Council; and the other from among the represented international institutions. A full time chief of staff would ensure that analysis and recommendations are delivered and communicated on a timely basis.

3. *Agreement on the Priority Areas for Review and Establishment of Task Forces*:   The list of nine challenges set out here plus a special China group could be used as the point of departure, subject to amendment by the central team. A total of ten task forces, plus a central oversight group (the core team), would thus be required. Task force members would be drawn from the leadership of public and private sectors of a full range of countries, institutions, and industrial sectors. Former heads of state and respected former ministers would be a logical pool of expertise to draw from.

4. *Timing of the Effort*: Provision of funds and staff could come from the G24 budgets to fund an initial twelve-month strategy diagnosis and design effort, with a significant public interim review at the six-month point. Implementation would take longer due to the complexity of the approvals process. A 36-month deadline, at which point the task force would be disbanded, would focus and intensify efforts during the life of the initiatives.

5. *SMARTER Goals and a Clear Vision*: Each effort would need to be driven by a clear and aspirational vision—the definition of success— and agree upfront on how to measure that success. Goals need to be SMARTER: Simple, Measurable, Achievable, Realistic, Tangible, Exhaustive, and Renewable. They would also need to be achieved.

Structure

Too often, in the past, institutions, or lack thereof, determined, defined or circumscribed strategy and limited strategic execution. If full potential is to be achieved in the management of critical global challenges, then this needs to be reversed—strategy should drive structure. Obviously, in the real world we start where we are and a wholesale redesign of the existing global architecture would be both impractical and inefficient. However, a thoughtful approach to global change could initiate a process of accelerated evolution in the direction of a more effective set of structures—temporary and permanent.

The point of arrival toward which progress will be measured is an effective set of successful international task forces and institutions, a more powerful set of intranational co-operative forums, and a fully enfranchised nation state underpinning a more effective and efficient integrated global structure. Achievement of this goal will require existing institutions to clarify their visions and objectives, and to reset their strategies to generate better results for their stakeholders. In some cases, new structures will need to be established in both the international and intranational arenas. The private sector, as already stated, will need to develop a more effective body for representation.

The lack of an established institutional presence in some critical areas highlighted above can actually be an advantage, since there is now an opportunity to create institutions which are modern, effective, efficient, and fully adapted to serve a clear purpose in the global architecture of tomorrow. That unique opportunity to rehabilitate and to build a set of global institutions which will underpin the global architecture of the next generation can operate as a first step in an improved management of a shared global enterprise.

Ability to Execute

It follows from the full nature of effective strategy that the structural approach will need to be executd in Next Generation Strategy at all levels—systemic, strategic, and tactical. Resources must be made available for diagnosis, strategic design, and aligned execution.

The structural approach must be both external—defining the relevant bodies, their authority, and their objectives—and also be internal—specifying roles, responsibilities, and processes. The model of Next Generation Strategy sets out an approach to structural optimization which will capture many of the relevant components of strategy and ensure their implementation.

The most appropriate approach to the design of a structure through which effective strategies can be defined and implemented is one which articulates both structure and operating principles. A purely structural approach will provide only a sterile outline of institutions, entities, and roles without a useful instruction manual—a set of operating guidelines which can give effective life to the structures outlined. Hardware and software need to operate in harmony in order for measureable results to be generated through a new, and more effective, global architecture.

Short- and Long-Term Approaches

A set of appropriate international institutions, fully formed, well funded and supported by nation states, is an essential part of a functional global architecture and a long-term goal of the effort. On the other hand, the urgency, importance, and cross-institutional nature of the problems set out above requires a complementary, more flexible and more immediate response. A set of dedicated task forces, each with a pre-set termination date and clear set of deliverables, could break the mold of bureaucratic deliberation and ineffective action by existing institutions. New organizational models will need to be developed and implemented to address the new paradigms and challenges we face in the future.

Resources will need to be carefully apportioned in order for investments to optimize yield. Strategic resource allocation will require conscious trade-offs based upon a clear understanding of return at all levels. The systemic element of a solution to a complex problem will specify the quantum of resource required and the nature of the investment—the allocation of human, financial, and intellectual capital—between contending claims. These allocation decisions are a common element in good strategy and aligned implementation. Investments and returns need to be carefully analysed and monitored for impact—essential feedback to optimize the corrective system.

At the most basic level, strategies for solutions will need to motivate and drive responses at a very fine level. Individual actions and co-ordinated implementation plans will need to be determined and executed. Even the most elegant of analyses and most convincing of visions will not create results if that vision is not engaged through effective action. In order to have any traction at all, strategic plans need to be engaged at an operating level and action taken to create specified changes. Effective actions, prioritized by strategy and aligned with a clear vision, are the levers which will move complex systems and solve practical problems.

Most systems contain within them a feedback mechanism or a series of feedback mechanisms which can provide opportunities for guidance and redirection. A systemic model of correction is no exception. In order to provide influence for change on the most effective basis, feedback systems will need to be developed and finalized to provide input to redirection and resetting of investment levels. The dynamic nature of systems will require a constant monitoring of the internal and external dynamics, of real-time assessment of the impact of initiatives and investments, and swift corrective action.

Just as the most appropriate structure and operating principles to determine and execute strategy are critical, a new model of leadership of the strategic effort of a wider Next Generation Strategy is essential.

Lack of Leadership

The gaps in the local global architecture are the source, and also the symptom, of a continuing level of satisfactory underperformance in global management. These gaps in the global architecture and the lingering state of satisfactory underperformance reflect a failure of our current global strategy and structure. They also underscore the shortfalls in global leadership to date. The following summary in the *Asian Wall Street Journal* of a meeting of world leaders at the World Economic Forum in Davos reflects the need for a better global strategy, a more effective global architecture, and more capable global leadership:

"If nothing else, the annual meeting, which brings together economic leaders and theorists from every corner of the globe, vividly highlighted that the US isn't alone at the drawing board for a new international financial system. And without a clear leader, the decade-long search for a new world order in the wake of the fall of the Berlin Wall has dissolved into buck-passing and a politically charged struggle for workable new ideas. Indeed, as the world's financial system is lashed by the forces of globalization, hair-trigger capital flows and continuing crises in Asian and emerging markets, there are no clear plans on the table, nor is there much in the way of real institutional progress, on what exactly to do…'We need a co-ordinated approach,' said Heiner Flassbeck, German state secretary for finance. '(We shouldn't) just let things go.'

But at the moment, that seems to be what's happening."

The path forward from this unacceptable situation will not be easy, for the challenges of systemic management, strategy, and leadership through the process are daunting.

There are two challenges presented by a vision of a more coherent set of global strategies and structures. The first, and more complex challenge, is to design and build the strategies, structures, and operating principles of an improved global architecture. The second is to employ these assets to realize a more aspirational vision for the future. This is a challenge for men and women of transcendent vision, statesmanship, and rugged political skills. It is a challenge that has, in the past, been mastered on more than one occasion.

The Early American Example

The founding fathers of the America State, for example, designed a constitution, set of institutions, and operating principles which have withstood two centuries of testing and evolution. The architects of tomorrow's world would do well to follow their example and aspire to the quality and endurance of their creation. The contributions of Jefferson, Adams, Madison, and their colleagues at the 1787 Constitutional Convention were not just that they designed efficient legislative, executive, and judicial branches with an effective balance of powers between them. The true genius of these architects of the America Republic was that the political structures and principles they captured in the Constitution and Bill of Rights institutionalized an entire Enlightenment philosophy—a clear vision of what could and should be built in America.

That philosophy was driven by a vision of what man was and a clear sense of the need to protect the natural rights inherent in the human condition. George Washingston's Circular Letter of 1783 captures the visionary foundations of the structures of the new nation: "The foundation of our empire was not laid in the gloomy age of ignorance and superstition, but at an epocha when the rights of man were better understood and more clearly defined than any former period; the researches of the human mind, after social happiness, have been carried to greater extent, the treasures of knowledge, acquired by the labors of philosophers, sages and legislatures through a long succession of years, are laid upon for our use, and their collective wisdom may be happily applied in the establishment of our forms of government."

Other countries which lacked the visionary leadership of the 18th century America often have struggled with less enduring structures and encumbering, rather than liberating, institutions. The unique sense of ownership of the future and enfranchisement in the present allowed the new American political system to be fully integrated with the social, cultural, and supporting political foundation of the country. In India, to pick but one contrasting example, a similar set of institutions and operating principles left behind by a departing colonial power have never achieved a similar level of adoption, relevance, and results due to a lack of this same sense of ownership and engagement. The burden of a socialist past is taking years to offset—confirming that the energy required to change the mindset of a country and operating environment can truly be enormous.

A New Nation State

The end of the Revolutionary War in America provided a rare opportunity to create a new nation state from an entirely new vision and approach to government. The principles of the Enlightenment, coupled with the practical character of the New World leaders, led to a new form of national best practice—enshrining the Universal Rights of Man from the Age of Reason within a robust set of balanced and effective governing structures.

It is often easier for new leadership to drive a program of change. The appointment of a new chief executive officer, election of a new national leader, or change in the head of an international agency creates an opportunity to capitalize on the spirit of change and navigate toward a different goal.

It is interesting to note that Jefferson and some of his colleagues at the 1787 Convention believed that every new generation should design its own government, institutionalizing a process of revolution, self-determination, redefinition, and creative change. The intention was to keep the spirit of revolution alive and to allow future generations to benefit from an opportunity to engage in a process to define its own vision, structures, and strategies. For better or worse, this concept was not adopted by the framers of the new nation, leaving future generations with a different kind of leadership challenge.

The Challenge of Change

It may be an even greater challenge today to build a new global order and architecture when there is no revolutionary or redefining opportunity, and where the major threats are both complex and have been accepted for too long at a level of "satisfactory underperformance." Crises, revolutions, new leadership, and periods of dramatic environmental shifts create a climate where progressive change is more easily accomplished. Truly great leaders will seize these opportunities to set out on a recharted course to a new, and more visionary, future. Yet, as examples in the business world demonstrate, opportunities for dramatic change can be created if not thrust upon the leaders of an enterprise.

Truly great leaders can drive change through the creation of opportunities where no single event or revolutionary change is creating major discontinuities around them. A lack of dramatic turbulence or revolution is no reason or excuse not to set out on a path to a better global architecture, nor to avoid setting a higher standard for global achievement.

The more capable the leadership team, the greater the potential for change and the more likely the realization of a new and more aspirational vision for the future.

In addition to the structural challenges of profound change, the human element of inspiration and motivation also needs to be addressed. Failure to engage the full combination of hearts and minds will ensure that the results will be less than fully acceptable and will perpetuate, at the best, a continuing state of satisfactory underperformance.

Today's Challenge

The first challenge facing the current group of world and national leaders is the challenge to agree on a broader set of aspirational visions and then to bring about the necessary major structural changes to realize those visions. This is especially difficult when the threats and risks are complex, not easily evident and not currently seen by the public at large to be at a crisis level. The challenges of peace time presidents and prime ministers are always to design and rally support for critical change programs without a single coalescing enemy, and in the absence of a neatly defined crisis or immediate threat. On the threshold of a new century and millennium, the challenge now is to take advantage of the opportunities presented by a period of relative peace and prosperity to build a sounder and safer world for tomorrow. Failure to capitalize on this opportunity can ensure that risks will unnecessarily become reality and many of the current levels of satisfactory underperformance will ripen into tomorrow's crises.

The second challenge, following the establishment of a new architecture, is to make the system work to achieve its initial goals—to keep the vision alive, refreshed, and renewed. National, international, and intranational leaders will all need to work together to ensure that the full potential of the improved structural approach is achieved.

Although the scale of the task is daunting and the complexity of the task high, there is also proven opportunity to move forward toward a more positive future. Application of the best model of strategic change and systemic redirection can significantly improve the odds of success, and can break down an apparently mountainous task into a series of manageable, and understandable, steps leading to the peak of an unclimbed summit. The content and process of Next Generation Strategy provide the roadmap to that summit, with a precise description of each step along the way. The schematic diagnoses of the three sequential phases of Next Generation Strategy can operate as a checklist of practical actions to be taken which serve as the steps upward in the generation of new and effective strategy.

Yet that strategic roadmap will be useless unless all relevant parties can be brought together to diagnose, design, and execute a shared strategy which is engaging at both a collective and individual level. A failure to identify, engage, and retain the interest of the relevant parties will ensure that the end result, no matter how well documented or how elegantly summarized, will not be substantial change in the real world. Ultimately, the challenge is one of leadership and will—a challenge to a very few individuals at the top of global organizations and the most powerful of nation states to come together in a common vision of what is possible today to make tomorrow a better place.

The art and science of leadership is driven by a mix of planning for the expected and preparing for the unforeseen. It is a test of skill and character, of personality and knowledge, of vision and action, and of position and capability. For a leader to lead, others must follow, and have a valid reason for following. What will create that reason on a sustainable basis? Only proven ability by our leaders to drive effective change through a process of foresight, motivation, redirection, and progressive improvement.

Today's leadership challenge, in the paradigm of Next Generation Strategy, requires that individual leaders have the capability to create a vision, design a better structure for implementation, pursue a change program, and motivate and inspire along the way. In a complex and fragmented new world, it creates a set of demands which can only be met through a new model of leadership.

Leadership in the Next Generation

Leadership in the next generation will be less about position and more about value added; less about hierarchy and more about influencing complex networks—formal and informal; less about control and more about enabling; and will be far more about engaging rather than employing or co-opting individuals in a collective enterprise. That new leadership model will be driven by a demonstration, personally and organizationally, of values, principles, aspirations, visions, and demonstrated capabilities to make change happen. The new model will need to be constantly reaffirmed through the addition of new insights, creative strategies and the generation of tangible results.

Leadership is also, in many ways, an act of faith. Faith in the individual. Faith in the vision. Faith in the value of one's individual and collective efforts. In order to accomplish truly great objectives, leaders must tap into the deepest motivations of those they lead. Fear of what may be is one motivator. But even more powerful are the positive motivators. On the other side of fear are love, aspiration and hope, and a desire to create something good and powerful for the future. The hopes and aspirations of individuals, translated into meaningful actions, will provide the most powerful of engines, and lead to the most significant of changes.

Future Renaissance of the State

Much has been written concerning the death of the nation state and the birth of a borderless world. Although there are many examples of systems globalizing and transcending national boundaries, the primary source of solutions, individual and collective, has to be the nation state. The inevitable rise of regional economies cannot be stopped as national economies converge and consolidate. Yet those same regions lack the political capacity and practical capability to bring about necessary change which is both urgent and important. The necessary funding, application of coercive force, ensuring of compliance with global or local standards, educating of the population, and other critical elements of global strategy can only come about through the existing network of nation states and the international institutions they control.

Next Generation Strategy restores and rejuvenates the role of the nation state, but also imbues that role with a much greater obligation as well. For the role of the state in Next Generation Strategy will be more complex, and more demanding. It will require more sophistication in each individual state's contribution to a collective global enterprise. The concept of sovereignty will need to evolve in a delicate balance of national and transnational interests. In most regions, the nation state is the highest order democratically sanctioned political entity. That legitimate sovereignty will need to be carefully and thoughtfully preserved where possible, and voluntarily subjugated to a greater good where appropriate. Even win-win options may require compromise and change at individual state level.

Perhaps the biggest challenge and responsibility of all is the requirement for the modern state to demonstrate the characteristics of a winning organization—being fast and flexible, long term in orientation, dissatisfied with the status quo, and externally oriented. Contrary characteristics or lack of national leadership commitment to global change will ensure that the current state of unsatisfactory underperformance lasts into the foreseeable future.

Crisis of the Spirit and a Search for Meaning and Value

Perhaps the greatest challenge we face in providing solutions for the critical problems of our times is not the mastery of a complex Chinese or Western model of dynamic systems behavior or a shifting environmental risk equation, but is something more personal, more individual, and, ultimately, more human. For at the heart of any program of new and deeper understanding, of strategic change and transformation, is a human element. Individual commitment, motivation, sacrifice, and determination will all be required to bring to bear sufficient energy to change patterns and systems which have too long been left unattended. In order to drive change, it will be important to capture the hearts and minds of the individuals involved, to engage those individuals in an effort which is, to them, transcendent.

From the time of Aristotle and Plato there has been a shared perspective between sages and prophets alike that a full human life contained an essential element of sacred behaviors and deep aspirations. A transcendent element has long been considered to be a natural part of the human condition.

Many people today are cut off from that feeling of transcendence, cut off from a feeling of purpose and belief which comes from engagement in the pursuit of a worthy goal which is greater than themselves. Across national boundaries, religious faiths, and economic classes there is now a broadly felt crisis of the spirit which flows from a common lack of sustaining purpose and belief. As the complexities and accelerating pace of life carry us forward into an uncertain future of escalating risk and seemingly declining personal control, more and more individuals are beginning to search for new meaning and value in their lives.

A lack of economic or social well-being may trigger a search for something deeper and more valuable than material wealth. But even in the affluent G7 countries, the accumulation of material wealth and increased standards of living seem to bring more stress, less enjoyment, more problems, and less satisfaction than ever before.

That dissatisfaction and a need for the achievement of something more fundamental, more meaningful, and more nourishing at a spiritual level is becoming so widespread, and so deep, that for many this dissatisfaction has become a personal crisis of the spirit, an awareness that the soul has become severed from a meaningful or sacred pattern of existence.

New connections, new systems of spiritual value and belief, and new motivations may be necessary to sustain a sense of purpose in both professional and personal lives. For many, less could be more and a re-balancing of priorities, values, and actions would re-establish a link to something more meaningful and more valuable to lives increasingly empty of true satisfaction.

Without a link to a sense of purpose, without a sense of personal integrity in the larger sense of the word, individuals can lose motivation, can lose a sense of deep achievement, and ultimately achieve for less than their own true potential.

Loss of Faith in the Old Holy Trinity

For many, it is as if the old pillars of our lives are falling apart under the pressure of the new world which is developing around us. There is a long-standing trend towards a loss of faith in the Old Holy Trinity— church, state, and family which stretches back over decades. All three of these institutions, which have for centuries provided a degree of stability and meaning to our lives, have been undergoing fundamental change, and erosion in their importance in the daily lives of their members. These three institutions, evolved over centuries, are now under pressure as never before.

Church

The role and importance of religion in the life of its citizens varies dramatically among countries. From a high of 85 per cent of individuals in Nigeria saying religion is "very important" in their lives to a low of 1 per cent in China, the role of established religion varies enormously. The percentage of respondents saying that religion was very important ranged from 50 per cent in the US, Poland, and South Africa to 34 per cent in Italy, and below 20 per cent in the United Kingdom, France, and Germany. Denmark and Japan scored below 10 per cent.

Although spiritual belief has held constant, and even grown in some countries, the decline in main-line church attendance and importance of established denominations as social and spiritual institutions has been visible for decades. Following a period of growth from the end of World War II to the middle of the 1960s, a 20-year decline in most leading religious establishments has been clearly demonstrated. The bestseller *Megatrends 2000* highlighted some of the impact on individual church groups in 1990. Over a 20-year period, the membership of the United Methodist Church dropped from a high of 11 million members in 1965 to 9 million in 1988. The Presbyterian church lost 25 per cent of its 4 million members. The Disciples of Christ fell from over 2 million to just above 1 million members and the Apothecarian church lost almost a million members in a decline to 2.5 million. The three largest Lutheran denominations lost more than half a million members.

These figures were also paralleled by a hemorrhage of nuns and priests from the Catholic Church and from other traditional vocations.

In the UK, the Church of England has long suffered from a decline in attendance and recent studies show that only 1 per cent of the population now attend the Church of England on a regular basis. A drop in the number of available ministers has also put pressure on church attendance. Some smaller parishes no longer have their own local priest. A consolidation of parishes and an accumulating collection of disused church properties has been a hallmark of the Church of England for many years.

At the same time that traditional religious institutions were failing to serve the renewed interest in spirituality and matters divine, and losing adherents as a result, religious establishments were becoming less concerned about the borders of their religion. Surveys of different religious communities over the last twenty years have shown a decline in hard borders between major religions. An accelerating consolidation of historically separate entities and an increase in humanitarian co-operation within local communities and across denominational borders reflects a familiar pattern of obsolescence, consolidation, and convergence, which further discards the old rigid model of the religious estalishment.

A Search for Something Different

A decline in traditional church attendance and structure in the US is not an indication of a lack of interest on the part of Americans in a spiritual element in their lives. Nor is the decline in attendance and relevance of the Church of England and the Catholic Church in Europe to be similarly interpreted as a lack of interest in spiritual affairs.

According to the Association of American Publishers, the sale of books in the category of religious studies and spirituality (including copies of the Bible) rose nearly 60 per cent between1992 and 1994. This is the same period which follows a decade-long decline in attendance at traditional establishments.

If anything, recent trends in the spiritual realm show an increasing degree of belief in a greater God and interest in the spiritual nature of life. The Pugh research center reported in 1997 that 91 per cent of Americans do not doubt the existence of God, an 11 per cent increase from a similar survey taken 10 years before. In Europe, the same percentage holds true for a belief in God—up 20 per cent to 90 per cent over the past decade.

Widespread atheism, agnosticism, and secularism appear to be fading, although the established religions are not benefiting from the surge in renewed spirituality. New options and smaller institutions have taken up the vacuum left behind by the decline in traditional institutional presence. In the US and other parts of the world, electronic churches, new denominations, and charismatic and evangelical groups are providing growth where the old leaders have faltered. The religious revival and rise in church attendance, like the US economy, is driven by more individualistic small to medium-sized spiritual enterprises in a new institutional paradigm.

While the established religious institutions in developed countries have shown a decline in the face of a continued and renewed interest in spirituality, countries emerging from under the yoke of communism have experienced a rebirth of attendance at traditional religious establishments. Once prohibited practices are now becoming more acceptable following the liberating perestroika in the former Soviet Union and other countries in Eastern Europe in 1989. The number of active churches in Russia rose from 50 to 250 by 1993. A similar revival in other parts of the former Soviet Union is equally positive. In central Asia in 1989 there were about 160 functioning mosques and one Medressah, or Islamic seminary. By 1993 there were about 10,000 mosques and 10 Medressahs.

In addition to the rebirth of churches in the former Soviet Union and Communist bloc countries, the Islamic awakening has emerged as a feature in the cultural, economic, and spiritual lives of citizens in the Middle East, Europe, and Asia. Led often by conservative clergy and supported by a younger, more educated population, the rebirth of fundamentalist Islam is a characteristic of Muslim countries from Northern Africa to Indonesia.

Many expert commentators cite the importance of the search for a new identity as part of the driving force behind this Islamic awakening. The post-Christian Western life style which is materialistic, sexually promiscuous, highly emancipated in terms of women's rights, and use of alcohol, embraces behaviors which threaten the traditional foundations of Islamic life. This new Western lifestyle has been increasingly rejected by a resurgent Islam. The reasons for this Islamic renaissance go to the heart of personal identity and values.

The controversial Islamic National Front leader Hassan al-Turabi has observed that Islam provides people with a sense of identity and a direction in life, something shattered in Africa since colonialism. In the

African context, it offers a unique sense of common allegiance. "Islam provides a focus for unity and a minimum consensus in the sense of regionalism and tribalism...The idea of the 'Nation' has offered nothing in this regard. Everyone knows African nations are the legacies of a product of colonialist cartographers...."

In the East, a more complex model of spirituality continues to unfold—blending new and old in unprecedented, and more potent, combinations of politics and religion. Islam and Hinduism have become more powerful forces in the Middle East, Malaysia, Indonesia, Pakistan, and India. Unfortunately, these religious movements have become increasingly militant in some of the more charged regions and cities.

The religious landscape in China is also far more fragmented and dynamic than ever before. The State Bureau of Religious Affairs reports that over 100 million followers could be counted in the five approved religions. Given that these five religions were banned during the period of the Cultural Revolution from 1966 to 1976, the numbers are surprisingly large and growing.

Even more surprising, and more threatening to the central state institutions, are the cults which have popped up all over the country. Over a four-year period starting in 1996, authorities in Hunan Province arrested cult leaders and suppressed nearly 10,000 local cults, according to a recent article in *Outlook*. The *International Herald Tribune* reported that 1,600 village-god temples were smashed by 264 "shock troops" made up of over 6,000 government officials.

This picture of concurrent growth in spiritual interest and rejection of traditional religious organizations only serves to underscore how complex, and dynamic the evolution of spiritual belief in China has become.

Although the rise of traditional religious establishments in newly liberated countries and in Islamic countries has demonstrated an ability to regenerate interest in traditional church structures, in most Western countries, the traditional church is no longer capable of addressing many of the sources of spiritual concern that have been generated by the modern world. The search for meaning and value, like so many other elements of modern life in the West, has assumed new, and more individualistic dimensions.

Family

The challenges to the family as an institution in the modern world have also come under pressure from a large number of sources and as historic trends show. In 1969, 9 out of every 1,000 marriages ended in divorce and only 5 per cent of children were born to unmarried women. Thirty years later, the divorce rate has tripled to greater than 20 per 1,000 and the percentage of children born to unmarried women has risen to 27 per cent. The impact of this disintegration of the nuclear family has an impact which will reverberate through future generations for decades. Children of one-parent families are historically far more likely to leave school, to be unemployed, and to have an unsustainable pattern with their own families. Some forecasters expect that the children of these single parent families, particularly in an economic downturn, may reverse recent positive trends in the US crime rate.

In England and Wales today, more than one and a half million men are fathers of dependent children who live in households other than their own. It is the traditional new pattern for the father in the divorced family to leave the family home, and mothers to continue to look after the children in the original residence. After departing from the residence, between one quarter and one half of male divorcees lose regular contact with their children after a five-year period. Absentee fathers are only one of the many negative after effects of divorce and decline in the family structure.

Within the family structure, there are other major changes which have emerged in recent times. The traditional role of father and husband as the unique breadwinner which has been described as "protector, provider, paragon of permanence" is no longer the operating model. Dual income families, the uncertainty of employment, and other challenges to the traditional male and female roles have increased pressure on the family and on roles within it. The decline of the traditional nuclear family reduces continuity, reliability, and a sense of belonging for individuals looking for stability and a home in a volatile and uncertain world.

Historic Decline of the Nation State

The modern state is under pressure at a level unprecedented since the emergence of the nation state as the primary source of political power in the 18th century. The nation state has shown itself to be less capable of addressing major threats to its economy, unable to guarantee the safety of its citizens, and apparently lacks desire or skill in defending the unique content of its cultural foundations.

The emergence of global systems and the rise of coherent and economically powerful regions have, in many areas, overtaken the state in power and influence. The modern state is atrophying as a result of a number of interrelated phenomena, from a declining capability to manage the risks and threats to the collective well-being of its citizens to a failure to provide a vision which fully engages individuals in their quest for meaning and value in their personal lives. The result has been a decline in relevance—a recognition that the nation state and its associated organs and institutions has relatively less impact on our lives than it has in the past.

Disillusionment and Disengagement in the American State

The net impact of this loss of faith in existing state institutions, values, and models is also a disengagement with the concepts of collective responsibility and individual engagement. It is no surprise that participation in American elections has been dropping steadily for over 50 years. The current level of participation at 27 per cent of the registered electorate, down from 61 per cent 25 years ago reflects the fundamental disillusionment with a political process which seems to offer little choice or has made little impact on the lives of American citizens.

The poor quality of debate, lack of difference between contending platforms, and uninspiring set of candidates have caused millions of voters to switch off politics and eschew participation in a process seen to be irrelevant to the daily lives of the voting population.

In another striking example of statistical decline in faith in the nation state in the US, the University of Michigan National Election Studies documented the response to the statement: You can trust the government in Washington to do what is right just about always or most of the time. In the early 1960s, over 70 per cent of the respondents agreed. By the 1990s, this percentage had fallen to below 20 per cent.

Emptiness of the Iron Rice Bowl

Just as the three traditional pillars of Western civilization are crumbling as we pass into a new millennium, the foundation stones of modern structures in the East are also coming under increased pressure. The Communist model which provided jobs, housing, and food for the masses in a centrally planned command economy is being left behind. The value of an autocratic leadership model has received severe blows in the recent crisis as the corruption, inefficiencies, and fundamental unfairness of an associated system of crony capitalism cracked under the pressure of a deep economic downturn in Indonesia.

Other national Asian institutions have also lost their credibility as guarantors of a better life. The Chinese Communist Party, Japan's MITI and Zaibatsus, North Korea's iron-fisted regime, Indonesia's Suharto, and other foundations of the Asian political and economic architecture for the last quarter-century have been discarded, discredited, or discounted.

In South Korea, the system of banks, *chaebols*, and labor working in harmony to drive growth temporarily collapsed in the recent crisis. In the old model, the state protected local industry and granted large loans to large conglomerates, the famous *chaebols*. These *chaebols*, in turn, invested the money into growth businesses, which were often unprofitable and heavily borrowed. The resulting growth (even unprofitable) in ship building, semiconductors, automobiles, and other industrial sectors provided jobs for the members of the trade unions. Members of these unions worked long and hard, putting aside 40 per cent of their salary as savings, which went into state banks, who in turn played their role in the national development spiral, lending it to the *chaebols* on a preferred basis.

With the crisis, this house of cards came tumbling down. The Kim Dae Jung government, trade unions, and *chaebols* are now involved in a contentious exercise to restructure the economy into a more consolidated, more sustainable, less leveraged and more profitable model for the future.

In the crisis, millions of Asian workers lost their jobs and thousands of businesses have been downsized or closed. The notions of unending growth, and jobs for life, have become further victims of the Asian crisis.

Where the Best are Indifferent

In the absence of a sustaining set of institutions or traditional structures, the restoration of a transcendent meaning and value to lives lost in a search for purpose and belief is perhaps the greatest challenge of this new era. Old models simply do not provide adequate foundations or direction to many individuals caught up in a confusing modern world. Change is needed, and in that process of change are opportunities for redefinition of the self and a change in systems of belief and the values that flow from those beliefs.

A renewed understanding, belief, commitment, and engagement in an effective program of action to drive positive change can also change our sense of who we are. It can also define what we do and how well we pursue our objectives. In our modern, fragmented, and increasingly individual world, that sense of purpose and belief must initially come from within, rather than from outside each individual. Before we can become fully engaged in any enterprise or initiative, we will need to see in that engagement a deeper value that completes our sense of who we are as human beings.

Without a deeper sense of engagement, without an individual feeling of ownership of collective action, we will never be able to reach our full potential and address fully the costs of underperformance in critical collective areas.

A Higher Synthesis Needed

In the end, successful Next Generation Strategy starts and ends with individual commitment and action: The actions of leaders, the support of followers; and the decisions and actions taken on a daily basis. Unless individuals have proper value systems, a proper set of motivations, and a full commitment to individual and collective change, there is no purpose or point in starting out on a journey of transformation and improvement. The pathway forward begins with a proper relation with the self—an inward step toward a long-term goal of external fulfilment.

Successful implementation of Next Generation Strategy will require the synthesis of many apparent antithetical elements—thought and action, national and global structures, internal and external systems, patterned and particular behavior—but of these the most essential is the bringing together of the individual self, expressed through meaningful actions, and collective potential, reflected in the state of affairs in the world we create.

Perhaps the best summary of this engagement of the individual and the collective in an effective synthesis was captured in a simple story told by many after-dinner speakers. A teacher tore up a magazine picture of the world into small pieces and asked each child to reassemble the pieces as quickly as possible. Many children labored long and hard to reassemble the picture of the blue and white sphere. But one child, when it was his turn, quickly completed the exercise in less than half the time of his classmates. When his teacher complimented him and asked how he had accomplished such a major task so quickly, he replied, "It was easy. I noticed there was a picture of a person on the other side of the page. When I put him back together, the world was also back together."

A Message of Hope

Many of the risk trends in the areas of greatest concern to us are moving in a dangerous direction, and have been for years, even decades. But those trends are not forever fixed. As the product of human design and action, they are also subject to human intervention and improvement. The past is only prologue, and does not determine an inevitable future. Even Nostradamus said to his son "The future is not fixed", and the gloomy Malthus admitted that human efforts resulting in technological breakthroughs could change the trends of a mounting population and resulting social catastrophe in a future for the Europe of his day.

Like Malthus, we have seen the opportunities created by technology, by discontinuities in complex systems, and from the turbulence created by the interaction of those systems. We have seen the opportunities created by an understanding of systemic management and redirection.

The challenges and scale of effort required to make progress against the negative momentum of complex global systems are not to be underestimated. Yet, the sustained effort required will be time consuming and costly. Results will not come overnight. Alignment of fragmented and divided political entities, well entrenched in an ineffective past, will not be easy to achieve. Nor can we expect our current leaders and existing institutions to drive change through status quo approaches to problems—approaches which have so often resulted in satisfactory underperformance and implicit denial of the true scale and nature of the threats we face.

The need for effective action in the most critical challenges of our time is rising in urgency and in importance. A continuing failure to address these challenges on a timely basis will dramatically increase the overall net risk assessment and ensure that positive opportunities for change are lost forever. One of the salient characteristics of systemic behavior is the accelerating nature of change. Newton's Second Law of Motion states that the force required to reverse the momentum of a dynamic system is equal to or greater than the momentum of the system at the time of application of the new force or energy. To create a meaningful change in direction or momentum will also require a relatively significant application of effort or force. If we wait too long to engage the change program, the cost of the eventual effort will grow and the likelihood of success recede.

However, through the adoption of a new and comprehensive systemic approach to analysis and solution of complex problems, we can indeed make great progress toward realizing new and more ambitious visions. Based on a thorough understanding of the new global paradigm and models of risk behavior, we can apply proven tools for systemic intervention and redirection. Even if those tools and approaches are still new and imperfect, the sheer capability of human effort, when properly motivated and directed, can bring renewed force to the efforts to reverse the negative pathways leading into our future.

As we look forward, there are already many signs of understanding, of progress and of hope for that future which lies so squarely in our hands.

Recognition of Interdependence

Increasingly, the interconnected nature of global systems is becoming apparent and acknowledged. A wide range of the great and the good at a global level has fully internalized the fundamental interconnectedness of global systems.

Peter Senge stated the essence of the case in response to a question on how organizations could come to terms with the increasing interdependency in the world:

"The first step is to realize that everything is interrelated. That the world is becoming more interconnected and interdependent, and that business is becoming more complex and dynamic. All of which means we have to change the way we think about learning and interacting with each other at all levels.

We have to develop a sense of interconnectedness, a sense of working together as part of a system, where each part of the system is affecting and being affected by the others, and where the whole is greater than the sum of the parts."

From Senge's rigorously analytical Massachusetts Institute of Technology (MIT) to the Dalai Lama's spiritual home in exile in Dharamsala, the message of interdependence in the modern world is gaining momentum and clarity. In 1991, His Holiness the Dalai Lama stated in a public address that:

"Our generation has arrived at the threshold of a new era in human history: the birth of a global community. Modern communications, trade, and international relations as well as the security and environmental dilemmas we all face make us increasingly interdependent. No one can live in isolation. Thus, whether we like it or not, our vast and diverse human family must finally learn to live together. Individually and collectively we must assume a greater sense of universal responsibility."

And from the political world Vice President Al Gore succinctly summed up the same issue in a few brief words: "seeing ourselves as separate is the central problem in our political thinking."

The recognition of this new global level of interconnectedness and functional interdependence is a tacit recognition of the underlying systemic nature of the world around us—business systems, economic systems, political and social systems, and other critical elements which make up the content of our businesses and shape the context of our lives.

Ultimately, the central observation emerges that these complex and dynamic global systems are themselves irrevocably combined in one increasingly seamless global paradigm. Each system has its own characteristics, presents its own challenges and requires separate responses to the risks and opportunities inherent within. Yet each individual system is interconnected. Each influences and in turn is influenced, by the nature and direction of the whole. Effective visions, strategies, and actions will need to consider this element of unity as well as the diversity of individual systems.

Statesmen and business leaders alike will need to recognize that reducing risk to the system as a whole will have a direct impact on the enterprises for which they are responsible, and that improvement in any one area contributes to the welfare of the whole.

Perfectibility and Performance

Theoreticians for centuries have extolled the perfectibility of man in abstract terms, describing in great detail the political, spiritual, and practical opportunities leading to advancement of the material and spiritual well-being of each individual on the earth. Enlightenment luminaries on both sides of the channel—Joseph Priestley and the Marquis de Condorcet among them—have described the path to enlightenment open to the newly liberated man of the 18th century. With the fall of monarchy and despotic institutions, the rise of democracy, and opening of new countries and frontiers, these essayists proclaimed that the perfectibility of man was without limit and that the world was well placed to advance toward a utopian state as we reached the next millenium.

Their optimistic exhortations stand in stark contrast to the concluding remarks of the learned Professor Kennedy in a book drafted two centuries after the hopes of the Enlightenment philosophers were so eloquently stated. As we actually broach the millennium threshold, the final words of *Preparing for the Twenty-first Century* say little of man's perfectibility and much of his follies and the dangerous threats he has created to his own human condition: "What is clear is that as the Cold War fades away, we face not a 'new world order' but a troubled and fractured planet, whose problems deserve the serious attention of politicians and publics alike...the pace and complexity of the forces for change are enormous and daunting; yet it may still be possible for intelligent men and women to lead their societies through the complex task of preparing for the century ahead. If these challenges are not met, however, humankind will have only itself to blame for the troubles, and the disasters, that could be lying ahead."

Practical Progress and Human Responsibility

Although the consolidated net risk assessments in the chapters above contain little in the way of systemic hope, there are offsetting opportunities for improvement. Already we can see some points of light in the darkness. In the environmental area, CFC production has plummeted. Harmful emissions per passenger vehicle are a fraction of former highs. Manufacturing pollution fell 2.3 per cent between 1995 and 1996 in the US and Canada. Paper and organic waste recycling are rising steadily. Engineers and inventors may be on the verge of a technology breakthrough which can provide a practical alternative to the internal combustion engine which runs off an ecologically neutral water supply or alternative emission-free source. Violent crime is declining in American cities. The education of women around the world is increasing. The Cold War is over and democracy restored to the former vassal states of the Soviet Union.

Admittedly, the negative trend information in some areas outweighs the positive many times over, but in these elements of progress there are profound signs of hope. When coupled with a systemic view which allows for positive discontinuous change or constructive systemic redirection, the chances for improvement in our world improve markedly. All of these positive accomplishments were the product of deliberate human intervention—acts of individual and common will to achieve a new vision of tangible improvement in the environment, in education, and in the social fabric of our cities.

Implicit in these changes is also the notion that all of us have the potential to drive or to contribute to positive change. We often speak of our human rights, but the proven potential for change underscores the need for us to accept our human responsibilities as well. We all face a conscious decision to drive change or to acquiesce in the downward spiral of our quality of life in its full measure, thus accepting the upward spiral of risk in all of its forms. No one is exempt from the choice. As Sartre posited, not to decide is to decide.

We clearly have an opportunity to drive effective change if we can rise above old antagonisms and discard myopic visions of what can and should be done. By combining individual visions and collective effort in the development of Next Generation Strategies for the most critical challenges of our times, we can find solutions to problems and create ever more stories of human victories in the Malthusian darkness.

Hope, Values, and the Human Spirit

Even without these proven success stories, the message of hope would still need to be promulgated. For a vision of a better world, a practical view of what can and should be, is not purely an effort of the mind. It is more than an analysis of past systemic behaviors and better approaches to strategic management. It is an effort of will and belief. The message of hope is as much spiritual as practical, as much driven by fundamental human values as it is by quantification of risk and opportunity. Vaclav Havel proclaimed that "Hope is a state of mind, not of the world. It is a dimension of the soul, and it's not essentially dependent on some particular observation of the world or estimate of the situation... It is the ability to work for something because it is good, not just because it stands a chance to succeed."

In these words we can find much which is relevant and uplifting in the face of great challenges and obstacles. Our engagement in the effort to make the world a better place will define better who we are and what we are here to do. Engagement of our individual and collective will in the pursuit of a vision based on hope as well as practical expectations will define us as individuals grounded by a laudatory set of values and characterized by an admirable sense of purpose.

Engagement will also increase our sense of belonging in the single united race of humanity, giving us a new sense of place, of purpose, and of substantial accomplishment. In the common struggle, some disengaged individuals may even find a sense of renewed spiritual integrity and a feeling of valuable purpose in their lives.

We are already at a great turning point on a road which is far from linear in its direction or even in its shape or consistency. We have arrived at a critical juncture, suspended between a past with unacceptable consequences and a threatening future with unknown prospects. The time is now to make the decision of engagement or acquiescence.

The Beginning of History

We are not, as Fukuyama stated, at the end of history, nor even at Thomson's edge of history. We are forever at the beginning of history, at the cutting edge of a process of transformation, rebirth, and renewal. Every day we begin afresh to craft the days beyond and to mark them in our own image. All of us live in a never ending moment of redefinition, in a constantly evolving and rejuvenating moment when everything is forever new, forever in the present, and full of the potential for change. At the ever fresh beginning of history we must constantly challenge ourselves to forget the past selectively, to reframe issues, and free ourselves from the limiting concepts and results of past strategies and initiatives.

We are not only here to learn the lessons of the past, but to learn and to apply the lessons of the future.

In many ways, there is nothing new in the content of this book. The higher synthesis proposed in the book is only another way to understand and respond to models of systemic behavior that predate this publication by millennia. Many of the systemic characteristics set out here are as old as time itself. And yet I hope that there is something new that emerges from these pages. For in every new perspective there is a potential for renewal, a rekindling of a sense of purpose, and an enhanced ability to create meaningful change.

Hearts and minds can be brought together in the sharing of effort and accomplishment in the struggle for a greater common good. In that effort we can not only find the integrity within ourselves, but also a unity that binds us all together in one great human family. That struggle is also an exploration of oneself, of one's true human potential, and of our collective capabilities as a united humankind. We must give of our best efforts and apply the most valuable of our learning. In that giving and in that application, we will, at last, rediscover the best of ourselves.

To return to T.S. Eliot in "Little Gidding", one of his Four Quartets:

"We shall not cease from exploration
And the end of all our exploring
Will be to arrive where we started
And know the place for the first time...
And all shall be well and
All manner of thing shall be well
When the tongues of flame are in-folded
Into the crowned knot of fire
And the fire and the rose are one".

We can learn more from the past. We can prepare ourselves better for the future. Through the application of our best knowledge and the engagement of our full individual and collective capability to master the most critical challenges of this volatile era, we can indeed make this a better world for the next generation.

Index

Bibliography

Armstrong, Karen, *A History of God,* New York, USA, Ballantine Books, 1994.

Bach, Richard, *Illusions The Adventures of a Reluctant Messiah,* New York, USA, Dell Publishing, 1977.

Bartlett, Christoper A.; Ghosal Sumantra, *Transnational Management Text, Cases & Readings in Cross-Border Management (2nd Edition),* USA, The McGraw-Hill Companies, Inc., 1995.

Bauman, Zygmunt, *Globalization The Human Consequences,* Great Britain, Polity Press, 1998.

Bennis, Warren (ed.), *Leaders on Leadership Interviews with Top Executive,* USA, Harvard Business Review, 1996.

Bernstein, Peter L., *Against All Odds,* USA, John Wiley & Sons, 1998.

Brown, David, *Cybertrends Chaos, Power, and Accountability in the Information Age,* England, UK, Penguin Books, 1998.

Brown, Lester R.; Renner, Michael; Flavin, Christopher, *Vital Signs, The Environmental Trends That Are Shaping Our Future,* USA, W.W. Norton & Company, Inc., 1998.

Capra, Fritjof, *The Web of Life A New Synthesis of Mind and Matter,* Great Britain, Flamingo, 1997.

Celente, Gerald, *Trends 2000: How to Prepare for and Profit from the Changes of the 21st Century,* USA, Warners Books, 1998.

Cimino, Richard; Lattin, Don, *Shopping for Faith: American Religion in the New Millennium,* San Francisco, USA, Jossey-Bass Publishers, 1998.

Collins, James C.; Porras, Jerry I., *Built To Last: Successful Habits of Visionary Companies,* New York, USA, HaperCollins, 1994.

Commager, Henry Steele, *Jefferson Nationalism, And The Enlightenment,* New York, USA, George Braziller, Inc., 1975.

Daniels, P.W.; Lever, W.F., *The Global Economy in Transition,* England, UK, Addison Wesley Longman Limited, 1996.

Davidson, Mike, *The Transformation of Management,* USA, Butterworth-Henenamn, 1996.

De Geus, Arie, *The Living Company Habits for Survival in a Turbulent Business Environment,* Boston, Massachusetts USA, Harvard Business School Press, 1997.

Delhaise, Philippe F., *Asia in Crisis: The Implosion of the Banking and Finance Systems,* Singapore, John Wiley & Sons (Asia) Pte Ltd, 1998.

Dent, Harry S. Jr., *The Roaring 2000s: Building The Wealth And Lifestyle You Desire in The Greatest Boom in History,* USA, Simon & Schuster, 1998.

Doz, Yves L.; Hamel, Gary, *Alliance Advantage: The Art of Creating Value through Partnering,* USA, Harvard Business School Press, 1998.

Drucker, Peter F., *Post-Capitalist Society,* USA, HarperBusiness, 1994.

Edelman, Marian Wright, *Families in Peril: An Agenda for Social Change,* USA, Harvard University Press, 1987.

Ehrbar, Al, *EVA: The Real Key to Creating Wealth,* USA, John Wiley & Sons, Inc., 1998.

Esman, Milton J; Telhami, Shibley (ed.), *International Organizations And Ethnic Conflict,* Ithaca & London, Cornell University Press, 1996.

Farkas, Charles M.; De Backer, Philippe, *Maximum Leadership,* New York, USA, Henry Holt & Company, Inc., 1996.

Finckenauer, James O.; Waring, Elin J., *Russian Mafia in America Immigration, Culture and Crime,* Boston, USA, Northeastern University Press, 1998.

Fooner, Michael, *Interpol Issues in World Crime and International Crime Justice,* New York, USA, Plenum Press, 1989.

Fuller, R. Buckminster (with Agel, Jerome; Fiore, Quentin), *I Seem To Be A Verb,* New York, USA, Bantam Books, Inc., 1970.

Gardels, Nathan (edited by), *The Changing Global Order World Leaders Reflect,* USA & UK, Blackwell Publishers, 1997.

Garrison, Omar V., *The Secret World of Interpol,* New York, USA, Ralston-Pilot, Inc.

Gates, Bill, *Business @ The Speed of Thought: Using A Digital Nervous System,* New York, USA, Warner Books, Inc., 1999.

Gersick, Kelin E. (ed.); *et al.*; *Generation to Generation: Life Cycles of the Family Business,* Boston, Massachusetts, USA, Harvard Business School Press, 1997.

Gibson, Rowan (edited by), *Rethinking the Future,* Great Britain, Nicholas Brealey Publishing, 1997.

Glazer, Nathan, *We Are All Multiculturalists Now,* USA, Harvard University Press, 1998.

Goold, Michael; Campbell, Andrew, *Strategies and Styles: The Role of the Centre in Managing Diversified Corporations,* United Kingdom, Blackwell Publishers, 1994.

Goudie, Andrew, *The Future of Climate,* London, UK, Phoenix, 1997.

Gouillart, Francis J.; Kelly, James N., *Transforming The Organisation,* USA, McGraw-Hill, Inc., 1995.

Gyatso, Tenzin His Holiness the Dalai Lama, *Ancient Wisdom, Modern World Ethics for a New Millennium,* London, Great Britain, Little, Brown and Company, 1999.

Hamel, Gary; Prahalad, C.K., *Competing For the Future,* Boston, Massachusetts, USA, Harvard Business School Press, 1994.

Hax, Arnoldo C.; Majluf, Nicolas, *Strategic Management,* USA, Prentice-Hall, 1984.

Hesselbein, Frances; Goldsmith, Marshall; Beckhard, Richard, *The Leader of the Future,* USA, Jossey-Bass, 1996.

Hesselbein, Frances; Goldsmith, Marshall; Beckhard, Richard, *The Organisation of the Future,* USA, Jossey-Bass Books, 1997.

Hirst, Paul; Thompson, Grahame, *Globalization in Question: The International Economy And the Possibilities of Governance,* Great Britain, Polity Press, 1996.

Hoffman, Bruce, *Inside Terrorism,* New York, USA, Columbia University Press, 1998.

Hunter, James Davison, *Culture Wars: The Struggle to Define America,* USA, BasicBooks, 1991.

Huntington, Samuel P., *The Clash of Civilization and the Remaking of World Order,* USA, Touchstone, 1997.

Independent Commission on Population and Quality of Life, *Caring For the Future: Making the Next Decades Provide a Life Worth Living,* Oxford, New York, Oxford University Presss, 1996.

Inglehart, Ronald, *Modernization and Postmodernization: Cultural, Economic And Political Change in 43 Societies,* Princeton, New Jersey, UK, Princeton University Press, 1997.

Jameson, Fredric; Miyoshi, Masao, *The Cultures of Globalization,* UK, Duke University Press, 1998.

Kaplan, Robert S.; Norton, David P., *The Balanced Scorecard,* Boston, Massachusetts, USA, Harvard Business School Press, 1996.

Kapstein, Ethan B., *Governing The Global Economy: International Finance and the State,* Cambridge, Massachusetts, London, Harvard University Press, 1996.

Katz, Michael B., *The Undeserving Poor: From The War On Poverty to the War on Welfare,* New York, USA, Pantheon Books, 1989.

Kelly, Robert J.; Maghan Jess, *Hate Crime: The Global Politics of Polarization,* USA, Southern Illinois University Press, 1998.

Kennedy, Paul, *Preparing for the Twenty-First Century,* New York, USA, First Vintage Books, 1994.

Kiplinger, Knight, *World Boom Ahead: Why Business and Consumer Will Prosper,* Washington, D.C., USA, The Kiplinger Washington Editors, Inc., 1998.

Kramnick, Isaac (ed.), *The Portable Enlightenment Reader,*New York, USA, Penguin Books, 1995.

Lama Surya Das, *Awakening To The Sacred: Creating A Spiritual Life from Scratch,* New York, USA, Broadway Books, 1999.

Landers, David S., *The Wealth And Poverty of Nations: Why Some Are So Rich and Some So Poor,* New York & London, W.W. Norton & Company, Inc., 1998.

Latouche, Serge, *The Westernization of the World: The Significance, Scope & Limits of the Drive towards Global Uniformity,* Great Britain, Polity Press, 1996.

Lipnack, Jessica; Stamps, Jeffrey, *The Age of The Network,* New York, USA, John Wiley & Sons, Inc., 1994.

Luftman, Jerry N. (ed.), *Competing in the Information Age: Strategic Alignment in Practice,* New York, Oxford University Press, 1996.

Mander, Jerry; Goldsmith, Edward (ed.) , *The Case Against The Global Economy: And For a Turn Toward The Local,* San Francisco, USA, Sierra Club Books, 1996.

McLaughlin, Corrine; Davidson, Gordon, *Spiritual Politics: Changing the World from the Inside Out,* New York, USA, Ballatine Books, 1994.

McRae, Hamish, *The World of 2020: Power, Culture And Prosperity,* Boston, Massachusetts, USA, Harvard Business School Press, 1998.

Montes, Manuel F.; Popov, Vladimir V., *The Asian Crisis Turns Global,* Singapore, Institute of Southeast Asian Studies, 1999.

Naisbitt, John; Aburdence, Patricia, *Megatrends 2000: New Directions for Tomorrow,* New York, USA, Avon Books, 1990.

Naisbitt, John, *Megatrends: Ten New Directions Transforming Our Lives,* USA, Warner Books, 1984.

Nakauchi, Isao, *Drucker On Asia: A Dialogue Between Peter Drucker & Isao Nakauchi,* USA, Butterworth Heinemann, 1997.

Ohmae, Kenichi, *Triad Power: The Coming Shape of Global Competition,* New York, USA, Free Press, 1985.

Ohmae, Kenichi, *The Borderless World: Power and Strategy in The Interlinked Economy,* Great Britain, Fontana, 1991.

Ohmae, Kenichi, *The End of the Nation State: The Rise of Regional Economies,* New York, USA, Free Press Paperbacks, 1996.

Peters, Thomas J.; Waterman Jr., Robert H., *In Search of Excellence: Lessons from America's Best-Run Companies,* USA, Harper & Row, Publishers, Inc., 1982.

Piasecki, Bruce W., *Corporate Environmental Strategy: The Avalanche of Change Since Bhopal,* USA, John Wiley & Sons, Inc., 1995.

Porter, Gareth; Brown, Janet Welsh, *Global Environmental Politics,* USA, Westview Press, 1996.

Porter, Michael E., *Competitive Strategy Techniques for Analyzing Industries and Competitors,* USA, The Free Press, 1980.

Porter, Michael E. (edited by), *Competition in Global Industries,* Boston, Massachusetts USA, Harvard Business School Press, 1986.

Porter, Michael E., *On Competition,* USA, Harvard Business Review, 1996.

Prahalad, C.K.; Doz Yves L., *The Multi-National Mission: Balancing Local Demands & Global Vision,* New York, The Free Press, 1987.

Reichheld, F. Frederick (ed.), *The Quest for Loyalty: Creating Value through Partnership,* USA, Harvard Business Review Book, 1996.

Ridley, Matt, *The Future of Disease,* London, UK, Phoenix, 1997.

Senge, Peter M., *The Fifth Discipline: The Art & Practice of The Learning Organisation,* USA, Currency Doubleday, 1994.

Schaler, Jeffrey A. (Ph.D.) (ed.), *Drugs: Should We Legalise, Decriminalize or Deregulate?,* USA, Prometheus Books, 1998.

Soros, George, *The Crisis of Global Capitalism: Open Society Endangered,* Great Britain, Little, Brown and Company, 1998.

Stares, Paul B., *Global Habit: The Drug Problem in a Borderless World,* Washington, D.C., USA, Brookings Institution, 1996.

Stewart, Thomas A., *Intellectual Capital,* Great Britain, London, Nicholas Brealey Publishing Limited,1997.

Thompson, William Irwin, *At The Edge of History And Passages About Earth: Exploration of the New Planetary Culture,* USA, Lindisfarne Press, 1990.

Vogl, Frank; Sinclair, James, *Boom,* USA, Irwin, 1996.